The Complete Idiot's Guide® to

Recording with Cubase

The Complete Idiot's Guide® to

Recording with Cubase

by *Michael Miller*

ALPHA
A member of Penguin Group (USA) Inc.

To Sherry—finally, and forever.

ALPHA BOOKS

Published by the Penguin Group

Penguin Group (USA) Inc., 375 Hudson Street, New York, New York 10014, U.S.A.

Penguin Group (Canada), 10 Alcorn Avenue, Toronto, Ontario, Canada M4V 3B2 (a division of Pearson Penguin Canada Inc.)

Penguin Books Ltd, 80 Strand, London WC2R 0RL, England

Penguin Ireland, 25 St Stephen's Green, Dublin 2, Ireland (a division of Penguin Books Ltd)

Penguin Group (Australia), 250 Camberwell Road, Camberwell, Victoria 3124, Australia (a division of Pearson Australia Group Pty Ltd)

Penguin Books India Pvt Ltd, 11 Community Centre, Panchsheel Park, New Delhi—110 017, India

Penguin Group (NZ), cnr Airborne and Rosedale Roads, Albany, Auckland 1310, New Zealand (a division of Pearson New Zealand Ltd)

Penguin Books (South Africa) (Pty) Ltd, 24 Sturdee Avenue, Rosebank, Johannesburg 2196, South Africa

Penguin Books Ltd, Registered Offices: 80 Strand, London WC2R 0RL, England

International Standard Book Number: 978-1-59257-499-5
Library of Congress Catalog Card Number: 2005910783

09 08 07 8 7 6 5 4 3 2 1

Interpretation of the printing code: The rightmost number of the first series of numbers is the year of the book's printing; the rightmost number of the second series of numbers is the number of the book's printing. For example, a printing code of 07-1 shows that the first printing occurred in 2007.

Printed in the United States of America

Publisher: *Marie Butler-Knight*
Editorial Director: *Mike Sanders*
Managing Editor: *Billy Fields*
Acquisitions Editor: *Tom Stevens*
Development Editor: *Ginny Bess Munroe*
Senior Production Editor: *Janette Lynn*
Copy Editor: *Ross Patty*
Cartoonist: *Shannon Wheeler*
Book Designers: *Trina Wurst/Kurt Owens*
Cover Designer: *Bill Thomas*
Indexer: *Angie Bess*
Layout: *Ayanna Lacey*
Proofreader: *John Etchison*

Contents at a Glance

Contents

Appendixes

Foreword

The most important asset to have on your side when writing music is freedom: freedom to experiment musically, freedom to experiment sonically, and freedom to experiment emotionally. The most important means to that freedom is the ability to capture it, develop it, refine it, and be inspired by it. As a television and film composer, record producer, songwriter, and recording engineer, I have enjoyed twenty years in the quest for this freedom. I found it in Cubase.

To get you started off in the right foot, I would first encourage you to adjust your perception of Cubase 4. Don't just think of this as "computer recording software," but instead think of it as a vast and limitless musical environment. Of course, it does have a technical side that this book will teach you, but the magic of Cubase is the creativity. The technical part of working with Cubase is much like ice-skating for a hockey player. It takes a little practice, but soon you won't even think about it, and all of your focus will be on playing music. Once you learn the basics of recording and manipulating audio and MIDI, Cubase will begin to lead you in endless creative directions. As you read and work through each chapter of *The Complete Idiot's Guide to Recording with Cubase*, you will find yourself flowing with creativity and exploring sounds and ideas that you couldn't possibly dream of when writing music with just a guitar or sitting at a piano.

Michael Miller's mastery of this software will walk you step by step from the basics of getting set up through the mastering of your final mix. You will work through a series of exercises to develop your skills in MIDI programming, recording techniques, audio editing, and working with the latest cutting-edge VST instruments and plug-in effects. Throughout the experience, you will discover that Cubase 4 is a multi-faceted program that includes deep feature sets for all areas of music from songwriting and album production, to film scoring and sound design. Cubase 4 will become the source of inspiration to develop your art, while offering the most reliable platform to record, edit, mix, and master your music.

All of this freedom is now yours, so experiment with everything, developing your own style and production techniques, and you will find yourself crafting rhythms, melodies, and sounds that are unique to everything you have created in the past. Start with simple things like using delay lines to inspire new rhythms, incorporating plug-ins to manipulate traditional sounds into groundbreaking new textures, and adding automation and dynamics to enhance the emotion of your piece. Soon you'll find yourself distorting your violin section and triggering it to play the hi-hat pattern of your song, or reversing your entire mix and playing it though a phase-shifted reverb to transform an uninspired film score into a unique, cutting-edge soundscape. Whether you are a classical guitarist or a contemporary film composer, the possibilities are endless, and the enhancement of your music will be refreshing and exciting. That is the magic of Cubase 4!

Doug DeAngelis

Doug DeAngelis is a well-known producer, composer, and recording engineer. His composing credits include the soundtracks for a number of hit television shows, including *CSI: Miami*, *The Evidence*, *Robbery Homicide Division*, *Third Watch*, and *L.A.X.*

Introduction

I've long been a fan of the golden days of studio recording. The days when Frank Sinatra would stand in front of a real live big band in the Capitol studios, hat cocked jauntily on his head, and rip through a record's worth of takes in a single evening. The days when Phil Spector would assemble a small army of seasoned musicians in Gold Star's humble 23' × 35' studio to record a veritable wall of monophonic sound on a state-of-the-art, three-track recorder. The days when George Martin would sit in the booth at Abbey Road, watching John, Paul, George, and Ringo reinvent studio recording in their own image. The days when all it took to get a great sound was some talented musicians, the right microphones, and a canny engineer behind the board.

Those days, of course, are long gone. Thanks to the advent of digital recording, we're no longer limited to two or three or four recorded tracks; when you're recording to hard disk, you can create as many tracks as you need. And you don't have to worry about getting everything perfect in a single take, either. It's a piece of cake to go back and punch in part of a part, or use digital editing techniques to cut out the clams and fix any unsteady tempos.

But the best thing about digital recording is that you don't need to invest in hundreds of thousands of dollars worth of equipment to do it. Thanks to Steinberg's Cubase software, all you need is a personal computer, a couple of monitor speakers, a MIDI keyboard or electric guitar, and a few microphones. You don't even need a fancy recording studio; Cubase lets you make professional-sounding recordings in your own bedroom or garage. The practical power of this technology is nothing short of amazing.

With all this power, however, comes complexity. Launch Cubase and you know what I mean; the interface is almost Byzantine, with all manner of knobs and sliders and pushbuttons filling the screen. It's downright daunting. Even if you manage to get all your instruments and microphones plugged in, how do you manipulate this interface to lay down professional-sounding tracks—and then make them sound even better with special effects and EQ?

Good questions, all—and all questions that I'll try to answer in this book. *The Complete Idiot's Guide to Recording with Cubase* is an attempt to show novice engineers and recording musicians how to create great-sounding recordings, using nothing more than a personal computer, the necessary microphones and musical instruments, and a copy of Cubase. Cubase may be powerful, but it doesn't have to be hard to use. You just have to know which buttons to push.

What You'll Find in This Book

My goal in writing *The Complete Idiot's Guide to Recording with Cubase* is to take a new Cubase user from setup to recording to mixing to mastering as quickly and as easily as possible and, in the process, help the user make better-sounding recordings.

With the exception of the first chapter, which is kind of a "quick start" to your first simple recording project, the book is organized the way you'll be working. I start with setup and configuration, work through the recording itself, proceed to some special techniques, and finish up with mixing and mastering. Start with the first chapter and end with the last, and you'll learn what you need to know to create your own Cubase recording projects.

The Complete Idiot's Guide to Recording with Cubase is composed of 15 individual chapters, organized into five general parts, as follows:

Part 1, "Getting Started," starts off with that "quick start" to your first recording project I mentioned. Then I go back and talk about what you need to set up your own home recording studio, and how to find your way around the somewhat complicated Cubase interface.

Part 2, "Recording," tackles the basics of recording music. One chapter is devoted to traditional audio recording (using microphones and guitars and such), another to MIDI recording (using MIDI keyboards and synthesizers). They're two different processes, and require slightly different techniques.

Part 3, "Editing," shows you how to edit the recordings you've made. Cubase offers a wealth of editing functions for both audio and MIDI recordings; I'll cover each type of editing separately.

Part 4, "Special Techniques," recognizes that not everyone records the same way. The first of these three chapters shows you how to use VST virtual instruments in your recordings, the second chapter discusses recording with loops and samples, and the third chapter teaches you several different ways to create a great-sounding drum track. It's all good.

Part 5, "Mixing and Mastering," brings you to the end of the recording process. You'll learn how to mix your multiple tracks down to stereo, how to add various types of plug-in effects, how to apply EQ, and how to export your master mix to a digital audio file for distribution on CD or over the Internet.

But that's not all. I've also included "The Complete Idiot's Recording Glossary" (otherwise known as Appendix A), which explains a lot of the technical terms used throughout the book. If you don't know an insert from a send, this is the place to look. And Appendix B details what's new in Cubase 4—and how Cubase 4 differs from Cubase Studio 4.

What You Need to Use This Book

I assume that you already have a copy of Cubase and a personal computer (Windows or Mac, it doesn't matter), and that you have the one installed on the other. That said, you should know that there are actually several different versions of Cubase available. This book is based on the features in Cubase 4, the full-featured version of the program. The book should also be useful if you're using the lower-priced Cubase Studio 4, which offers the same basic features as Cubase 4 but lacks some of the higher-end, more professional bells and whistles.

As to version numbers, this book is written on Cubase 4. If you're using a prior version of the program, such as Cubase SX2 or SX3, most of what's discussed here should still work for you. The techniques are the same, in any case, even if a few of the menu items have changed.

To make a recording with Cubase, of course, you'll need the appropriate computer hardware, musical instruments, microphones, and auxiliary devices. I won't detail all those requirements here; turn to Chapter 2 to find out exactly what you need.

In terms of experience, I don't assume that you know a whole lot about recording coming into this book, although any prior knowledge is always good. This book is ideal for musicians who want to record their own work, or for budding recording engineers looking to learn more about their craft. I'll try not to get too technical, and to guide you gently through the tasks involved.

How to Get the Most Out of This Book

To get the most out of this book, you should know how it is designed. I've tried to put things together in such a way that you don't need instructions on how to read it, but still …

The best way to approach this book is to read it front to back, at your own pace. Each subsequent chapter builds on the ones previous, so you might miss something if you skip around. Still, I understand the temptation; that's why books have indexes.

Throughout the entire book you'll see a number of little boxes (what we in the publishing profession call *margin notes*) that present additional advice and information. These elements enhance your knowledge or point out important pitfalls to avoid. Here are the types of boxes you'll see scattered throughout the book:

Note

These boxes contain additional information about the topic at hand.

Tip

These boxes contain advice, tips, and tricks on how to better do what you're trying to do.

def•i•ni•tion

These boxes contain definitions of words or terms discussed in the main text.

Caution

These boxes contain warnings and cautions about what to avoid when you're working on your recording project.

In addition, most chapters have one or more sidebars. These are short text pieces set apart from the main text, focusing on a particular recording-oriented topic. These sidebars are where I put forth my personal opinions and advice on how to make better recordings. Recording is a personal business, after all; like it or not, I felt I owed you my thoughts on some important topics.

Beyond This Book

As much as I know you'll find this book useful, I offer a slight caution. Cubase is a very full-featured program, and there's a lot that the program can do that I don't cover in the book. (For example, you can use Cubase to create surround-sound mixes for movies and video; I don't cover that at all, sorry.) I limit the coverage to those operations likely to be used by the average recording musician or novice engineer. This is done in part to keep from complicating things and confusing you, the reader, and in part because there are only so many pages in this book. To cover every single feature and option in Cubase would require at least a 1,000-page book, and you probably wouldn't want to read it. For now, I'm sticking to common tasks and operations—and to standard recording projects.

If you want to do anything fancier than what's presented here, I recommend several additional resources. Chief of these are the Cubase.com and Cubase.net forums, located online at www.cubase.com and www.cubase.net, respectively. These sites are where the true Cubase gurus hang out; these folks are generally quite helpful in assisting their fellow Cubase users.

And if, like me, you're fascinated with the golden age of recording, I recommend you check out a book called *Temples of Sound: Inside the Great Recording Studios* (Jim Cogan and William Clark, Chronicle Books, 2003). It's a terrific tour through all the legendary studios of the 1950s and 1960s, from Sun to Capitol to Gold Star to Stax to the Snake Pit at Motown. Many of these studios are long gone or little used these days, but the great sounds remain, recorded for posterity on vinyl and CD.

Let Me Know What You Think

I always love to hear from my readers. If you want to contact me, feel free to e-mail me at cubase@molehillgroup.com. I can't promise that I'll answer every e-mail, but I will promise that I'll read each one.

If you want to learn more about me and any new books I've written, check out my personal website at www.molehillgroup.com. This is also where you'll find any corrections or clarifications to the book. Check it regularly.

Acknowledgments

I had assistance from dozens of individuals in the creation of this book and would like to thank the following for their help:

Thanks to the usual suspects at Alpha Books, including but not limited to Marie Butler-Knight, Tom Stevens, Billy Fields, Ginny Bess Munroe, Janette Lynn, and Ross Patty, for helping to turn my manuscript into a printed book.

Thanks also to composer Doug DeAngelis, for taking time from his busy schedule to contribute the foreword to this book, and to Angus Baigent of Steinberg, for his assistance in providing software for evaluation.

Special Thanks to the Technical Reviewer

The Complete Idiot's Guide to Recording with Cubase was reviewed by an expert who double-checked the accuracy of what you'll learn here, to help us ensure that this book gives you everything you need to know about composing music. Special thanks are extended to Brian McConnon for his review and comments in this regard.

Brian runs MTECH Marketing Communications, a public relations and marketing communications firm that happens to have Steinberg as a client. Brian has more than 15 years of musical instrument and pro audio industry experience; before forming MTECH, Brian worked directly for Steinberg, which is why he knows so much about the product.

My heartfelt thanks to Brian for his assistance and advice—and for helping to make this a better book.

Trademarks

Part 1

Getting Started

We'll start things off with a bang by launching you directly into your first recording project. (It's a simple one, but it's a good way to get your feet wet.) Then you'll learn how to put together your own recording studio, and find your way around the Cubase interface.

Chapter 1

Your First Recording Project

In This Chapter

- Connecting your instrument to your PC
- Opening a new project
- Configuring Cubase for recording
- Setting the recording levels
- Making the recording—and listening to playback

If you're a new user of Cubase software, you're probably eager to get everything set up and start recording. Well, there's a lot to learn about Cubase (that's why you bought this book!), but you can get up and running fairly quickly. In fact, that's what you do in this chapter. Just follow the step-by-step instructions to complete your first simple recording project.

Note the word "simple" in the previous sentence. What we do here is learn how to make a basic one-track recording—no overdubs, no editing, no special effects, no MIDI. We cover all those advanced operations in subsequent chapters; right now, all we're doing is the easy stuff. It's the fastest way to get productive with Cubase.

What You Need

Before you begin your first recording project, here's what you need:

- A personal computer (Windows or Mac)
- Cubase 4 or Cubase Studio 4 software, already installed
- A set of monitor (powered) speakers, connected to your computer
- A set of headphones
- An electric guitar (no amplifier necessary), electronic keyboard, or microphone

Caution

As tempting as it is, you can't just plug your instrument into your computer's existing mic in jack. Not only is the jack the wrong size (you want something with a ¼" jack, to match the ¼" plug on your guitar or microphone cable), the sound quality of most PCs' default connectors is unacceptable for serious recording.

- Some sort of audio input device connected to your PC
- The necessary cables to connect your instrument to the input device, and the input device to your PC

A quick note: I cover how to set up various types of recording studios in Chapter 2, but for now I'll point out that you need some sort of interface box to connect your instrument to your computer. If you're on a tight budget or only need to record one instrument at a time, you can get by with something simple, such as M-Audio's low-cost Fast Track USB. On the other hand, if you plan on recording an entire band at the same time, you'll need a device with multiple line inputs. I assume you have some sort of input device, and that you have it properly installed and configured to work with your computer and with the Cubase program.

Step 1: Make the Connections

Tip

Depending on the type of mic you're using, you may need to run it through a preamplifier before connecting it to your computer, to boost the signal to an acceptable level. Many audio input boxes include built-in preamps, just for this purpose.

The first step in making a recording is to get everything connected. In essence, you want to connect your instrument to an audio input device, which in turn connects to your computer. It sounds pretty simple, and in most cases it is.

If you're using a guitar or electronic keyboard, you use a standard guitar cable to make the connection from your instrument to the input box, as shown in Figure 1.1. If you're connecting a microphone (to record an acoustic instrument or vocalist), the type of connector you use depends on the microphone. Professional-quality microphones use a balanced XLR connector, such as that shown in Figure 1.2. Lower-quality microphones, as well as many mics designed for stage use, use a standard ¼" connector, such as the kind used on guitar cables. Make sure your input box has the proper connector for your microphone.

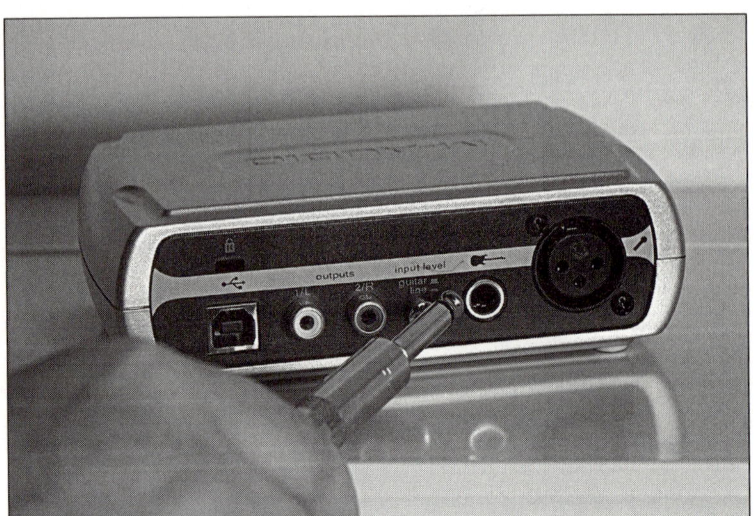

Figure 1.1 *Connecting a guitar cable to an input box.*

Figure 1.2 *Connecting an XLR cable to an input box.*

The input box, of course, should already be connected to your personal computer. Most input boxes connect via USB; some higher-end devices connect via FireWire (sometimes called IEEE 1394). Either type of connection is good.

Your computer should also have a set of powered speakers connected. For now, you can use the standard speakers that came with your PC—although, when you get more serious about the whole recording thing, you may want to invest in a pair of monitor-quality speakers. (I talk more about this in Chapter 2.) You use the speakers to listen to the playback of your recording.

The final connection is that of a pair of good-quality headphones, preferably the close-ear type. You'll use the headphones to listen to your instrument while you're recording.

> **Caution**
>
> You don't want to listen to yourself while recording through your PC's main speakers, especially if you're recording via microphone. The sound from the speakers will get picked up by the microphone, thus corrupting the sound you're trying to record. You use headphones to isolate the sound you're hearing from the sounds you're recording.

Step 2: Launch Cubase

After you've made all the physical connections, it's time to launch Cubase and configure it for your new recording project.

Let's start by making sure the USB copy protection key that came with your software is inserted in an open USB port, and then you can launch the Cubase program itself. From within Windows XP, click the Start button and select **All Programs > Steinberg Cubase 4 > Cubase 4.**

> **Note**
>
> If you're using a version different from Cubase 4, make the appropriate name-based changes to the computer menus.

After a few moments, the Cubase program opens on your desktop. As you can see in Figure 1.3, the Cubase workspace itself is currently empty, except for the transport panel at the bottom of the workspace.

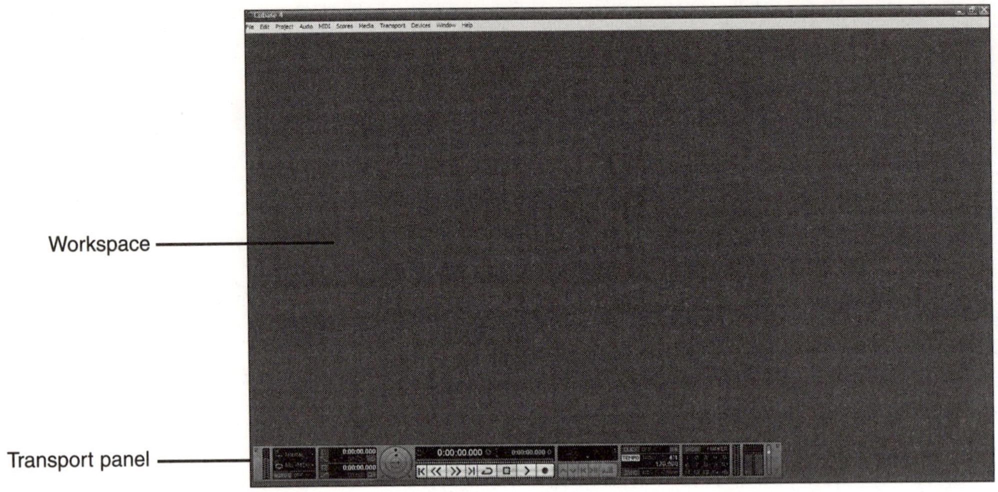

Figure 1.3 *Launching Cubase with an empty workspace.*

Step 3: Create a New Project

Now we want to create a new recording project. Cubase lets you create all sorts of projects, with varying numbers and kinds of tracks. You can start with a blank workspace and work your way up, or you can start with a pre-designed project layout, called a template. Unfortunately, Cubase doesn't have a template for "simple single-track recording," so we'll start with an empty template and add everything else we need.

Open your new project by selecting **File > New Project.** When the New Project dialog box appears, as shown in Figure 1.4, select **Empty,** then click **OK.**

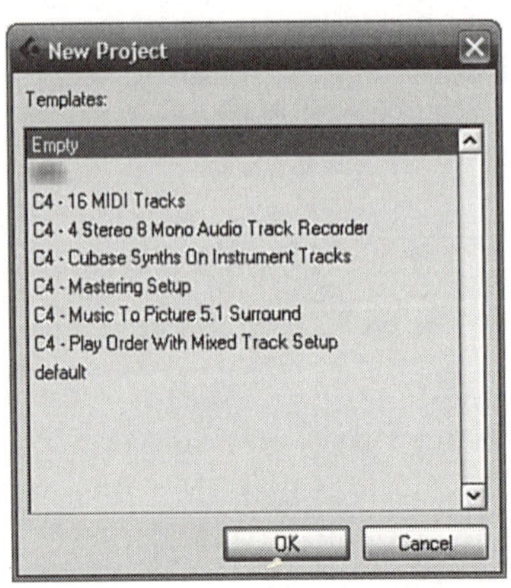

Figure 1.4 *Opening a new project with an Empty template.*

Cubase now displays a dialog box that prompts you to select a directory for your new project; I recommend creating a Cubase folder in your My Documents folder, although you can place this directory anywhere on your hard disk. Select the folder you want, then click **OK.**

Step 4: Add an Audio Track

As you can see in Figure 1.5, a new project window opens in the Cubase workspace—but it's empty. No problem; all you have to do is add a recording track to the project.

Figure 1.5 *Your new project, with an empty project window.*

You do this by selecting **Project > Add Track > Audio.** When the Add Audio Track dialog box appears, as shown in Figure 1.6, pull down the Configuration list and select **Mono,** then click **OK.** (You select the Mono option because your guitar or keyboard outputs a single audio channel; later in the process you can send that single channel to both the left and right channels of your recording.)

Figure 1.6 *Creating a new mono audio track.*

Now we're cooking. The project window now includes a track labeled Audio 01. We'll also want to display a *track inspector*, as shown in Figure 1.7, which includes various settings for the selected track. You display the track inspector by clicking the Show Inspector button in the upper left corner of the toolbar, at the top of workspace.

Figure 1.7 *Your project with a single audio track added.*

Step 5: Configure the Input

Even though you have a new audio track in Cubase's project window, you're not quite ready to start recording yet. You first have to set up the proper input for the track, so that what you play is recorded onto the Audio 01 track.

You configure this audio input routing from the track inspector area at the left of the project window, as shown in Figure 1.8. Click the **Input Routing** field to display a pop-up menu of available input devices. Select your input box from this list. (On my system, the correct choice is Mono In 1; it may be different on yours.)

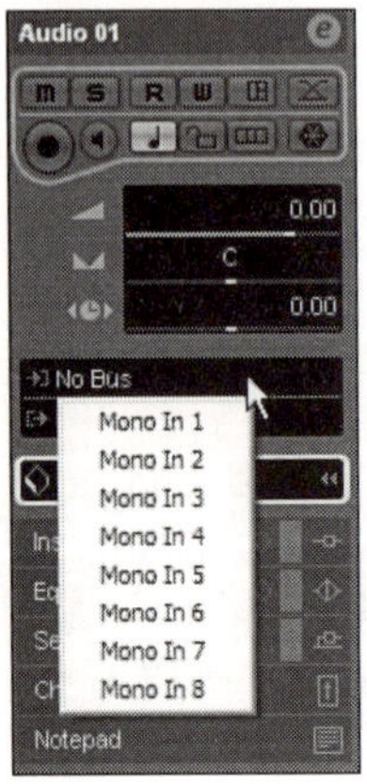

Figure 1.8 *Configuring the proper input for the audio track.*

Step 6: Display the Mixer

Many of the recording functions in Cubase are controlled by means of a virtual audio mixer called, appropriately enough, the mixer. You open the mixer window by selecting **Devices > Mixer.**

As you can see in Figure 1.9, the mixer window contains a number of vertical channel strips, each of which control volume, recording, monitoring, and other functions. For this particular project, there are three channel strips—the input channel (which controls the input from your audio input device), the Audio 01 channel (the track to which you're recording) and the Output channel. (If you don't see the input channel strip, click the Hide Input Channels icon in the common panel, on the far left of the mixer.)

Tip

You can also open the mixer by clicking the **Open Track Mixer** button in the Cubase toolbar, or press the F3 key on your computer keyboard.

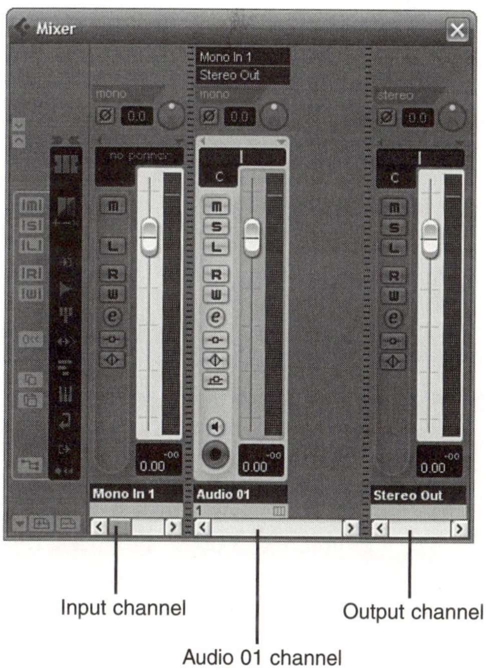

Figure 1.9 *The mixer window, with various input and output channel strips.*

Step 7: Enable Monitoring

Now that the mixer window is open, we want to make sure that you can hear your instrument while you're recording. You enable this monitoring capability by clicking the **Monitor** button for the Audio 01 track in the mixer, as shown in Figure 1.10. When clicked on, the button should light up orange.

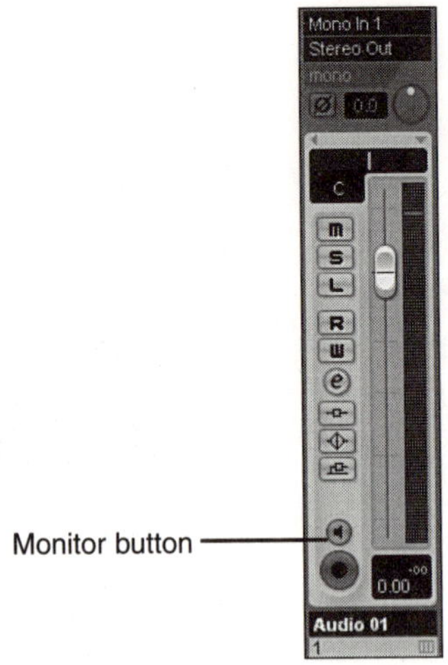

Figure 1.10 *Click the Monitor button to hear what you're playing.*

Now you can turn down (or turn off) your system's speakers and plug in your headphones. When you play your instrument, you should be able to hear what you're playing through the phones. You can adjust the monitor volume level by using the level fader for the Audio 01 track in the mixer.

Step 8: Set the Recording Levels

We're just about ready to start recording. But first we need to set the proper recording level for your track. We do this in the mixer window.

The concept behind recording levels is fairly simple. You want to record at as high a level as possible without distorting the sound. Set too high a level and the audio will "clip," or sound distorted and buzzy. Set the level too low and the audio will sound too soft, without the necessary punch. (And possibly with some soft details lost.) The clipping threshold is 0 dB; if this level is exceeded, the red clipping indicator will light up.

Setting the recording level is a bit like performing your own private sound check. That is, you need to play your instrument while you adjust the control. Start by setting the volume control on your guitar or keyboard to a moderate position—then start playing. Play as loud as the loudest you intend to play on the recording. Let it rip!

While you're playing, watch the level meter in the input (Monitor In 1) strip. Use your mouse to slide the level fader up and down to adjust the input level. You want the loudest notes you play to just tap the 0 dB level, without causing the clipping indicator to light up. This will require a bit of trial and error; make sure you err on the side of playing too loud, or else you could end up with some distortion if the levels are louder in your actual recording.

Step 9: Enable the Track for Recording

The next thing you need to do is activate your audio track for recording. This is an easy enough task, accomplished from within the mixer. Go to the channel strip for Audio 01 and click the **Record Enable** button, as shown in Figure 1.11. When recording is enabled, the entire button should light up red. (When recording isn't enabled, only the very center of the button is red.)

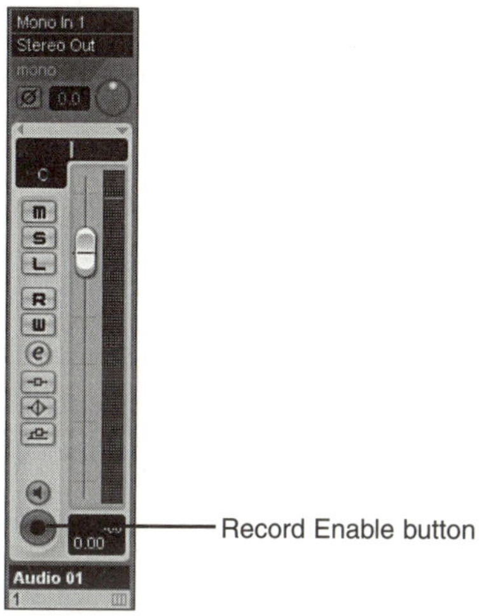

Figure 1.11 *Enabling recording for the Audio 1 track.*

> **Note**
>
> There are many more recording options available in Cubase than we're using in this example project, all of which I'll discuss throughout the course of this book. All of these options should be turned off by default when you start with the Empty template, so you don't have to worry about them here.

Step 10: Record!

I know what you're thinking—that's a lot of prep work for a simple recording. I agree. But now that it's all out of the way, it's time to rock and roll.

The actual recording is the easiest part of the process. (Technology-wise, that is; you still have that whole issue of playing the right notes on your instrument!) All you have to do is click the **Record** button, play your song, and then click the **Stop** button.

That sounds almost *too* simple, doesn't it? Let's go through the process, step by step:

1. With your instrument in hand, use your mouse to click the **Record** button on the transport panel, as shown in Figure 1.12.
2. Begin playing. As you play, an audio waveform will be created in the project window, in the Audio 01 track position, as shown in Figure 1.13.
3. When you're done playing, use your mouse to click the **Stop** button in the transport panel.

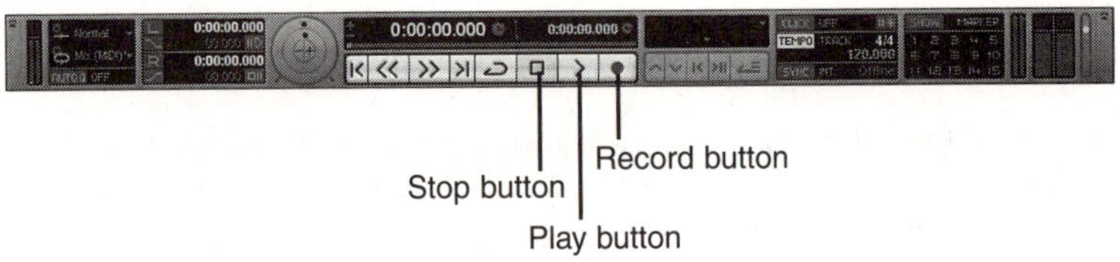

Figure 1.12 *Use the transport panel to start and stop recording.*

Figure 1.13 *A recording in process—note the waveform in the Audio 01 event.*

That's it—you've just completed your first audio recording!

Step 11: Play Back the Recording

Want to hear what you've just recorded? Of course you do! Well, take off your headphones, turn up the speakers, and click the **Monitor** button for channel Audio 01 in the mixer. (That is, you want to turn off the monitoring function, so that the button changes from orange to gray.) Next, click the **Rewind** button on the transport panel, as shown in Figure 1.14, to return to the very beginning of your recording. Now click the **Play** button, and listen to your recorded brilliance. When the recording is over, click the **Stop** button. Repeat as many times as necessary.

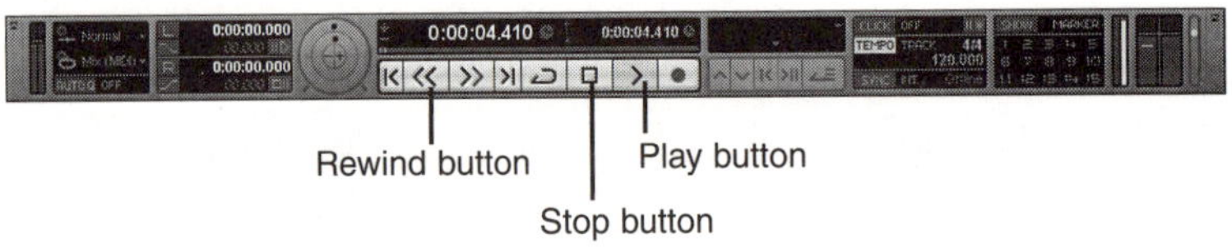

Figure 1.14 *Use the transport panel to rewind and play back your recording.*

Of course, few recordings are this simple. You may want to add sections to this track, or overdub portions of the track, or include other instruments on additional tracks. You may even want to edit your recording, or rearrange sections of the piece, or even delete part of the recording. And then there's the whole process of employing audio effects, reverb, equalization, and so on. You learn about all these things as you progress through this book. But it all starts with recording a single track—which you now know how to do!

The Least You Need to Know

- Start by connecting your instrument to your PC, using some sort of audio input box.
- Open a new project in Cubase, select the Empty template, and then add a single stereo audio track.
- Turn on the monitoring function.
- Set the recording level as loud as possible without clipping.
- Enable the audio track for recording, click the **Record** button, and start playing; click the **Stop** button when you're done.
- To play back your recording, click the **Rewind** button to return to the beginning of the track, then click the **Play** button.

Chapter 2

Setting Up Your Cubase Recording Studio

In This Chapter

- Determining what type of computer you need
- Evaluating monitor speakers
- Selecting the right recording equipment
- Soundproofing and configuring your recording space
- Choosing the right microphones

Before you can start recording with Cubase, you have to assemble, install, and configure your computer system, and then set up your recording studio. On the computer side, that means determining what types of equipment you need, and then figuring out how to get it to work with Cubase. On the studio side, it could mean anything from setting up a simple MIDI keyboard in a spare bedroom to assembling a full-fledged, acoustically perfect, professional recording space. It all depends on what types of music you'll be recording, and how.

Although I can't go into all the possible permutations of computer systems and recording studios here, I discuss some of the most common types of systems—and how they should be configured.

What Kind of Computer Do You Need?

Because Cubase is a computer-based recording program, we'll start with the computer. The first consideration, of course, is choosing what computer platform to use. Here we run into the first instance of "personal choice," because Cubase can run on either a Windows PC or an Apple Macintosh, and there's really no advantage to using one platform over another. Whichever platform you use, however, you need to make sure that your computer has the technical "oomph" to run the program without bogging down at critical moments.

Here's the deal. If you're serious about recording your music, you need to invest in the most powerful computer you can afford. Processing digital audio files is CPU-intensive work, and the faster and more powerful your computer's microprocessor, the easier things will be.

> **Tip**
>
> Steinberg lists both minimum and recommended system requirements for computers running Cubase 4. In my experience, I've found the minimum requirements unsatisfactory; instead, follow Steinberg's "recommended" requirements, which are the ones listed in this chapter.

It's a simple fact that computing power is one area where you shouldn't pinch pennies; you need as much horsepower as possible to edit large digital music files, and to play MIDI and VST instruments in real time. With an underpowered computer, you'll experience long wait times while processing files and (more important) unacceptable latency when using MIDI and VST instruments, and when monitoring your playback. This latency—a slight delay between what you play and what you hear—makes it extremely difficult to play and record in real time. You can diminish the latency effect by using a computer with a relatively fast processor, lots of random access memory (RAM), and a big, relatively fast hard disk.

Whether you're using a Windows PC or a Mac, your system needs to meet or exceed the following specifications:

> **Note**
>
> ASIO drivers enable direct communication between the audio card and the Cubase program. Audio cards or interfaces with ASIO drivers typically have lower latency (input-output delay) than traditional audio cards.

- For Windows systems, a Pentium or Athlon microprocessor running at 2.8GHz or faster; for Mac users, a G5 dual processor running at 1.8GHz or faster
- 512MB RAM or higher
- 200GB or more dedicated hard disk space
- Monitor and graphics card that support at least 1024 ∞ 768 resolution; the bigger the monitor, the better—and a 16:10 aspect ratio widescreen display is better yet
- Audio card or interface that meets or exceeds 16-bit stereo recording/playback and 44.1 kHz sampling; for Windows users, the card should come with either an ASIO driver or a DirectX- or Windows Multimedia-compatible driver; for Mac users, the card should be supplied with the proper Mac OS X (Core Audio) drivers
- Powered speakers (for listening to playback)
- Enough free USB and FireWire ports to support Cubase's copy protection key and any audio input devices you connect to your system
- DVD drive (for loading the program)
- CD-R/RW drive (for burning your completed audio discs)
- Internet access (for license registration)
- Windows XP Home or XP Professional operating system (for Windows users) or Mac OS X Version 10.4 or higher (for Apple users)

> **Tip**
>
> To calculate how much hard disk space you'll need, know that one minute of CD-quality mono audio requires 5MB of hard disk space. That's 10MB for a minute of stereo, or 120MB for a minute of 24-track recording.

Optionally, you should consider going with an external hard drive (dedicated solely to storing your audio files) and a dual-monitor setup (so you can display the project window on one monitor and the Mixer window on a second monitor). And it's definitely worth your while to bump up your system's memory as much as possible; a system with 2GB or more memory will perform a lot faster than one with the bare minimum 512MB RAM.

Setting Up Your Recording System

The computer may be the centerpiece of your recording setup, but it's still just one component of the system. Depending on the type of recording you do, you may need to add a variety of outboard components, from MIDI interface boxes to multi-channel control surfaces. Next, we'll look at some common types of recording, and typical equipment considerations for each.

Recording from CDs

Hip hop, techno, and other loop-based music relies on music sampled from other recordings—typically recordings on compact disc. After the samples are ripped from CD to your hard disk, they can be imported into Cubase for editing and playback.

If you're ripping tracks or sampling sounds from CDs, you can probably use the CD drive built into your PC. Alternately, you can connect an external CD player to your computer; to do this, you'll need both a CD player and a sound card or audio input box that has L/R audio inputs or an S/PDIF digital audio connection.

> **Note**
>
> Learn more about loop-based recording in Chapter 11.

Figure 2.1 diagrams a typical setup for this type of system.

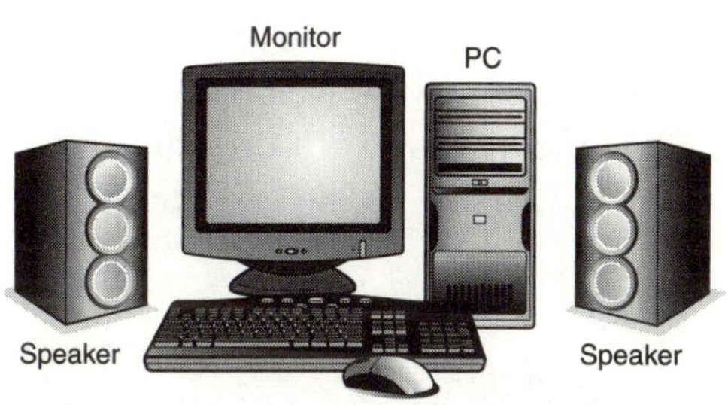

Figure 2.1 *A system designed for sampling CD tracks.*

MIDI Recordings

Many musicians do their composing and recording using MIDI instruments. With MIDI, you can use a single instrument, typically a MIDI keyboard, to input all the music for all the tracks; the sounds for each track are then assigned via a MIDI sequencer. MIDI input can also drive Cubase's VST virtual instruments.

> **Note**
>
> Composers who use Finale, Sibelius, Notion, or other music notation programs can save their scores as MIDI files, and then import those MIDI files into Cubase for recording.

For MIDI recordings, you'll need some sort of MIDI instrument as well as a MIDI interface to your computer. The MIDI interface is typically an external device; you connect your MIDI keyboard to the MIDI interface, and then connect the MIDI interface to your PC, via either USB or FireWire. Figure 2.2 diagrams a typical setup for a MIDI-based recording system.

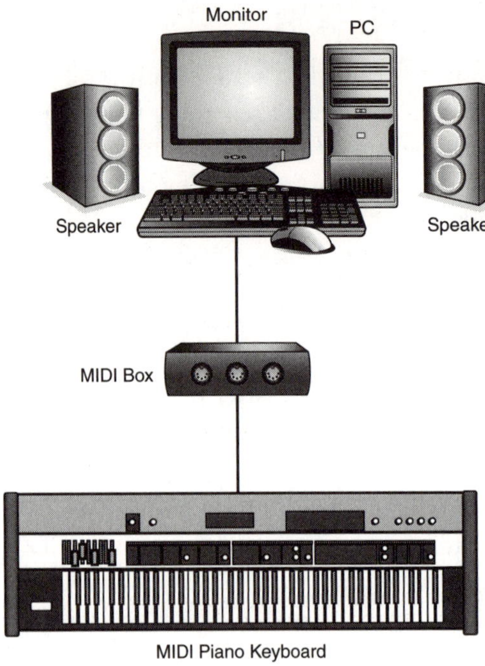

Figure 2.2 *A system designed for MIDI recording.*

> **Note**
>
> Learn more about MIDI recording in Chapter 5.

Most MIDI interface boxes have just one or two MIDI inputs, and a corresponding number of MIDI outputs (to connect back to your MIDI instrument). Some popular MIDI interface devices include the M-Audio UNO (shown in Figure 2.3), Edriol UM-1X, MOTU Fast Lane USB, M-Audio MIDISport 4x4, and Yamaha UX16.

Figure 2.3 *The M-Audio UNO MIDI interface device.*
(Courtesy of M-Audio.)

Single-Track Recording

Many great recordings have been made in the privacy of small home studios with the instruments being laid down one track at a time. If this describes the way your musical genius works, you can put together a very effective Cubase recording system at a relatively low price.

If you're only recording one track at a time, you don't need a big, expensive mixing board with tons of inputs. You can probably get by with a simple audio input box with a single input. Just connect your instrument (guitar, keyboard, or microphone) to the input box, then connect the input box to your PC, via either USB or FireWire. Figure 2.4 diagrams a typical setup for a single-track recording system.

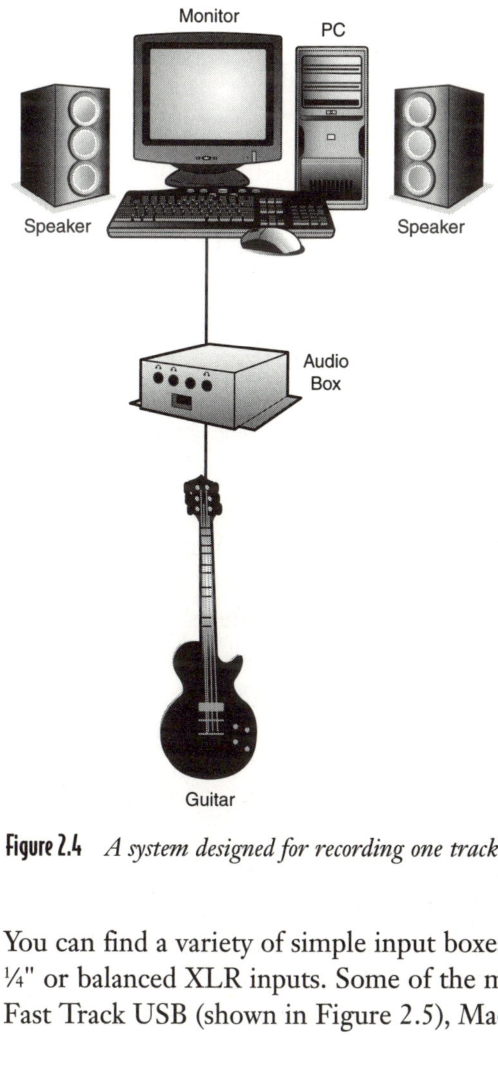

Figure 2.4 *A system designed for recording one track at a time.*

You can find a variety of simple input boxes, with anywhere from one to four ¼" or balanced XLR inputs. Some of the most popular include the M-Audio Fast Track USB (shown in Figure 2.5), Mackie Spike, and Griffin iMic.

> **Tip**
>
> Some manufacturers offer combination audio/MIDI interface boxes. A good example is TASCAM's US-122, which offers two ¼" line-level audio inputs, two balanced XLR inputs, and MIDI input/output connections. It connects to your PC via USB.

Figure 2.5 *The M-Audio Fast Track USB audio input box.*
(Courtesy of M-Audio.)

Multi-Track Recording

Larger home studios (and all professional studios) have the capability to record multiple audio tracks simultaneously. You need this multi-track capacity when recording a live drum kit (mics on the snare, the bass drum, all the toms, and above the cymbals), a chorus of background vocals, large wind or string sections, or a rock or jazz band playing live in the studio.

For this type of system, you need an external mixer—called a *control surface*—that can connect to your computer and handle anywhere from 4 to 16 to 24 inputs or more. You'll connect the appropriate instruments and microphones to the mixer, then connect the mixer to your computer, typically via FireWire (which is faster than USB).

> **Note**
>
> Don't confuse a computer control surface with a free-standing digital audio workstation (DAW), which includes its own hard disk for recording—and doesn't need a computer to operate.

When you use an external mixer/control surface, you have the option of adjusting the volume faders and other controls on the mixer itself, or in Cubase's virtual mixer interface. You can also connect external effects processors directly to the control surface, and manage them as Send or Insert effects in Cubase. Figure 2.6 diagrams a typical setup for this type of multi-track recording system.

There are a number of different mixer/control surfaces available, at a variety of price points (depending on number of inputs and other features). Some of the most popular include the TASCAM FW-1082 (shown in Figure 2.7), JL Cooper CS-32, and Mackie Control Universal.

> **Tip**
>
> If you're shopping for recording equipment, some popular online retailers include Pro Audio Solutions (www.proaudiosolutions.com), Sweetwater Sound (www.sweetwater.com), and zZounds.com (www.zzounds.com).

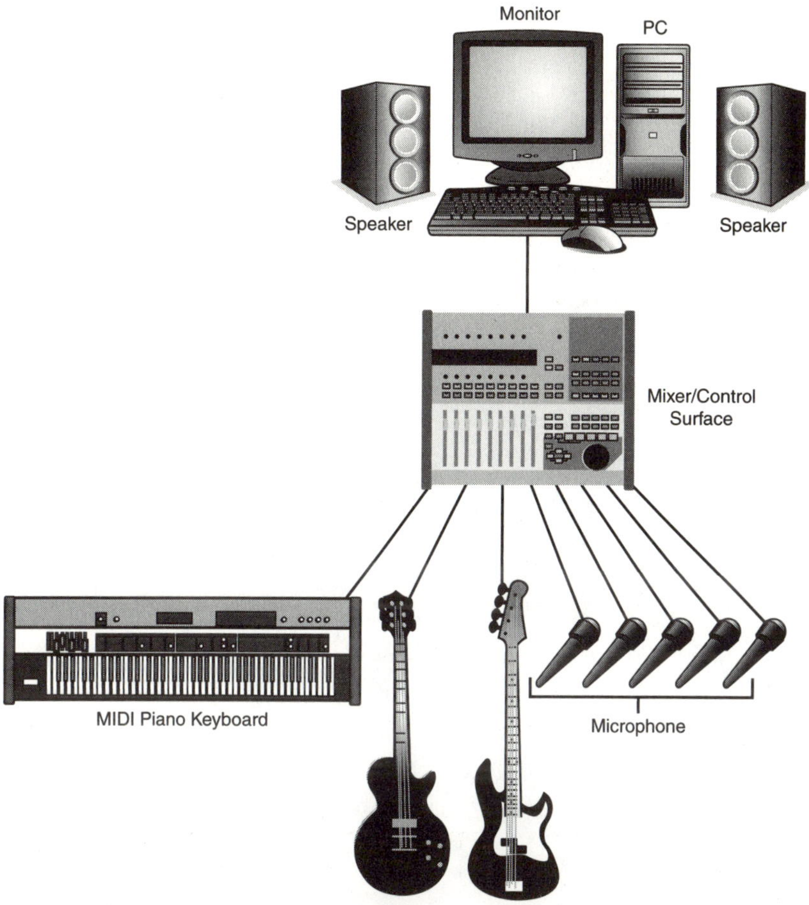

Figure 2.6 *A multi-track recording system using an external mixer/control surface and external effects processing.*

Figure 2.7 *TASCAM's FW-1082 8-channel external control surface.*
(Courtesy of TASCAM.)

Adding Monitor Speakers

Note

Studio monitor speakers are often called *nearfield monitors,* because you sit quite near them when you're listening. The audio qualities of nearfield monitors are necessarily different from traditional floor-standing or bookshelf speakers used in home audio systems.

In addition to your main computer, you also need a set of speakers with which to listen to your recordings. Although you can use the standard PC speakers for this purpose, they really don't deliver the kind of audio performance that accurately reproduces the music you've recorded. In other words, the speakers that came with your PC simply aren't good enough to use for professional monitoring purposes.

To accurately reproduce high fidelity audio, you need a set of studio-quality monitor speakers, such as the ones shown in Figure 2.8. Monitor speakers are bigger and better than typical computer speakers; they'll reproduce the full dynamic range of your music as accurately as possible, without any distracting shadings.

Figure 2.8 *Right and left monitor speakers from Samson.*
(Courtesy of Samson Technologies Corp.)

Most monitor speakers are powered speakers, just like your PC's normal speakers. That means you don't need an external power amplifier; the amplifier is built into each speaker cabinet. You connect monitor speakers to your computer's normal speaker output connections, and then plug them into a nearby power outlet.

Note

The powered monitor speakers I describe are also called *active* speakers. You can also find *passive* monitor speakers that require external amplification; as you might expect, you'll spend a lot more money for this sort of setup.

From this description, you've probably gotten the impression that monitor speakers are quite expensive. Well, they are—at least compared to the cheap computer speakers on sale at your local Best Buy. You can spend anywhere from $100 to $1,500 and up for a good pair of powered monitor speakers. You'll also need to spend a few bucks for stands to elevate the speakers for ear-level listening.

Don't go looking for monitor speakers at your local computer or consumer electronics store. Instead, you'll need to visit a music store that specializes in recording and sound reinforcement products, or shop at a similar online retailer. Popular speaker brands include ADAM, Event, Genelec, JBL, M-Audio, Mackie, Roland, Samson, and Yamaha.

Recording on Location

Of course, not all recordings are done in the controlled environment of a recording studio. Live recordings have long been an important part of the music scene, although in the old days that meant trundling expensive tape recorders and mixing consoles out to a club or auditorium. Today, any notebook computer can function as a self-contained portable recording studio; just ensure that Cubase is installed and you carry an audio interface box or two with you.

I can't give you much specific advice for location recording, because every location will be different. What becomes especially important, however, is the choice and position of your microphones. We're not talking MIDI or direct-injection recording, here; it's all live into the mics. You can choose to close-mic individual instruments, or set up a few mics at the front of the stage to catch the entire performance. (This latter approach is how most orchestral and choral recordings get made.) If you have time, experiment with mic placement before the performance you're recording; small changes can have a big effect.

Setting Up Your Studio Space

When one discusses computer-based recording, the tendency is to focus on the computer part of the equation, which is well and good. But it doesn't matter how easily you can edit and process your digital audio if what you first record to disk doesn't sound so hot. For this reason, you should pay at least as much attention to the creation of a performer-friendly recording studio space, with proper-sounding acoustics.

Choosing Your Space

Many home recording enthusiasts set up their studios in a spare bedroom or garage, which is fine for the engineering part of the process. However, most untreated bedrooms are not acoustically ideal. No matter how small (or how large) your recording space, you probably need to do some work to bring it up to spec, acoustically.

And the size of the space matters, too. If you're just recording yourself on acoustic guitar, a small space might be fine. But if you're recording a four-piece rock band, complete with drums, you're going to need a bit larger space. In addition, different-sized spaces have different acoustical properties; don't expect to get that big Phil Spector Wall of Sound effect when you record in an 8' × 10' bedroom.

If your recording projects consist almost exclusively of MIDI instruments or direct-injected guitar and bass parts, you don't need too big a recording space—and you don't have any acoustical issues to consider. That's because your recordings do not involve microphones; your MIDI instruments are recorded directly to your computer, as are your guitars and bass, so room acoustics simply don't factor into the equation. For most home recordists, that translates into using a spare bedroom as your studio—much like the home project studio shown in Figure 2.9.

Figure 2.9 *The author's home studio—HP computer, Gateway widescreen display, Tascam control surface, Samson speakers, and Alesis MIDI keyboard.*

> **Tip**
>
> Can you make a room *too* dead? Yes, especially when recording vocals. As discussed previously, you can always use another room with livelier acoustics (such as a bathroom or garage) to record your vocal tracks, or you can simply add digitally processed reverb or delay after the fact, from within Cubase.

When it's more than just you and a guitar or keyboard, you need to think about expanding to a larger recording space. You need enough space to hold you and the other musicians, but you don't have to overdo it; you're not looking for big-sounding rooms with cathedral ceilings and such. That might mean turning your basement into a studio, or maybe even your garage. Whichever you choose, you'll definitely need to soundproof it, to create a relatively "dead" sound. (A dead room lets you record purer signals, without worrying about ambient sounds and reflections; it's easier to add effects to a dry sound than it is to deal with complicated sound reflections and such.)

Many large studios have a separate drum room or booth to better isolate the drums, which tend to leak into all the other mics. You might also want to consider a separate vocal booth; this one doesn't have to be super-roomy, just large enough to hold a single vocalist and a microphone.

Soundproofing Your Space

One thing a recording space has to be is quiet. You don't want to lay down a gentle vocal track and then find out you also recorded your neighbor's lawn mower in the background.

To soundproof a room, you need to use your ears and be a little creative. Short of building an acoustically soundproof room from scratch with double drywall and insulation (which is a whole other thing), there are several things you can do to keep outside noise out of your recordings.

First, make sure you close all the doors and windows. (You'd be surprised how many amateur musicians forget to close the bedroom door when recording!) If you have a noisy air conditioner or furnace, turn it off—at least when recording. (It's okay to turn it back on between takes.) Have a fish tank in the room?

Turn it off, too; those filters and pumps all make a lot of noise. And don't forget the computer itself; most computers are fairly noisy, so you may need to bury it in sound-deadening material.

In addition, much of the material you might use to deaden a room will also help to soundproof the room. Read on to learn more.

Deadening the Room

A dead room, which many recordists prefer, is one that doesn't generate any unwanted acoustical reflections, echoes, or reverberation. You hear the sound of the instrument or vocalist, and nothing else.

Deadening a room means eliminating as many hard, reflective surfaces as possible. If the floor isn't carpeted, lay down area rugs. Cover all windows, mirrors, and other glass surfaces with quilts or blankets. Consider hanging tapestries from the walls, or attaching acoustical foam or even Styrofoam egg cartons to help deaden the sound. And don't forget the ceiling; that's another hard surface you need to deal with, one way or another.

The goal is to minimize the reflective surfaces. Soft wall and floor coverings of any sort will absorb sound waves, which is what makes the sound go dead. You want as much sound absorption—and as little reflection—as possible.

Tip

A good source of acoustical foam and other sound control products is Auralex (www.auralex.com). Visit the company's website to obtain a personalized room analysis and see what type of sound control you need.

Additional Studio Resources

Whole books have been written on designing and building recording studios, home or otherwise. This isn't one of them, but here are a few I recommend:

- *Basic Home Studio Design* (Paul White, Sanctuary Publishing, 2002)
- *Building a Recording Studio* (Jeff Cooper, Synergy Group, 1984)
- *How to Build a Home Recording Studio from Scratch* (Michael Shea, TAB Electronics, 2002)

In addition, several websites offer articles, reviews, and user forums of use to the budding home recordist:

- Home Recording Connection (www.homerecordingconnection.com)
- HomeMusicRecording.com (www.homemusicrecording.com)
- HomeRecording.com (www.homerecording.com)
- Recording Studio Design Forum (www.johnlsayers.com/phpBB2/)
- The Recording Website (www.recordingwebsite.com)

Finally, *EQ* (www.eqmag.com), *MIX* (www.mixonline.com), and *Recording* (www.recordingmag.com) are three magazines targeted at the home recording market. They're all worth a read, and their websites also contain much useful information.

Recording Vocals

Even if you're setting up a simple MIDI studio, you still have to figure out how to record your vocal tracks. And recording vocals isn't quite the same as recording most acoustic instruments.

First, you probably don't want to record your vocals out in the middle of everything else. Most vocalists prefer a little privacy when they're singing, which you can achieve by sectioning off your main recording space with baffles, or by putting the singer in a separate room or vocal booth.

Some engineers prefer a vocal space to have some degree of reverberation. To this way of thinking, it's better to record vocals with a little natural reverb than to lay down totally dry tracks; the sound of a "live" room adds presence to the vocals, filling them out. (This is why you like the sound of your voice singing in a shower stall or stairwell; a full voice sounds better than a thin one.)

If you're going for a sound with natural reverb, don't rule out recording your vocals in a stairwell, garage, or bathroom. (Don't laugh; many professional studios use some variation of this technique.) That's because these areas have a very "live" sound with lots of reflections and reverberation from all the hard surfaces. You want some of that reverberation to make its way back to the microphone, to mix with the vocalist's natural singing voice.

Other engineers prefer to minimize the effect of the room on the vocal tracks. This means recording in a relatively dry room, without any natural reverberation or reflections. Reverb and other effects can then be added later in the mixing process.

To record this type of neutral vocal track, position the microphone in the middle of the room, away from any reflecting walls or surfaces. You may also need to use some acoustical foam, screens, or room dividers to soak up any stray reflections.

Whatever type of sound you're going for, you need to place the mic in front of the vocalist on a sturdy stand. You definitely don't want the singer to hold the microphone when recording; you also don't want to tempt the singer to grab the mic stand as she would during a live performance. (Any movement of the mic or the stand will be heard on the recording—not ideal.) The best approach is to use a tall boom stand that lets you hang the mic down in front of the singer. And always use a windscreen or pop filter to reduce sibilance.

Then there's the recording process itself. Vocalists can sometimes be maddeningly inconsistent, not only in their pitch and vocal inflections but also in how they approach the microphone. Don't be surprised to see the vocalist backing up and leaning forward throughout the recording, which plays havoc with your input levels. If she's too close to the mic, the meters go into the red; if she's too far away, the meters might not move at all. Short of nailing the vocalist in place precisely six inches away from the mic (a near-perfect distance), how can you cope with this?

One solution, of course, is to work the sliders mercilessly throughout the entire recording. This requires a lot of skill and no little amount of effort, but good engineers can make it work. A better solution, however, might be to invest in an outboard compressor unit, which is inserted into the chain between the mic (or mic preamp) and the mixing board/input box. The compressor automatically lowers the volume when the input exceeds a certain threshold, thus guarding against level peaks when the vocalist leans too far forward or turns up the volume. The compressor can also be set to boost low volume levels, thus evening out any dynamic flux. (Of course, you can also use Cubase's built-in compressor plug-in after the fact, but it's nice to have a trouble-free track to work with during the mixing process.)

Choosing Microphones

Garbage in, garbage out. That old adage applies particularly to recording vocals and acoustic instruments. A recording made with a low-quality microphone is going to sound mediocre, no matter how much post-recording processing you apply within Cubase. Start with a recording from a high-quality mic, however, and your mixing job gets a whole lot easier.

In other words, to create a high-quality recording, you have to start with a high-quality mic.

Choosing a microphone can be a tad confusing, however, as there are quite a few different choices available. We'll look at the available choices next.

Different Types of Microphones

There are two primary types of microphones used for recording today: dynamic and condenser. Each has its own particular acoustical characteristics.

Dynamic Microphones

Dynamic mics record via electromagnetic induction. A dynamic mic actually works like a backwards speaker; a small diaphragm inside the mic vibrates under sound pressure. The diaphragm is connected to a wound coil that moves within a magnetic field, which then generates a small amount of electricity. The electric signal represents the original audio waveform, and is sent to the mixer or recording console. Because the diaphragm generates its own electricity, dynamic mics do not require any outboard power.

Dynamic mics are best suited for recording acoustic instruments, rather than vocals. They're especially good for louder instruments, such as brass and woodwinds, and for mic'ing guitar amplifiers. (Figure 2.10 shows the workhorse Shure SM57, an affordably priced dynamic mic.)

Note

A high-end type of dynamic mic is the *ribbon microphone*. Ribbon mics use a corrugated metal "ribbon," similar to a filament in a light bulb, to generate electricity. These mics are very fragile and sensitive to loud sound pressure levels.

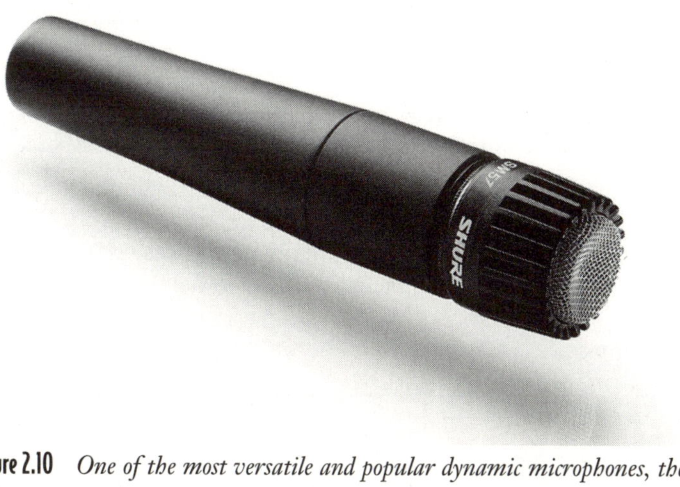

Figure 2.10 *One of the most versatile and popular dynamic microphones, the Shure SM57. (Courtesy of Shure Incorporated.)*

Condenser Microphones

Condenser mics are powered by an outboard power source (sometimes called *phantom power*), and are more sensitive than dynamic mics. Again, a diaphragm inside the mic vibrates under sound pressure; the resulting electric signal is generated via electrostatic induction. Within the family of condenser mics, those with larger diaphragms are more sensitive (and more expensive) than those with smaller diaphragms.

Condenser mics are best suited for recording vocals and some softer acoustic instruments, such as strings. They are not well suited to recording loud instruments, such as trumpets or trombones. (Figure 2.11 shows the Neumann TLM103, a popular condenser microphone.)

Figure 2.11 *The Neumann TLM103, a condenser mic often used to record lead vocals. (Courtesy of Georg Neumann GmbH.)*

Note

A *tube microphone* is a specific type of high-end condenser mic. A tube mic contains its own power supply, which is used to charge its diaphragm and back plate. The output signal is generated by the difference in capacitance between the diaphragm and the back plate. A vacuum tube is used to amplify the signal before it is sent to the mixer or recording console, resulting in a warmer sound than with other types of mics.

Different Pickup Patterns

Both dynamic and condenser microphones are available in a number of different response patterns. This refers to what sounds are picked up from which sides of the mic.

As shown in Figure 2.12, there are three different types of pickup patterns:

- **Omnidirectional**—picks up equally well from all directions.
- **Cardioid**—picks up sound in a heart-shaped pattern in front and to the sides of the mic.
- **Bidirectional**—picks up sound in a figure-eight pattern in front of and behind the mic

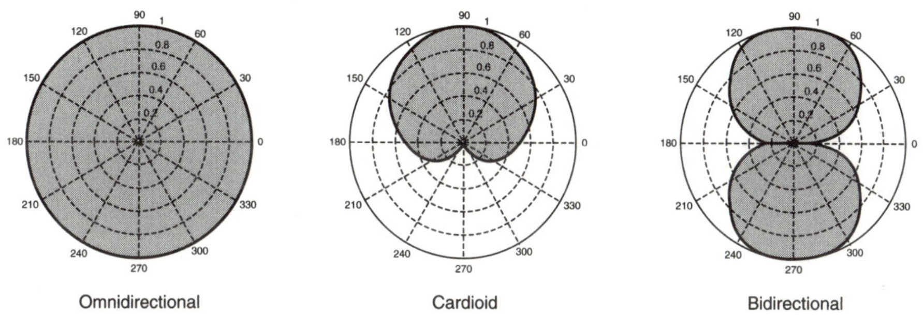

Figure 2.12 *Omnidirectional, cardioid, and bidirectional pickup patterns.*

To record a relatively dead sound in the studio, use a cardioid mic. To record a sound with some room reverberation, consider using an omnidirectional mic.

> **Note**
>
> In addition to the standard cardioid pattern, super-cardioid and hyper-cardioid mics also pick up highly directional sound from directly behind the mic.

Cables and Plugs

Lower-priced microphones, and those designed for live performance, typically come with ¼" plugs, as shown in Figure 2.13. As you've probably already noticed, you can't plug a ¼" plug into the ⅛" jacks found on the back of your personal computer. This is why you need some sort of audio breakout box, with ¼" jacks, when you're doing serious recording.

Higher-end microphones come with balanced XLR connectors, such as that shown in Figure 2.14. These connectors are more resistant to rough handling, and (more important) less likely to pick up electrical buzz and hum from other instruments. Most higher-end audio interface boxes come with XLR jacks.

Obviously, you should make sure that your mics, audio input devices, mixers, and such all use the same type of input—and that you have enough (and long enough) cables to connect all the instruments you'll be recording.

> **Tip**
>
> When choosing a microphone, don't forget a proper microphone stand (a sturdy boom stand is versatile enough to use with almost all instruments) and some sort of windscreen/pop filter, to cut down on hissy s's and popping p's.

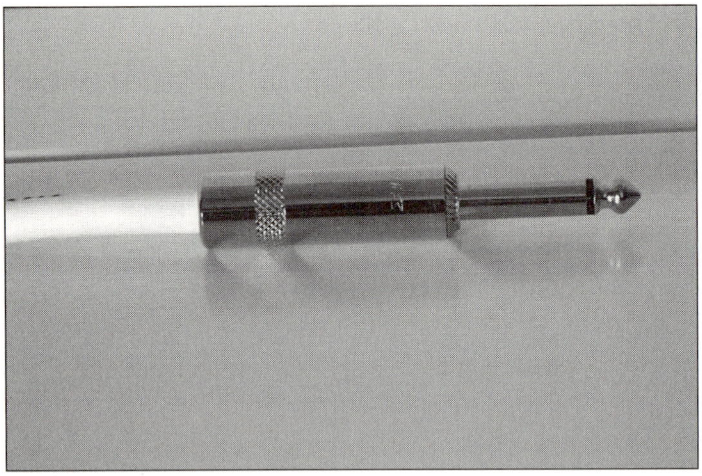

Figure 2.13 *A ¼" microphone plug.*

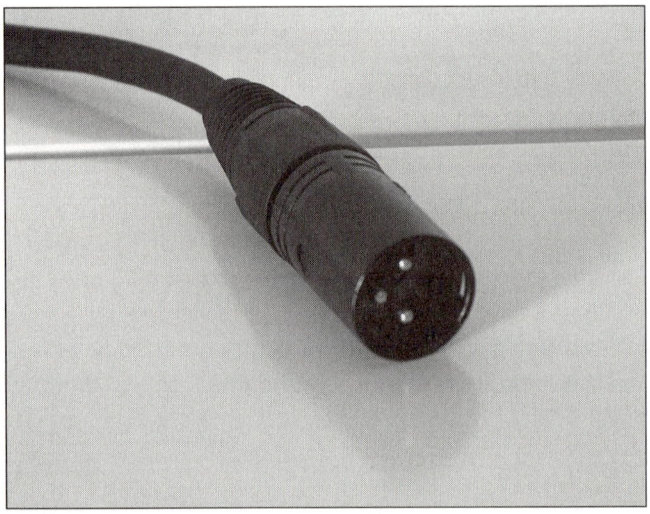

Figure 2.14 *An XLR microphone connector.*

Power and Pre-Amplification

As you learned previously, some types of mics have their own built-in power, and some require what is called *phantom power*. In particular, all condenser mics require some sort of power. Some condensers are battery powered (using one of those little watch-type batteries), while others receive phantom power via the mic cable. These mics have an extra prong on the XLR connector, and receive power from your sound card, audio input device, or mixer. In addition, many microphones require some sort of pre-amplification to generate a strong enough signal for recording. This is typically not an issue with dynamic mics, but is something to consider with condenser mics. If you need to boost your mic's signal (and you'll know when you start to record), you'll need to invest in a separate pre-amplifier. Many different models are available, from single-input units to 4- and 8-input boxes that also perform rudimentary mixing functions. Check them out before you record.

Tip

Some electric instruments don't need to be mic'ed. Electric guitars, basses, and keyboards can be recorded via "direct injection," where the instrument is plugged directly into the computer or mixing console. With this approach, effects can be added later to achieve different types of sound. (Or, as some engineers prefer, you can mix the sound recorded via direct injection with that recorded by placing a microphone in front of the instrument's amplifier, getting the best of both worlds.)

What Mics Should You Use?

If you're just starting out with your Cubase recording studio, you're no doubt asking the question, "How many mics do I need?" Well, it all depends on what you're recording, how you're recording it, and what kind of budget you have.

If you're recording one instrument or vocal track at a time, you can get by with a single mic. In spite of what you might think about stereo recording, you don't need two mics to record one instrument; your single input can be routed to stereo within Cubase.

That said, certain types of live recordings do benefit from using two microphones. Let's say you're recording a group of singers; setting up two mics lets the vocals pan across the entire stereo sound field. (Stereo recording is also recommended when recording live orchestra, concert band, and choral performances.)

If you're recording a pop, rock, or country band live in the studio, you'll need enough mics to go around for all the musicians who are playing at the same time. While you can direct inject guitars and keyboards, you'll still need mics for acoustic guitars, acoustic piano, drums, and vocals.

Speaking of drums, there are a number of ways to approach recording an entire drum set. The basic approach puts two mics overhead and slightly in front of the kit, to capture the total sound. This is often augmented by a single mic positioned between the snare drum and hi hat (to beef up the backbeat) and another mic placed inside or in front of the bass drum (to capture the basic pulse). Moving beyond this four-mic setup, many professional engineers put a separate mic on each tom and over each cymbal. This might be overkill for home recording, but it does offer the most isolation and flexibility.

If you're on a budget, a good all-around microphone is the Shure SM57 (~$100). This dynamic mic (with a cardioid pattern) is a long-time standard for both live and recording purposes, and can be used to record just about any kind of instrument, from acoustic guitars to drums. (In a pinch, you can also use the SM57 to record vocals.) If you have a bigger budget, consider the Sennheiser MD 421 (~$400) or, moving into the condenser category, the Neumann KM183 (~$800).

For recording drums, the Shure SM57 works well for overhead, snare, and tom use. For the bass drum, you want a mic designed specifically for this purpose, such as the Shure Beta 52 (~$200).

Probably the most important microphone in your setup is the main vocal mic; save a big part of your budget for this. You want a large diaphragm condenser mic with a cardioid pattern, such as the Neumann TLM103 (~$1,000) or Shure KSM44 (~$700).

Finally, for voiceover work you don't have to go quite as expensive. Consider the Electro Voice RE20 (~$400) or the Shure SM7B (~$350), both good-quality dynamic mics with very smooth response curves.

The Least You Need to Know

- For best results, you need a relatively fast computer with lots of memory and hard disk space. Both Windows and Macintosh models work equally well.
- For accurate playback of your recordings, you should invest in a pair of powered monitor speakers.
- If you're recording one track at a time, you'll need a simple audio input box and (if you're recording via MIDI) a MIDI interface box; if you're recording multiple tracks all at once, you'll need an external multi-track mixer, called a control surface.
- The type of studio space you create depends on the type of recording you'll be doing, as well as your available space. It's easy to convert a spare bedroom, basement, or garage into a serviceable home studio; you'll want to make the room as dead as possible, using sound-absorbing materials.
- You'll need to assemble an assortment of microphones for all the acoustic instruments and vocals you'll be recording. Dynamic mics are fine for recording most instruments, but you'll want a good-quality condenser mic to record lead vocals.

Chapter 3

Mastering the Cubase Workspace

In This Chapter

- The parts of the Cubase workspace
- Navigating the project window
- Using the transport panel
- Operating the mixer
- Opening and saving recording projects

Back in Chapter 1 you saw what the Cubase workspace looks like when you first start the program, before you load or create a recording project. As you remember, it's empty—except for the transport panel at the bottom. There's the standard set of pull-down menus at the top of the screen, of course, but other than that there's nothing there.

The Cubase Workspace

When you look at the Cubase window as a whole, you're looking at the Cubase workspace. Everything you do in Cubase is done somewhere within this workspace; all the windows and controls are displayed here, either side by side or in some sort of overlapping fashion.

Tip

Given all the individual windows and controls you can display within the workspace, it makes sense to maximize the workspace so that it fills up your entire screen. It's also a good idea to set your computer monitor's resolution to its maximum setting, so that you can fit as much on the screen as possible. (At a minimum, you'll want to display 768 × 1024 resolution; 1024 × 1280 is even better.)

When you first start the program, before you load or create a recording project, the Cubase workspace is completely empty—except for the transport panel at the bottom. There's the standard set of pull-down menus at the top of the screen, of course, but other than that there's nothing there.

After you load a project, however, everything changes. As you can see in Figure 3.1, the workspace is now filled with three main windows/controls—the project window, the transport panel, and the mixer.

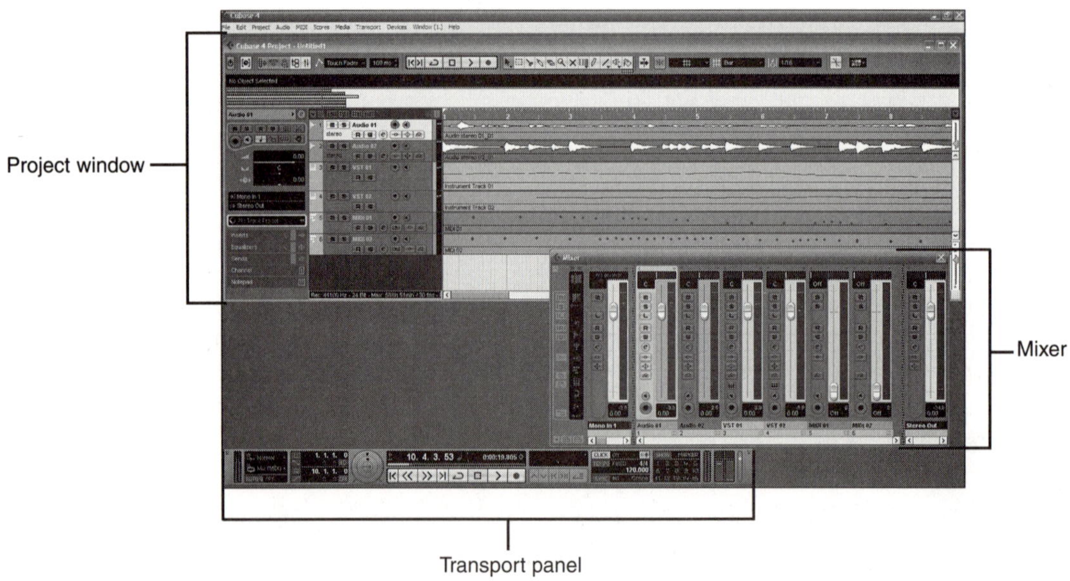

Figure 3.1 *An active Cubase workspace.*

Organizing the Workspace

In fact, the workspace can get quite crowded; when you have windows sitting on top of windows, it's sometimes tough to get to the part of the program you want to use. Fortunately, Cubase lets you organize your workspace however you like it, and then save that layout for use in the future.

You can rearrange and resize the various windows manually, or you can choose to automatically tile or cascade the windows. The automatic option is located on the Window menu; just pull down the menu and select from Tile Horizontally, Tile Vertically, or Cascade.

After you have your workspace organized to your satisfaction, you can save this layout by selecting **Window > Workspaces > New Workspace.** When the New Workspace dialog box appears, enter a name for the workspace, then click **OK.** The layout is now saved.

To use this layout in the future, select **Window > Workspaces** and then choose the workspace by name.

Customizing the Interface

Cubase also lets you customize the program interface, to some degree. You can brighten or dim various parts of the interface, select certain items to hide or display, and even change the color of the recording meters. I'll let you explore these options on your own; you do the customization from within the Preferences dialog box, which you display by selecting **File > Preferences.**

Using Cubase's Controls

All of Cubase's main windows contain an assortment of sliders, knobs, buttons, and other controls. Many of these controls are very small and might appear to be difficult to use. If nothing else, some are difficult to figure out; do you click or turn or press or what?

Here's one key point to remember. You operate all Cubase's controls—no matter what they look like—by using your mouse. If it's a button, you use your mouse to click it. If it's a slider, you use your mouse to drag it. If it's a knob, you use your mouse to turn it (sometimes while holding down the Shift key on your computer keyboard).

Many of Cubase's controls don't look like controls. They may look like icons, or flat graphics, or arrows. In most instances, these controls activate when you click them; click a down-arrow, for example, and you might expand a panel or display a pop-up menu.

If you're not sure whether something is a functional control or just a decorative part of the interface, just hover your cursor over it. If it's a control, Cubase will display a tooltip with its name. If no tooltip appears, you're hovering over nothing important.

The Project Window

The big window in the middle of the Cubase workspace is called the *project window*, and it's where most of the action takes place. Each recording project has its own project window, which provides you with an overview of the project. You use the project window to examine your recordings, both while you're recording and afterward. The project window is also an area where you can make adjustments to your tracks (adding effects, EQ, and the like), as well as initiate any editing that's necessary.

As you can see in Figure 3.2, the project window is divided into several individual sections, many of which you can turn on or off. We'll look at each section in turn.

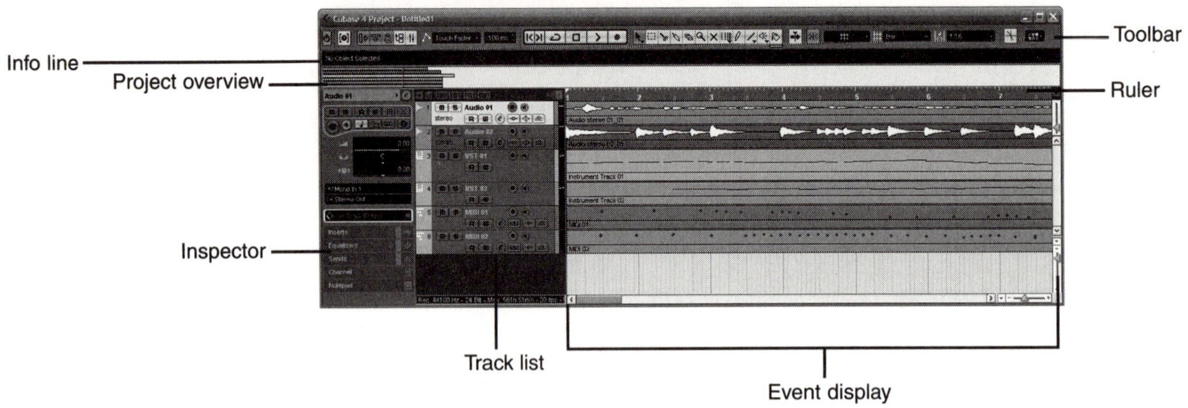

Figure 3.2 *The parts of the project window.*

Toolbar

The *toolbar*, shown in Figures 3.3 and 3.4, is displayed at the very top of the project window. It contains a series of controls and buttons that initiate key operations. Included in the toolbar is a set of transport controls that duplicate the same controls found in the transport panel.

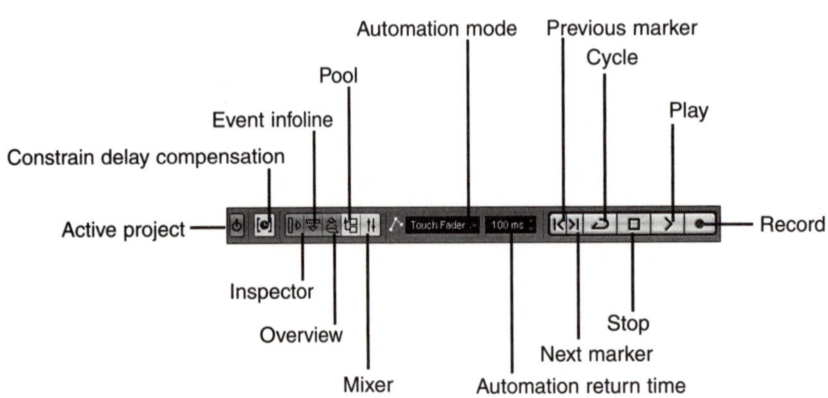

Figure 3.3 *The left side of the Cubase 4 toolbar.*

We'll discuss the various parts of the toolbar as the related topics arise throughout the book. For now, remember that you can display the name of each tool by hovering your cursor over that part of the toolbar.

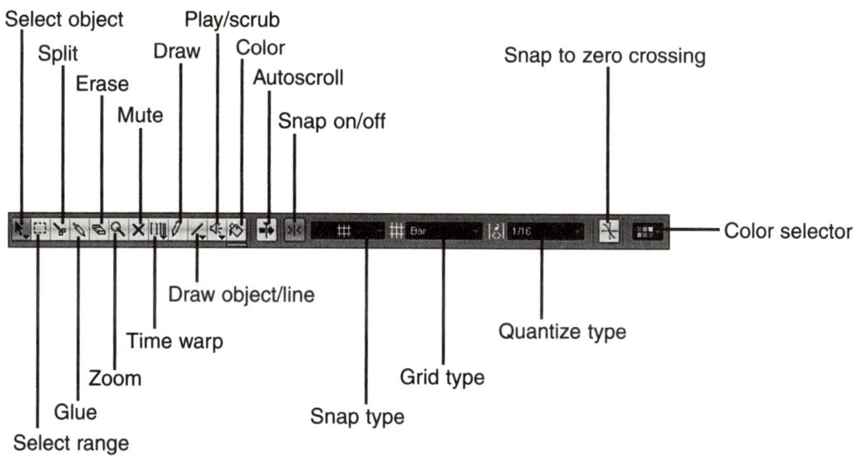

Figure 3.4 *The right side of the Cubase 4 toolbar.*

Info Line

The info line (Figure 3.5) displays information about the currently selected event—start time, end time, length, and so on. You display the info line by clicking the **Info Line** button on the toolbar.

Figure 3.5 *The info line.*

Overview

The overview (Figure 3.6) displays a reduced view of all the recorded events on all the tracks. The blue rectangle illustrates what part of the overview is currently shown in the event display. You display the overview by clicking the **Overview** button on the toolbar.

Figure 3.6 *The overview.*

Ruler

The ruler (Figure 3.7) appears over the event display area of the project window and displays the timeline of the project. You use the ruler to track the length of your recording over time.

You can change what the ruler measures if you right-click on the ruler and select a new measurement from the pop-up menu. You can opt to have the ruler display the following:

- Bars+Beats (measure bars, individual beats, sixteenth notes, and ticks)
- Seconds (elapsed time in hours, minutes, seconds, and milliseconds)

- Timecode (for video projects; displays hours, minutes, seconds, and frames)
- Samples (individual sound samples)
- User (similar to Timecode for video use; displays hours, minutes, seconds, and frames, with a user-definable frames per second)

Figure 3.7 *The ruler, displaying Bars+Beats.*

Inspector

The track inspector (Figure 3.8) is the area to the left of the track list. In essence, the inspector displays additional controls and settings for the selected track. When you click a track in the track list, the inspector displays information for that track. Click a different track, and the inspector changes to display information for the new track.

The information displayed in the inspector is divided into individual sections, and is somewhat different for different types of tracks. For audio tracks, the bottom half of the inspector includes sections for Inserts, Equalizers, Sends, Channel (a duplication of the channel strip in the Mixer), and Notepad. To display the full panel, click the icon to the right of the section name.

Figure 3.8 *The inspector for an audio track.*

Track List

The track list (Figure 3.9) displays all the available tracks in your project, from top to bottom. Naturally, the number and type of tracks displayed depends on your individual project. A simple project, such as the one we did back in Chapter 1, might only have one or two tracks. A more ambitious project, such as the one shown here, might have 16 or 24 or more tracks, each devoted to a specific instrument or microphone.

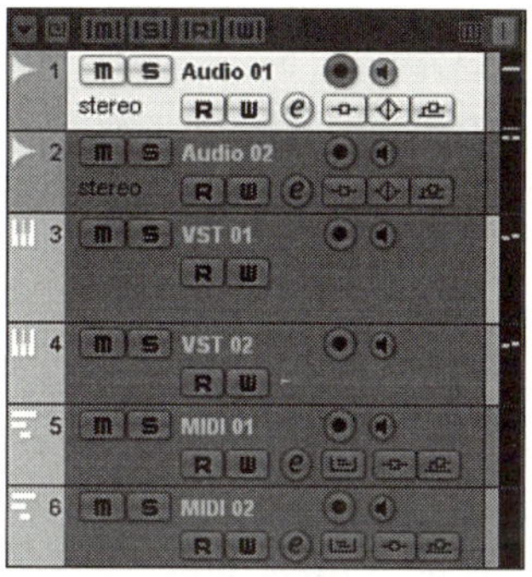

Figure 3.9 *The track list.*

Within the track list area are various settings for each track. In the default configuration, you'll find an area for the track name (which you can edit) and buttons for Mute, Solo, Record Enable, Monitor, and so on. You can opt to display specialized subsets of these controls by clicking the down arrow above the track list; your options include Recording—Minimal, Editing, and Mixing.

Tip

To view more (or fewer) of the controls in the track list, you can make the entire track list area wider or narrower. Just drag the right-hand border of this area right or left, as necessary.

Types of Tracks

Cubase's project window displays several different types of tracks. These track types include:

- **Audio,** which is used for audio recording.
- **MIDI,** which is used for MIDI recording.
- **Instrument,** used to record Cubase's VST instruments.
- **Folder,** which contains multiple other tracks.
- **FX channel,** which contains send effects created by Cubase's various audio processors.
- **Group channel,** which contains multiple audio channels for the purpose of applying the same effects to all channels.
- **Marker,** which displays positioning markers for the project.
- **Play order,** which enables you to mark out sections of the project for playback in a particular order.
- **Ruler,** which contains a timeline of the project.
- **Video,** which contains video events.

Editing Track Names

Cubase gives each track a rather unimaginative name—Audio 01, MIDI 02, and so on. It's much more useful to name each track for the instrument that it's recording. So Audio 01 might be better named Lead Guitar, and MIDI 02 could be labeled String Section.

Renaming tracks is one of the easiest things you can do in Cubase. To rename a track, just double-click on its label in the track list, then type in the new label. That's it.

Rearranging and Color-Coding Tracks

By default, tracks are listed in the track list in the order that they were first added to the project. If you're making a large multi-track recording, however, you may want to group your tracks in a different order. For example, you may want to group all the drum tracks together, or all the vocal tracks together, or all the guitar tracks together, and so on.

You can change the order of the tracks by dragging any track to a new position within the track list. Just position your cursor in any blank area of the track controls, hold down the left mouse button, and drag that track to another position within the track list. As you move the cursor up or down the list, you should see a green line move from track to track; this shows the position of the track you're dragging. When the green line is where you want the track positioned, release the mouse button.

> **Tip**
>
> The horizontal zoom slider (just around the window corner from the vertical zoom slider) is used to expand or contract the length of the elements in the event display. Move the slider to the right to expand the ruler and view more fine detail; move the slider to the left to contract the ruler and fit a longer period on-screen.

Another way to organize your tracks is to color-code them. Again, you may want all drum tracks colored red, all keyboard tracks colored blue, and so on. To recolor a track, activate the show track colors feature by clicking on the multi-colored boxes just left of the ruler. Then click the colored bar to the right of the track in the track list; this displays a rainbow-like color menu. Select the color you want from this list.

Resizing Tracks

There's one last bit of reconfiguring you may want to do with your track list. By default, the tracks in the list are only a single line tall, which means that most of the controls extend well over to the right—and are thus hidden from view. If you want to view more of the track controls, you can expand the height of each individual track. You can make this area two, three, even four lines tall.

To adjust the height of your tracks, use the vertical zoom slider at the lower right of the project window.

Event Display

To the right of the track list is the event display (Figure 3.10). This part of the project window is divided into a series of horizontal *events* for each track. An event is simply one instance of recording. When you record on an audio or MIDI track, you create a recording event; a project that hasn't yet been recorded will have an empty event display area.

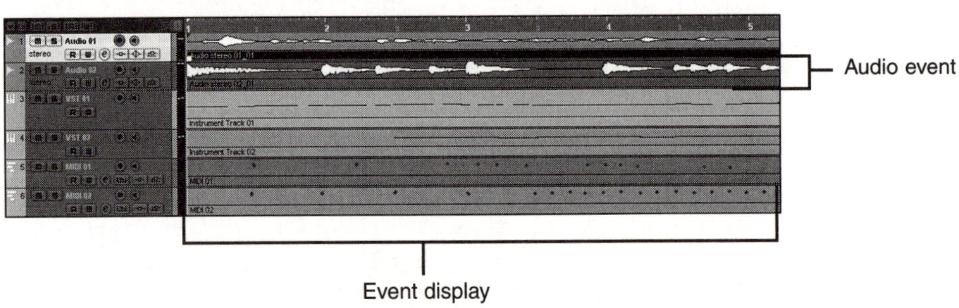

Figure 3.10 *The event display, with recorded events for several tracks.*

A single track can contain multiple events, each recorded at a different point in time. You can layer events on top of events, as you rerecord over an existing track. And if you connect multiple events together, you create what Cubase calls a *part*.

Note

Audio events display a waveform of the recording. MIDI events display a bar of the MIDI information.

The Transport Panel

The transport panel, shown in Figure 3.11 and 3.12, is exactly as described; it contains the transport controls you use to stop and start recording and playback. The controls are very similar to those you might find on any tape recorder or DVD recorder, with several more specialized controls added.

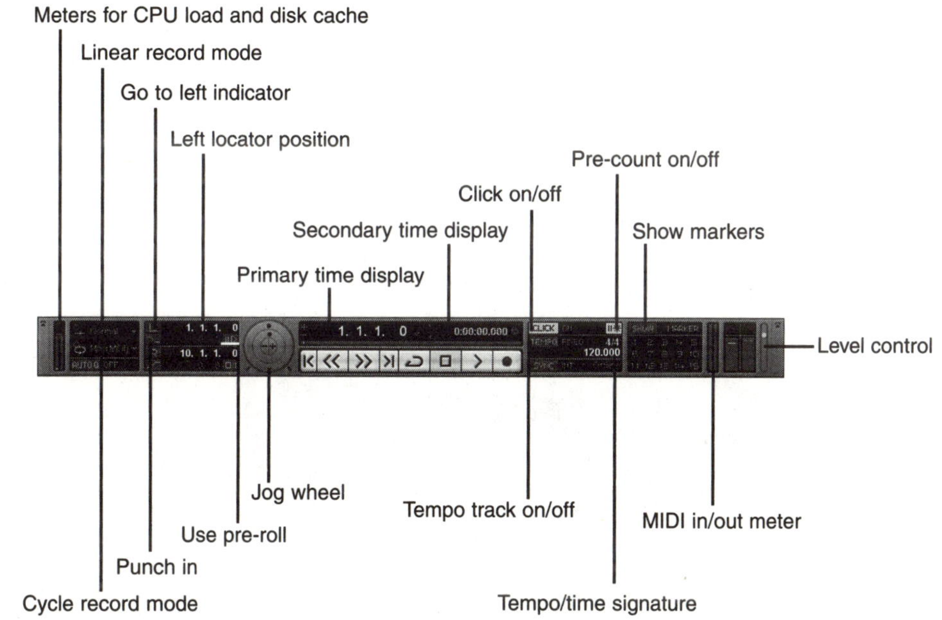

Figure 3.11 *The transport panel.*

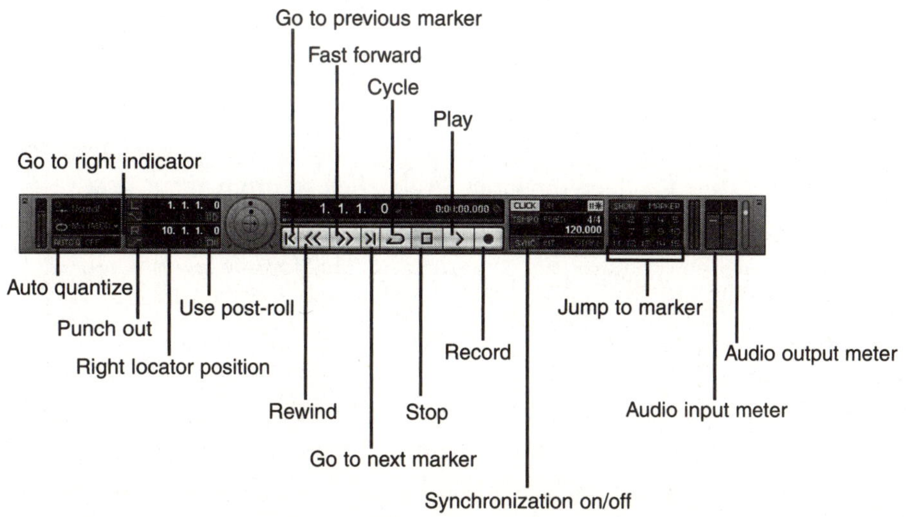

Figure 3.12 *Transport controls on the transport panel.*

Tip

If the transport panel is ever closed by mistake, you can redisplay it by selecting **Transport > Transport Panel,** or pressing F2.

You can customize which controls are displayed in the transport panel if you right-click anywhere in the panel and then check and uncheck the available features. I discuss the individual controls as the related topics arise throughout the book. For now, know that you can use the transport panel not only to control your recording and playback, but also to monitor and control a variety of recording activities.

The Mixer

The mixer, shown in Figure 3.13, is a virtual version of the physical track mixers you find in professional recording studios. You use the mixer to adjust recording levels and other controls while you're recording, mixing, and mastering.

There are three ways to display the mixer window. You can click the **Mixer** button on the project window toolbar; you can select **Devices > Mixer** from the pull-down menu; or you can press F3 on your computer keyboard.

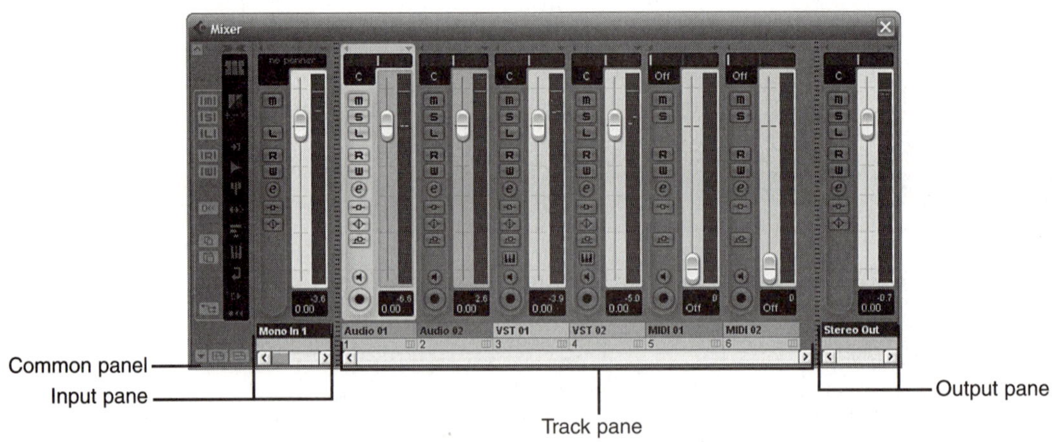

Figure 3.13 *The mixer window in routing view.*

Note

If you have more tracks than the mixer can display at one time, scroll bars will appear below each pane. You can then scroll left to right through the channel strips of that particular type.

The mixer contains a series of *channel strips,* each representing an input, output, or recording channel or track. The channel strips in the mixer are arranged by type in four separate panes, as follows:

- **Common panel,** containing global settings for all channels.
- **Input pane,** containing controls for each individual input on your system. You use this pane to adjust the input levels when recording.
- **Tracks pane,** containing channel strips for each audio and MIDI track in your recording. You use this pane to adjust the volume levels when mixing.
- **Output pane,** containing a channel strip for your system's output.

Each channel strip contains a variety of controls for a specific channel or track. As you can see in Figure 3.14, these controls let you adjust the track's input level, enable/disable recording and monitoring, edit channel settings, enable read and write automation, and so on.

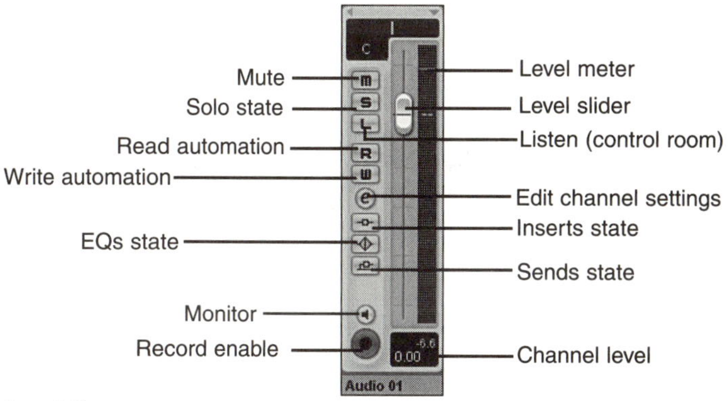

Figure 3.14 *An audio channel strip in the mixer.*

By default, the mixer is displayed in a somewhat compact view called the routing view. If you want to display even more controls for each channel, right-click at the top of the mixer and select **Window > Show Extended View** from the pop-up window. As you can see in Figure 3.15, you now have a larger top area in which to display additional controls. You can choose which controls to show by clicking the down arrow above each channel strip, and then selecting what you want from the pop-up menu. This lets you display different information for each channel.

Figure 3.15 *The mixer window in extended view.*

All these controls for all these channels let you control the sound of your recordings. You adjust the level sliders in real time as you record, or when you mix the tracks you've recorded. Get to know the mixer; you'll be using it a lot.

Display Tips

Given that both the project window and the mixer are equally important and should both be displayed when you're making a recording, you're faced with the issue of how to fit them both on the screen at the same time, in a usable manner. This is no small problem.

One solution is to use as big a monitor as possible, and set your display for the highest resolution possible, in order to fit more information on screen. Here is where a 20" or larger monitor, perhaps with a widescreen display, is ideal. (I recommend Apple 23" and 30" Cinema HD displays, which will work with both Apple and Windows computers.)

Another solution is to install two video cards in your computer and use a dual monitor setup. With this type of configuration, you can put the project window and transport panel on one screen, and the mixer on the other.

Opening and Saving Projects

As you know now, neither the project window nor the mixer is active until you've loaded a *project*—either a new one or one you've previously recorded. When you create a new project, you can start from scratch or you can get a jump-start by using a pre-designed template.

If you choose to start from scratch, you start with an empty project window (no tracks) and build your project up from there, one track at a time. If you choose to start with a template, you start with a predetermined track layout. Either method is good, although using a template is often faster.

def•i•ni•tion

Cubase calls each master recording you make a **project**. A project consists of one or more recorded tracks, in either audio or MIDI format, as well as all the effects and processing associated with those tracks. If you were recording an album of ten songs, you would create ten separate projects—one for each song on the album.

Creating a New Blank Project

When you created your simple project in Chapter 1, you used the start-from-scratch approach. With this method, you take an empty project window and add as many tracks as you need for your recording. If you're just recording acoustic guitar and vocals, you would add two tracks. If you're recording a big band, you might add 24 tracks or more. You tailor your project to what you're recording.

To create a new project from scratch, follow these steps:

1. From within Cubase, select **File > New Project.**
2. When the New Project dialog box appears, as shown in Figure 3.16, select **Empty,** then click **OK.**
3. When the Select Directory dialog box appears, select where you want to save your project, then click **OK.**

You now have a blank canvas from which to work. You add tracks to your project by selecting **Project > Add Track,** then choosing the type of track to add (typically Audio or MIDI).

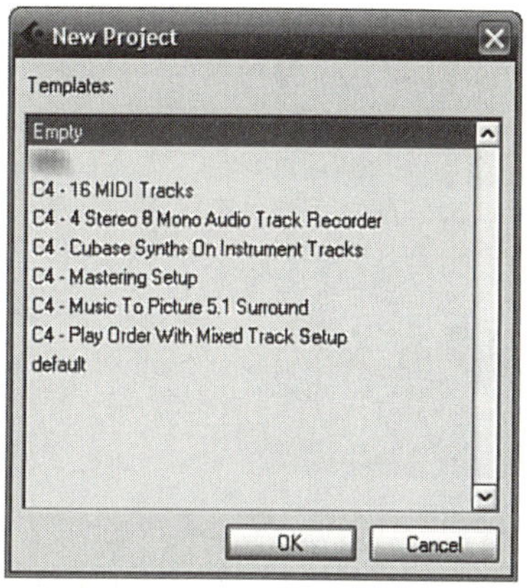

Figure 3.16 *Opening a new project from the New Project dialog box.*

Creating a New Project from a Template

When you create a new project from a template, everything you need is already there—all the tracks, all the settings, and so on. You can start recording almost immediately.

Cubase 4 comes from the factory with five pre-defined templates installed:

- **16 MIDI Tracks,** ideal for MIDI-only recordings
- **4 Stereo 8 Mono Audio Track Recorder,** ideal for multi-track audio-only recordings (shown in Figure 3.17)
- **Cubase Synths on Instrument Tracks,** ideal for recording Cubase's VST instruments
- **Mastering Setup,** ideal for final CD mastering
- **Music to Picture 5.1 Surround,** with 4 audio tracks for surround sound recordings
- **Play Order with Mixed Track Setup,** with 4 audio tracks, 4 MIDI tracks, and 4 VST instrument tracks

To create a new template-based project, follow these steps:

1. From within Cubase, select **File > New Project.**
2. When the New Project dialog box appears, select the desired template, then click **OK.**
3. When the Select Directory dialog box appears, select where you want to save your project then click **OK.**

As with any other project, you're not limited to the number or types of tracks included in the template. After the project is open, you can add or delete tracks as necessary.

Figure 3.17 *A new project based on the 4 Stereo 8 Mono Audio Track Recorder template.*

Saving Your Own Templates

Let's assume that Cubase's built-in templates won't always meet your own personal recording needs. Maybe you prefer a 16-track recording. Maybe you need a mix of 24 audio tracks and 16 MIDI tracks. Maybe you prefer a minimalist environment with just two tracks for recording.

However you like to work, you can set up Cubase accordingly—and then save that setup as a template for future use. Follow these steps:

1. Set up your project with the desired number and types of tracks. (But don't record anything yet—you only want to save empty tracks!)
2. Select **File > Save As Template.**
3. When the Save As Template dialog box appears, enter a name for your template, then click **OK.**

The next time you want to create a new project, your newly created template will be included in the template list.

Saving Your Project

After you start working on a new project, you need to save your work. To save a new project, follow these steps:

1. Select **File > Save As.**
2. When the Save As dialog box appears, enter a name and location for the project.
3. Click **OK.**

After you've initially saved and named your project, you can save your continuing work by selecting **File > Save.**

Re-opening an Existing Project

Few projects are created and completed in a single session. Cubase lets you re-open existing projects to continue your work; you can take as long as you want to finish your recording.

To re-open an existing project, follow these steps:

1. Select **File > Open.**
2. When the Open Project dialog box appears, navigate to the folder where the project is stored.
3. Select the project to open.
4. Click the **Open** button.

Just remember—when you start editing your project, you should always (and frequently) save your work!

The Least You Need to Know

- You can arrange the windows in the Cubase workspace in any fashion you like, and then save that layout for future use.
- The main window in the workspace is the project window, which contains the track list, event display, and track inspector.
- The transport panel contains the controls you use to start and stop recording and playback.
- You use the mixer to set recording levels and mix the tracks for your final recording.
- When you create a new recording project, you can start with an empty workspace, or use one of Cubase's predesigned templates.

Part 2

Recording

This is what Cubase is all about—recording! There are actually two different ways you can record in Cubase, traditional audio recording or MIDI recording. You'll learn how to do both.

Chapter 4

Recording Audio Tracks

In This Chapter

- Configuring Cubase for audio recording
- Monitoring the recording and creating a monitor mix
- Using a click track
- Making the recording
- Recording additional tracks
- Overdubbing an existing track

Cubase accommodates two similar-but-different types of recording—the recording of traditional audio tracks and the recording of MIDI tracks. I talk about MIDI recording in Chapter 5; in this chapter, I focus on traditional audio recording. Of course, I'm not sure how traditional recording can be when you're doing it on a computer. Instead of recording to reel-to-reel tape, you're recording to a computer hard disk; a Cubase recording is 100% digital, as opposed to the analog recording that held sway until the 1980s. But those (major) changes aside, Cubase's audio recording features let you record any instruments and vocalists that can be mic'ed or connected directly to your computer or mixer—just like they did it in the reel-to-reel days.

When you make an audio recording with Cubase, you get to "work the board" just like you would in a professional recording studio. You can slide the level meters to adjust the recording volume, twiddle the knobs to apply equalization, even punch in and punch out edits on previously recorded tracks. But because you're recording digitally, you also have the option of editing your recording in a number of ways, including copying and deleting sections, speeding up and slowing down the tempo, even raising or lowering the pitch. When you make a digital recording, what you end up with are bits and bytes on a hard disk; editing is as easy as manipulating those digital ones and zeros. This is, of course, a good thing; in the old analog reel-to-reel tape days, editing involved splicing the tape, and the only way to change pitch or tempo was to play the tape faster or slower. Digital audio recording is definitely a good thing.

I talk more about editing and processing your audio recordings in Chapters 6 and 7; right now, I'm going to focus on the recording process itself. And, as you've probably come to expect, making an audio recording with Cubase starts with a fair amount of prep work, in the form of setting up your project and configuring some important settings.

Configuring Cubase for Audio Recording

> **Caution**
> The ASIO Multimedia driver has higher latency rates than the other drivers, which means that there may be a noticeable delay between what you play and what you hear when recording MIDI and VST instruments. This is why you want to choose one of the other drivers, if available.

When you're recording straight audio (in other words, not MIDI), you have to tell Cubase what audio device(s) you're using. You do this from Cubase's Device Setup dialog box. Just follow these steps:

1. Select **Devices > Device Setup;** this displays the Device Setup dialog box, shown in Figure 4.1.
2. From the tree list in the Devices pane (on the left side of the window), click **VST Audio System.**
3. In the right-side pane, pull down the ASIO Driver list.
4. All available drivers should be listed. You need to select the best driver for your system. If your audio card supports ASIO, an ASIO driver for that card will be listed, and should be selected. (This card-specific driver will give the best performance.) The next-best choice is the ASIO DirectX Full Duplex driver, if available. Of course, if you're using an external control surface or audio input device, select the driver for that device. If none of these options are available, you can select the ASIO Multimedia driver.
5. Click the **Apply** button, then click the **OK** button.

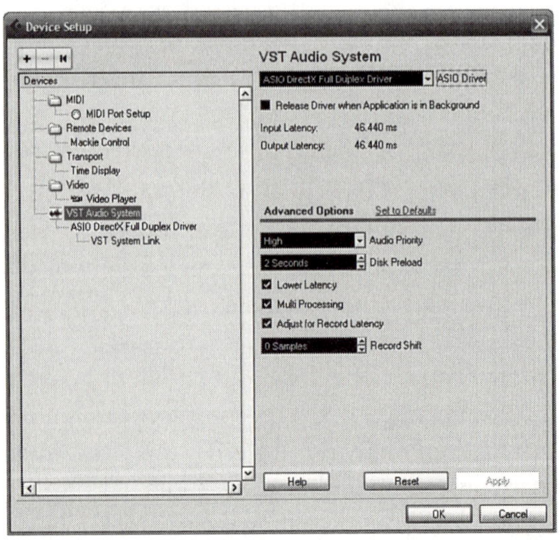

Figure 4.1 *Selecting an audio device from the device setup window.*

In some instances you may need to configure the settings for this driver. (This is necessary if you get an error when running the automatic device test, or if the device's manufacturer recommends specific settings.) If so, you'll need to return to the devices pane and select your ASIO driver. Then, in the right-side pane, click the **Control Panel** button. (Or, on a Mac, open the control panel from the System Preferences menu on the Apple menu.) Configure the settings as directed by the device's manufacturer.

> **Note**
>
> Space doesn't permit the discussion of all of Cubase's configuration options, or the topic of troubleshooting problem setups. If you have questions or problems connecting and configuring any specific piece of equipment, go to the Cubase operation manual or to Steinberg's website and online knowledge base (www.steinberg.de).

Before You Record: Do Your Homework!

Think that's all you need to do to prepare Cubase for recoding? Think again. Before you make any type of recording in Cubase, you have to create a new project and set up the workspace for what you're recording. Not that you can't change things in mid-process, but you probably should do a bit of homework beforehand to get the workspace set up properly.

What do you need to know before you start recording? Here's a brief checklist to go through:

Pre-Recording Checklist for Audio Recordings

- ❏ What type of music are you recording?
- ❏ How many different instruments and voices will you be recording, and how many separate audio tracks will you need?
- ❏ How many musicians will be playing at the same time?
- ❏ Will you be recording the entire recording live, or will some parts of the recording be overdubbed later?
- ❏ Is the tempo constant throughout the piece, or does it vary at all?
- ❏ What is the destination media for this recording, and what level of recording quality will you need?

Important questions, all—and here's why.

The type of music you record affects your entire project. As you might imagine, recording a classical string quartet is a much different job than recording a four-piece rock band—even though the same number of instruments is involved. Recording classical music requires different mic'ing strategies than does recording rock music; you might only use two mics to record the four strings, whereas the rock band might require 16 or more mics (multiple mics on the drums!) with some instruments plugged directly into the computer or mixing console. In addition, you have different dynamics to worry about; classical music can vary considerably between loud and soft passages, where rock music is mainly loud. This is why you need to know what you're recording up front, so you know what to expect and prepare for.

Obviously, knowing how many instruments you're recording determines how many tracks you need to record—and you need to set up your track arrangement before you press the record button. Of course, the number of instruments/vocalists doesn't always translate into a like number of tracks;

mic'ing a drum set might require anywhere from four to eight mics, whereas you might have two or three background singers singing into a single mic. Again, plan it out ahead of time.

If you have multiple musicians playing live, you'll need to arrange monitoring for all those musicians. Recording one musician at a time is easier in this regard.

Tempo is another important consideration. If the tempo is constant throughout the piece, you probably want to record to a *click track*. On the other hand, if you have a lot of shifting tempos (or if you're playing more fluid types of music, such as classical or jazz), a click track will probably just get in the way. Whichever you choose, you need to do it up front; you can't go back and add a click after you've made a recording with a more flowing tempo.

def•i•ni•tion

A **click track** is a metronome-like click that sounds on every beat of each measure, in time to the selected tempo. You use a click track to help all the musicians play to the same steady beat.

Finally, it's important to know why you're making this recording—that is, what the destination media is. If you're making a quick-and-dirty recording for web-only downloading, you don't need to record at audiophile-level quality. On the other hand, if you're aiming to release your recording on CD, you want to record at the highest quality level possible. Know, however, that the higher quality level you select, the more disc space you use; it's a trade-off.

Setting Up Your Audio Recording Project

After you've worked through the pre-recording checklist, it's time to get started. And you get started by creating a new project, and configuring the workspace to your specific needs.

Creating a New Project

I discussed this before, but I'll go ahead and do it again, just in case you slept through those chapters. Your audio recording will be made within a unique recording project, and you create a new project by following these steps:

1. From within Cubase, select **File > New Project.**
2. When the New Project dialog box appears, select **Empty,** then click **OK.**
3. When the Select Directory dialog box appears, select where you want to save your project, and then click **OK.**

Tip

Remember to save your new project and to give it a unique and functional name.

These instructions assume you want to create an empty project and add the specific tracks you need, rather than working from a pre-designed recording template. If you find that one of Cubase's templates perfectly suits your needs, feel free to go that route, instead. Just remember—you can customize any workspace for the number and type of tracks you actually need.

Adding Tracks

The project now created, it's time to customize it for your specific recording needs. First and foremost, that means adding tracks for each instrument or vocalist you'll be recording.

Before you add tracks, of course, you need to plan out what instruments you'll be using, how you'll be mic'ing them (or, with guitar, bass, and keyboards, if you'll be recording them directly into the computer/console), and in what order you want to place the tracks. Order within the Cubase mixer is arbitrary, but it helps to group like instruments when you later add EQ and effects during the mixing process.

One of the most useful new features in Cubase 4 is the ability to add pre-configured audio tracks. These *track presets* (also available for MIDI and VST instrument tracks) are templates that include pre-selected inserts, effects, and equalization that define a particular sound. Using a track preset is a quick way to add a ready-to-use track, without having to tweak the settings yourself.

To add a new track to your project, follow these steps:

1. Select **Project > Add Track > Audio.**
2. When the Add Audio Track dialog box appears, pull down the Configuration list and select **Mono.**
3. Check the **Browse Presets** option, and the dialog box expands to display the list of presets, as shown in Figure 4.2.
4. Select an instrument type from the **Category** list, then select a **Sub Category, Style,** and **Character** for that instrument (if desired—the more you filter, the fewer choices you'll see).
5. Available presets will now appear in the Viewer pane of the dialog box. Select the preset you want from this list, then click **OK.**
6. The new track now appears in the track list, labeled with the preset you selected. If you want to change the track name, double-click the label and enter a new one.

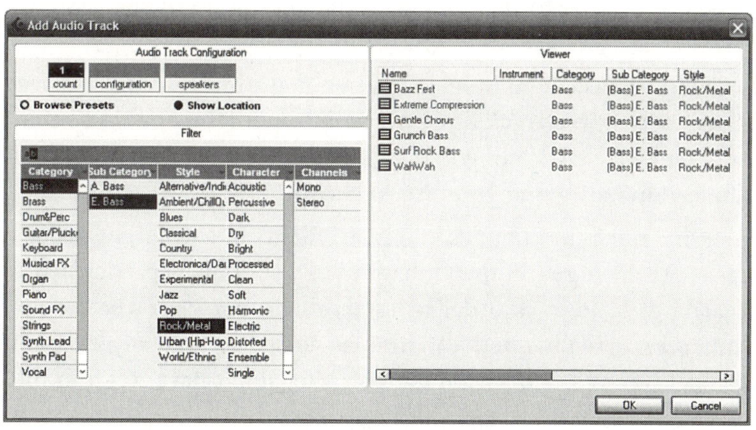

Figure 4.2 *Adding a new track with preset information.*

Now repeat this process as many times as necessary to add all the tracks you'll need for your recording. (But don't worry; if you later decide to add another instrument to the mix, you can add new tracks at any time in the process.)

Tip

It helps to color-code similar tracks within the mixer. For example, you might configure all the vocal tracks the same color, or all the rhythm tracks the same color, or all the guitar tracks the same color, and so on.

Note

Why select mono input when adding a new track? It's simple; practically every microphone or direct instrument you record is in mono. You can choose to send that mono input to two stereo channels during the mixing process, but you're only recording a single-channel signal to begin with.

You can also change track presets for any existing audio track. All you have to do is select **Media > Open SoundFrame Browser.** This opens the SoundFrame Browser, shown in Figure 4.3, where all of Cubase's track presets are stored. Select the **Category** tab and make sure only the **Show Track Presets** button is selected, then start browsing through the presets you want. To apply a preset, use your mouse to drag the preset from the SoundFrame Browser to the selected track in the track list. When you drop the preset on the track, the track is reconfigured with all the preset settings. (You can also use the SoundFrame Browser to select presets for MIDI and VST instrument tracks.)

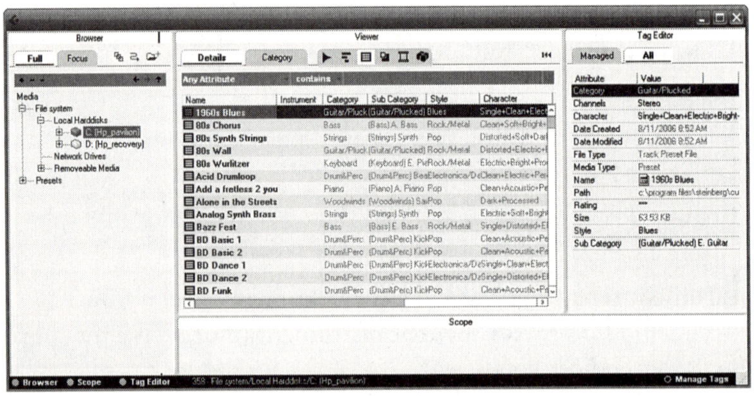

Figure 4.3 *Browsing for track presets with the SoundFrame Browser.*

Configuring Input and Output Busses

All those tracks sitting in your track list don't mean a thing until you tell Cubase what inputs are to be recorded on which tracks. You do this by assigning a distinct input *bus* to each track.

You'd think this would be easy. The first channel on your mixer/control surface is routed to the first track in the track list, the second channel is routed to the second track, and so on—right? Well, you *can* do it that way in theory, but in the real world things don't always align quite so cleanly.

First, you may plug in your microphones and instruments in a different order from how the tracks are arranged in the Cubase track list. This is particularly likely if you've rearranged the track order to something other than what you started with. In any case, it really doesn't matter, as you can assign any channel in your physical mixer to any track within Cubase; they don't have to go in the same order.

Second, your mixer/control surface might not have the same number of inputs as you have tracks. This is likely if you're recording from a home studio, where you plan to layer multiple tracks to create your recording. Depending on your equipment, you may only have a single input channel to work with. How, then, do you use one input channel to record on more than one track?

def•i•ni•tion

Audio is transferred between external devices and the Cubase program via a series of **busses.** Input busses route audio from your hardware to Cubase; output busses route audio from Cubase to your hardware. So when you record audio, you're using one or more input busses, and when you play back audio, you're using one or more output busses.

What you have to do in this instance is reassign the input bus for each pass of your recording. For example, if you lay down the bass track first, you first assign your input bus to that bass track. If you then choose to lay down a guitar line, you reassign the input bus to the guitar track. And on and on and on. (Alternately, you can assign the same bus to multiple tracks, since you'll only be recording on one track at a time.) This is how you record multiple tracks from a single input.

Assigning input busses is relatively easy. Here's how to do it:

1. Select a specific track in the track list.
2. In the selected track's inspector, click the **In** field, as shown in Figure 4.4.
3. The pop-up menu will display all available input devices; select the input you want to assign to this track from the list.

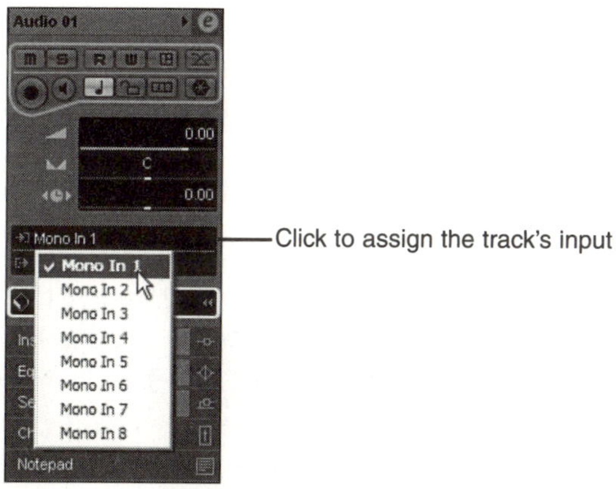

Figure 4.4 *Assigning input for a specific track—click the In field in the track inspector.*

If you're using a mixer/control surface with multiple inputs, you should repeat these steps for every channel of the mixer you'll be using. As noted, you can also reassign inputs to other tracks during later recording passes—or, even easier, assign the same input to multiple tracks during a single pass.

Setting the Recording Quality

Cubase doesn't limit you to a single recording quality level. You can create lower-quality recordings for web distribution, or higher-quality recordings for CDs or movie soundtracks.

You set the recording quality for your project in the Project Setup dialog box, shown in Figure 4.5. You open this dialog box by selecting **Project > Project Setup.** There are three settings in this dialog box that affect recording quality, and they're all grouped together at the bottom of the dialog box.

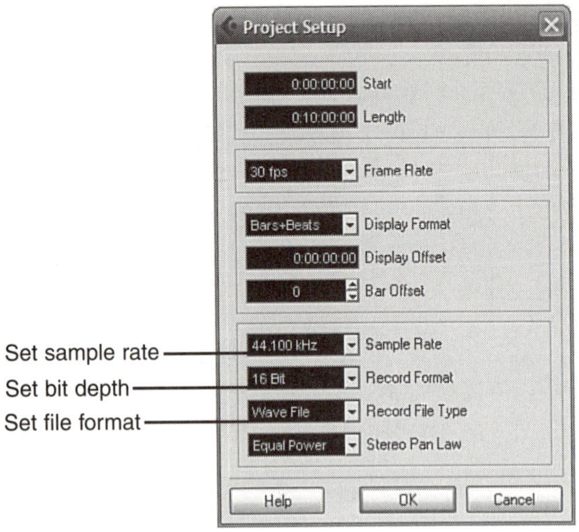

Figure 4.5 *Configuring recording quality in the Project Setup dialog box.*

The first setting to configure is the *sample rate*. The sample rate determines how many times per second the analog input is sampled into digital format. The higher the sample rate, the more samples that are used to create the digital recording; the more samples used, the greater the accuracy to the original sound, and the higher quality the recording. Note, however, that the higher the sample rate you choose, the more disc space you use. (Sample rate is measured in thousands of cycles per second, or kilohertz.) The sample rate used for compact disc audio is 44.1 kHz, so you might think that any higher rate would be overkill. This is true to a point, although some recordings targeted at the audiophile market are sampled at higher rates.

The next setting in the dialog box is *record format*. This selects the *bit depth* of your recording—that is, the detail and resolution that is recorded when the analog signal is sampled to digital. A higher bit depth produces a higher-resolution, higher-quality recording. Historically, most digital recordings have been made with 16-bit resolution. However, many higher-fidelity recordings are now being made at 24-bit and 32-bit levels. Not all sound cards support these higher bit depths, however; you should choose the bit depth that your computer's sound card supports.

Note

You can only record at as high a bit depth as your computer's sound card supports. For example, if you have a 16-bit sound card and select 24-bit recording in Cubase, your recording will be made at the 16-bit level. The only time you might choose a higher bit depth is when your card's bit depth falls between Cubase's selected levels; for example, if you have a 20-bit sound card, you should choose 24-bit recording in Cubase.

The final setting to configure is the *record file type*. This selects what type of audio file you create when you make a record. Cubase can record to four different file types, but the one you almost always want to use is the Wave (.WAV) format. This is the industry standard audio format for all professional recordings.

The last setting in this dialog box, Stereo Pan Law, has nothing to do with recording quality, and can be left in its default position (Equal Power).

Tip

When you're recording for ultimate mix-down to CD, know that whatever quality levels you use for recording, the standard CD format supports only 44.1 kHz, 16-bit stereo files. (SACD and DVD-Audio support higher sample and bit rates, however.) This doesn't mean that you shouldn't record at higher levels; the higher quality your initial recording, the better the final CD will sound. Just know that whatever recording quality levels you set, you'll need to convert your recording to 44.1 kHz, 16-bit during the CD mastering process. (Learn more about mastering in Chapter 15.)

Preparing to Record

All your tracks created, labeled, and assigned? Quality levels set? Then it's time to prepare your individual tracks for recording.

Setting Input Levels

One of the most important skills for a recording engineer is that of setting the proper input levels. Set the input level too high and the recording will overload and distort; set it too low and the audio will sound too soft, without important details.

As you recall from Chapter 1, you need to set the input level for each input before you start recording. You do this from the mixer, using the level fader control—the little slider that moves up and down in the input channel strip, as shown in Figure 4.6. You adjust the fader with your mouse.

The way it works is simple. Before you start recording, you have the musician sing or play his part, with the specific instructions to play as loud as he plans to during the actual recording. As he plays, you adjust the fader for that particular input so that the green level indicator just bumps up against the 0 dB level, which is the level you never want to exceed. In other words, you want to set the input level so that the loudest sections of your recording come as close as possible to 0 dB, without going over. (And you'll know when that happens; the red clipping indicator will light, as a warning.)

Tip

The input level isn't the only thing that affects the quality of the sound you record. When you're recording acoustic instruments, microphone choice and placement is at least as important as how hot you run the levels—as you learned in Chapter 2.

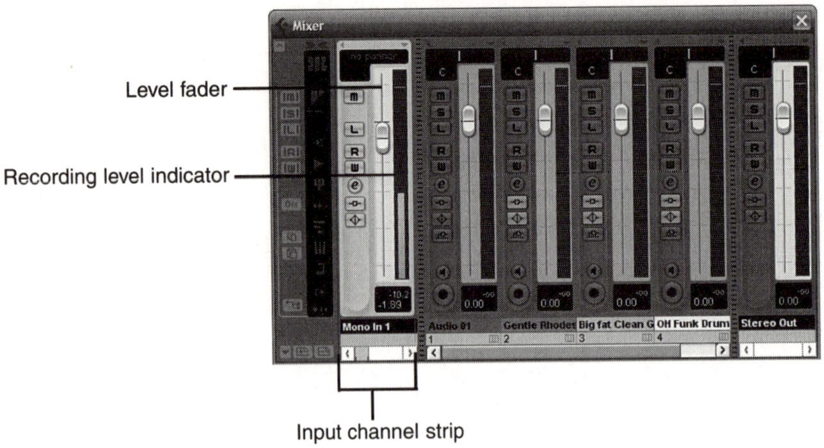

Figure 4.6 *Setting input levels in the mixer.*

> **Tip**
>
> You can obtain a wider range of input levels by switching the mixer to Routing View, which activates an Input Gain knob above the fader control. Just left-click on the input channel in the mixer, then select **Window > Show Routing View.** From here you can use the Shift key to adjust the Level Gain knob with your mouse.

You'll need to set input levels for every input you're recording. At this point, don't worry about the relative balance between inputs; it's okay if the rhythm guitar sounds louder than the lead guitar, or if the bass drum sounds louder than the bass guitar. You'll set the final volume balance during the mixing process; for now, you want to record as "hot" as possible for each and every input, to get the maximum sound possible. (After all, you can always make a loud instrument softer; you can't turn up the volume any louder than what you originally recorded.)

Enabling Tracks for Recording

Ask yourself a simple question—what tracks will you be recording first? The answer to that question determines which tracks you need to enable for recording.

Until you enable a track for recording, it just sits there in your track list, silent and mostly harmless. You can do all the prep work you want, but until that track is enabled, you can't record on it. (Which is good to know when you're recording multiple tracks in multiple passes; if a track isn't record-enabled, you can't accidentally record on it!)

> **Tip**
>
> You don't have to enable all your available tracks at the same time. Cubase makes it easy to record multi-track recordings in multiple passes. For example, you would enable only the bass and drum tracks if you wanted to record the rhythm section first; you would then enable the other tracks on subsequent recording passes. (We discuss the multi-pass recording process in the "Recording Additional Tracks" section, later in this chapter.)

After a track is record-enabled, it *will* be recorded—just as soon as you click the Record button in the transport panel. That is, when you click Record, any and all record-enabled tracks will record. No disenabled track will record. You get the idea.

To enable a track for recording, follow these steps:

1. From within the mixer, go to the channel strip for the track you want to enable.
2. Click the **Record Enable** button, as shown in Figure 4.7.

That's it. When recording is enabled, the entire button should light up red.

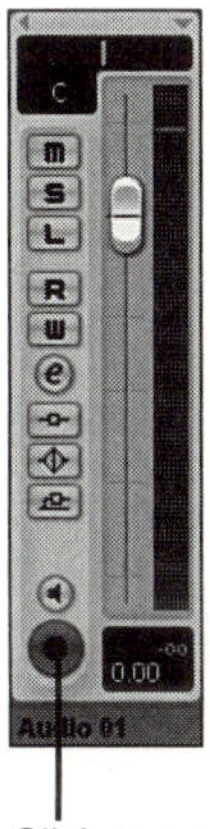

Figure 4.7 *Enabling recording from a mixer channel strip.*

Monitoring the Recording

You really wouldn't want to make a recording without hearing what's being recorded. To listen in during the recording process, you have to activate and configure Cubase's monitor function.

Setting the Type of Monitoring

Cubase offers a lot of flexibility when it comes to monitoring—which also means that all the choices can sometimes be a tad confusing. I'll help remove some of the confusion. The type of monitoring you want to use is called *tapemachine style*, because it works just like you'd expect monitoring on a traditional tape recorder to work. When Cubase is recording or stopped, it monitors the input. When Cubase is playing back a recording, it monitors the output. There's no manual switching necessary. To configure Cubase for tapemachine-style monitoring, follow these steps:

1. Select **File > Preferences.**
2. When the Preferences dialog box appears, as shown in Figure 4.8, scroll down through the selection in the left-hand tree and select **VST.**
3. In the right-hand panel, pull down the Auto Monitoring list and select **Tapemachine Style.**
4. Click the **Apply** button.
5. Click the **OK** button.

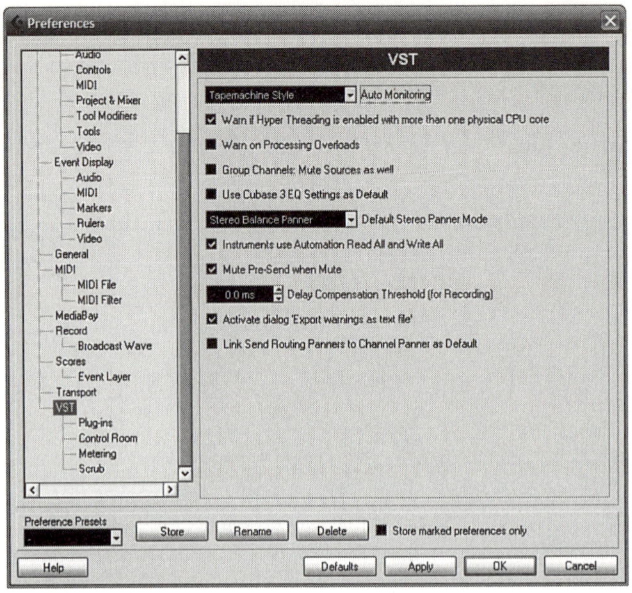

Figure 4.8 *Setting up tapemachine-style monitoring.*

> **Tip**
>
> Cubase 4 (*not* Cubase Studio 4) includes a new monitoring function called the Control Room. This function is designed for use in professional recording studios, with separate studio and control room areas. The Control Room function is turned off by default; if you want to use this function for monitoring in your home studio, consult the Cubase 4 manual for more information.

Activating Track Monitoring

You decide what you want to monitor on a track-by-track basis. For example, if you're recording four tracks out of eight, you need only activate monitoring for those four tracks. Here's how you do it:

1. From within the mixer, go to the channel strip for the track you want to activate.
2. Click the **Monitor** button, as shown in Figure 4.9.

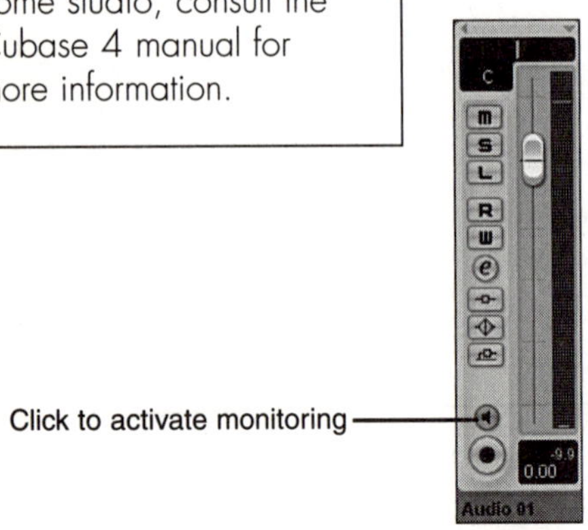

Figure 4.9 *Activating monitoring for a specific channel.*

When activated, the Monitor button should light up as orange.

Tip

You don't have to listen to every track when you monitor a recording. For example, a drummer might want to monitor only the electric bass track; he might not want the vocals in his monitor mix. Accordingly, you as an engineer might sometimes want to hear how one or two tracks sound by themselves, without being distracted by the other instruments. This is why you can turn monitoring on or off for individual tracks.

Creating a Monitor Mix

Remember when I said not to worry about the volume mix between tracks when recording? Well, that advice stands, but you may not like what you hear if you monitor this raw mix. For this reason, many engineers prefer to create a separate monitor mix that musicians can play to when recording. You still record all the tracks at their maximum individual levels; you simply mix the levels differently to send to the monitor speakers or headphones. Even better, you can apply EQ and effects to the monitor mix, without actually recording them on the tracks themselves.

You create a monitor mix using the audio channel strips in the mixer. Raise and lower the level faders for each channel to raise and lower the volume sent to the monitor.

And that's not the only adjustment you can make to the monitor mix. You can add equalization to any selected track by displaying the mixer in extended view, displaying the EQ controls at the top of the mixer, and then adjusting the equalization accordingly. You can also add send effects by displaying the sends at the top of the mixer and making the appropriate selections. You can also mute any track in the mix by clicking the Mute button, or listen to any track by itself by clicking the Solo button. (Learn more about EQ in Chapter 13; learn more about plug-in effects in Chapter 14.)

Just remember—the adjustments you make in the audio channel strips (*not* the input strips!) apply only to what you're hearing in the monitors. Cubase is still recording the raw audio input as configured in the selected input channels.

Caution

If you have a slower computer with a high latency rate, the monitor mix may be slightly out of sync with the actual recording/playing—which is not a good thing. To use Cubase's internal monitoring, make sure your computer has the horsepower to deliver low latency when recording.

The Importance of a Good Monitor Mix

Because the monitor mix applies only to what you hear in your studio monitors or headphones, not to what you actually record, why is a monitor mix important? There are a number of reasons.

For musicians, the monitor mix is what you hear in your headphones when recording. If you're a musician, you know that how clearly you can hear the other instruments affects your own playing. If you're a keyboardist following a vocalist, you need to hear the vocals up front in the monitor mix. If you're a drummer, hearing the vocals isn't near as important as hearing what the bass player is doing. If you're a rhythm guitarist, you might only want to hear the drums and bass. And whatever you need to hear, you need to hear it clearly; there's nothing worse than trying to play along to a muddy monitor mix.

For engineers, the monitor mix serves several functions. First, it helps you hear everything that's going on—and gives you a heads-up to any mistakes being played or recorded. Second, it provides a rough first pass on how you might want to mix, process, and equalize your final mix; in other words, it lets you experiment with your final sound. In any case, you want to be able to hear each instrument clearly, to ensure that what you're recording is worth keeping.

How you listen to the monitor mix is also important. In the booth, you want a pair of monitor speakers that accurately represent what's being recorded. In the studio, you need closed-ear headphones that let the musicians hear the mix without any interference from other sounds around them. And however you monitor the recording, you want the sound to be clear and accurate, without any artificial coloration. The better your monitoring equipment, the better your recording will be.

Using a Click Track

A steady tempo is the hallmark of many different types of recordings. And the best way to ensure a steady tempo is to have the musicians play along to a click track, which provides a precise metronome-like click dialed in to a specific beats-per-minute rate. When the musicians play to the click, the tempo won't speed up and slow down, like it might in an unregulated live performance.

To Click or Not to Click—That Is the Question

That's not to say that you want to force all your musicians to use a click track. Certain types of music need that rock-solid beat, although other types need to breathe a bit more, tempo-wise. When and how you use a click depends on the type of music you're recording and the musicians you're working with.

Most of today's popular music is expected to have a very steady beat. That includes rock, pop, country, R&B, hip-hop, and the like. For these types of music, you definitely want to provide a click for the musicians to lock into.

Jazz music, on the other hand, typically has a more fluid tempo. Jazz tends to ebb and flow throughout the course of a performance, and forcing jazzers to lock into a rigid beat might result in a wooden recording. With jazz musicians, the best course of action is often to let the "tape" roll and catch the magic as it occurs.

Classical music is also ill-suited to using a click track. Like jazz, most classical music is fluid in terms of tempo, with the conductor earning his pay by urging the musicians ahead or reining them in as necessary. In addition, many classical pieces feature numerous changes in tempo and time signature, which would make it difficult to provide a constant click throughout the entire piece. As with jazz, the best approach for classical music is to press the Record button and let the musicians play.

Finally, musicians who are new to the studio might find playing to a click somewhat disconcerting. If you're working with inexperienced musicians, you may want to turn off the click and let them find their own way, at least for the first several takes. It's all too easy for a nervous musician to focus solely on the click and lose all spontaneity in their playing. It's okay to let the tempo vary a little, if that means recording a more lively performance.

Setting the Click

Cubase provides its own built-in click track for use when you're recording. When you activate the click, you also set the recording's time signature and tempo. In addition, you can also turn on a precount, which provides two measures of clicks to set the tempo before the recording starts. Just follow these steps:

1. In the transport panel, click the **Click** control on, as shown in Figure 4.10. (The control will "light," and the word ON will appear next to it.)
2. Click the **Precount** control on.
3. Click the **Tempo** control on.
4. Click the **Time Signature** control and enter the time signature for this recording (4/4, 3/4, and so on).
5. Click the **Tempo** control and enter the tempo for this recording, in beats per minute.

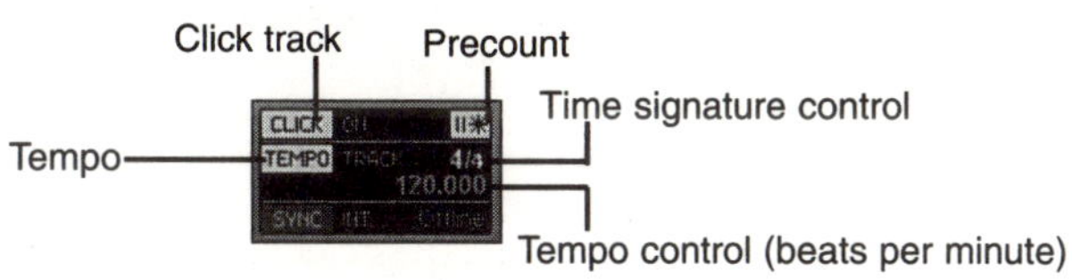

Figure 4.10 *Activating the click track in the transport panel.*

You can adjust the sound and the pitch of Cubase's electronic click by selecting **Transport > Metronome Setup.** The Metronome Setup dialog box, shown in Figure 4.11, lets you select from Cubase's standard beep or any external sound (in WAV or other audio file format) for the click. If you use the built-in beep, you can adjust the beep's pitch and volume level. You can also select how many measures are in the precount, and whether the click sounds in recording, playback, or both.

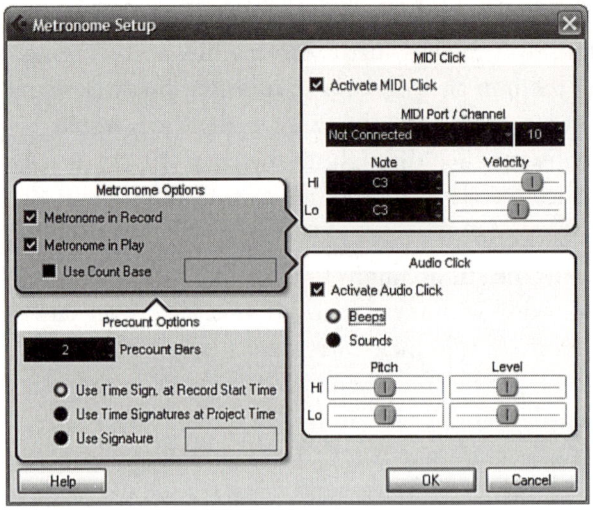

Figure 4.11 *Configuring Cubase's click track.*

With these controls set, the click track will play throughout your recording. When you press the record button, you'll hear two measures of clicks in the monitor mix; the recording will start with the third measure.

The only other thing you probably want to do is configure the ruler in the Project window to reflect bars and beats, rather than elapsed time. Because all the musicians will be playing to a set tempo, viewing your recording in terms of measures and beats within measures will help you identify individual sections, which is useful when it comes to editing and mixing the recording. You configure the ruler in this fashion by right-clicking on the ruler and selecting **Bars+Beats** from the pop-up menu.

Playing to a Click Track

Most professional musicians are used to playing with a click track. Clicks are used not only in the recording studio, but also onstage to ensure steady tempos during live performances.

Even amateur musicians shouldn't find the click track totally foreign. After all, the click track is nothing more than an electronic metronome, and almost all musicians have played along to a metronome at one time or another. A click track is just a very persistent metronome.

That said, musicians who are new to the studio might have trouble playing along to a click track. Some musicians find the click too rigid and intrusive, and actually pay too much attention to it—which typically results in jerky rhythms as they try too hard to play exactly on the beat.

The key to playing with a click is to treat it as just another instrument. After all, most musicians don't have any trouble playing along with a drummer, or a bass player, or a percussionist playing a cowbell or woodblock. How is a click track any different?

If the click is treated as just another instrument, then musicians can learn to play *around* the click, rather than playing *to* it. That means you can rush or drag the beat a little, knowing that the beat of the click will always remain constant. If you play a little ahead of the beat for a period, you then come back to the click to reinforce the tempo. It's not necessary to always match your downbeat with that of the click; weaving in and around the click produces a much more human-sounding performance.

As the recording engineer, you want to adjust the volume of the click so that it's subtle in the mix, not overpowering, just like a cowbell or woodblock would be. You may also want to use the Metronome Settings dialog box to change the click from the robot-like beep to something that sounds more like a real instrument, such as a cowbell or shaker.

In addition, you may choose to have the click play on every other beat (good for fast numbers, or to give the musicians a bit of leeway during the recording) or on each half-beat (almost necessary when recording slow ballads). You do this by adjusting the Count Base setting in the Metronome Settings dialog box.

Making the Recording

Alright, enough with the preliminaries. By now you should have everything set up for recording; the only thing left to do is make the recording itself.

At this point, I'll assume that you're recording to a click track, that you've enabled each of the inputs that you'll be using for this recording pass, and that you've activated monitoring and set an appropriate monitor mix. Assemble your musicians (or prepare yourself, if you're recording your own playing), get the room perfectly quiet, and signal everyone that you're ready to "roll the tape." (Yeah, I know there's no tape involved with digital recording, but old phrases never die.)

Here's what comes next:

1. Click the **Record** button in the transport panel.
2. Listen to the two measures of clicks in the precount.
3. Begin playing when the recording commences with the third full measure.

4. Monitor the recording levels in the input channels in the mixer, as shown in Figure 4.12. Make on-the-fly adjustments to the input level sliders as necessary.
5. When the performance is over, let the recording continue for a few seconds to catch any trailing resonance. Make sure the musicians stay perfectly quiet until you signal them that the "tape" has stopped.
6. Click the **Stop** button to end the recording.

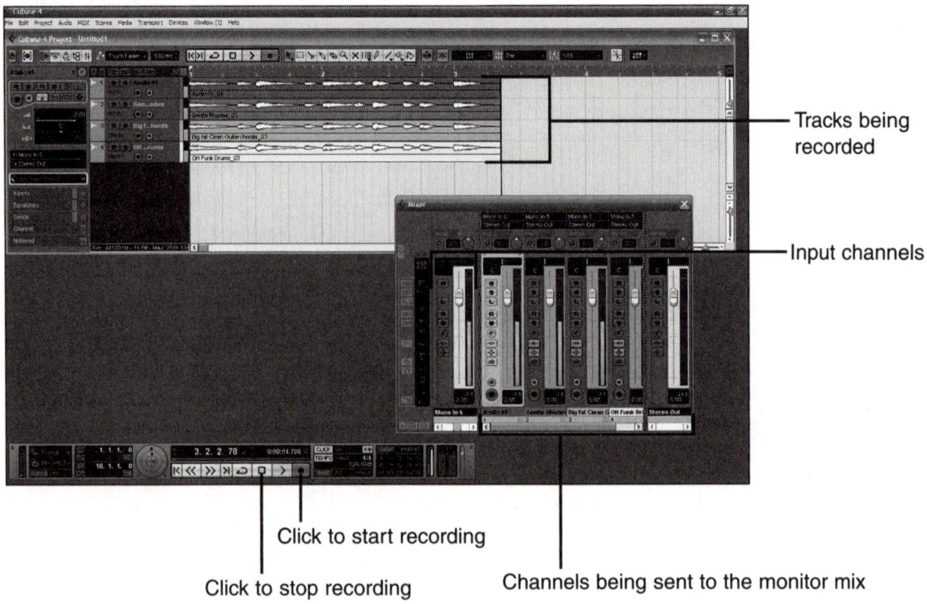

Figure 4.12 *Monitoring a recording in progress.*

After all the prep work, the actual recording seems pretty easy. Well, it is—from the engineer's standpoint, anyway. (All the pressure is now on the musicians to perform without making any mistakes.) Most of the engineer's magic comes in the mixing process, when you add equalization, reverb, and other effects processing. (Learn more about mixing in Chapter 15.)

Tip

Don't feel as if every recording you make is a "keeper." If the recording doesn't sound right, or if the musicians are making a lot of mistakes, feel free to stop the recording, regroup, and then make a second (or third or fourth) pass. One of the joys of computer-based recording is that you can record as long and as often as you want, without incurring additional tape cost.

Creating a Conducive Studio Atmosphere

Recording can be a stressful process—not just for the engineer, but also for the musicians in the studio. Unfortunately, when musicians get stressed and nervous, they don't always play their best. How do you reduce the stress and create an atmosphere that encourages those magic moments that make for a quality recording?

Although it's important for musicians to have a professional attitude about recording, it's also important for them to not be too tight. You can loosen things up by making the studio environment as comfortable as possible. Depending on the musicians, that might mean providing food and drink, comfy pillows, candles, maybe even a videogame machine to play during breaks in the process. You want the musicians to be as relaxed as possible, while still being alert and ready to perform their parts.

Knowing that musicians will feel some self-imposed pressure to play their parts as perfectly as possible, you don't want to add to their stress. This means that you should adopt an encouraging attitude, and try not to be too critical or judgmental of their playing. If someone plays a clam, don't yell out "That really sucked!" Instead, try something like "Okay, that was good, but let's see what we can get on another take." Don't be afraid to offer suggestions, as long as they're positive in nature. You want so subtly push the musicians to a higher performance level; it's more of a carrot approach, without the stick.

This also means that you should be as accommodating as possible to the needs of the musicians. You might want to record every instrument individually, for the best possible separation, but if the band insists on playing live together, go along with it. You're there to capture the best possible performance on disc, which you can't do if you antagonize the musicians. You depend on them to deliver their parts, just as they depend on you to lay down the great-sounding tracks. Work together and you can create magic.

Playing Back the Recording

Listening to what you just recorded is even easier than making the recording. Just follow these steps:

1. Click the **Rewind** button on the transport panel to return to the start of the recording.
2. To listen to the playback without the click track, click the **Click** control off.
3. Click the **Play** button.
4. When the recording is over, click the **Stop** button.

Easy enough. The mix you hear during playback will be the same mix you created for monitor use. You can alter this mix by adjusting the individual channel controls in the mixer.

Tip

You don't have to listen to every track you recorded. To focus on a particular instrument or vocal track, click the Solo button in that track's channel slice in the mixer. Alternately, you can mute individual tracks that you don't want to listen to during playback; just click the Mute button on the selected tracks.

Recording Additional Tracks

Few recordings these days are accomplished in a single recording pass. You can add other instruments and vocals to your base recording by making additional recording passes, adding new tracks to your recording as you go.

Assuming that you've already added the new tracks to the track list in the project window, recording additional tracks is a relatively easy process. You can add tracks that last the entire length of the recording, or that pop in during specific segments of the recording.

Recording a Full-Length Track

To add an instrument or vocal that exists through the entire length of the recording, follow these steps:

1. Disable recording for those tracks you've previously recorded by clicking the red **Record Enable** button off for those channels in the mixer.
2. Enable recording for your new tracks by clicking on the **Record Enable** button for those channels in the mixer.
3. Set the input levels for the new tracks you'll be adding.
4. Activate monitoring for those channels you want to hear in the monitor mix for your new recording pass.
5. Turn on the click track by clicking on the **Click** control in the transport panel.
6. Ready your musicians for recording.
7. Click the **Record** button in the transport panel.
8. The click track counts off the two-measure precount, then recording starts.
9. When the musicians have finished recording, click the **Stop** button.

Multi-pass recording is really pretty easy, especially when the musicians are playing throughout the entire piece. For the musicians, it's just like playing along to the recording. When you're done, your original recording has been enhanced by the new tracks you've added.

Recording from a Specific Point

> **Note**
>
> When you first create a recording project, the project cursor is positioned at the start of the project—which is why your main recording always starts at the beginning.

Oftentimes you don't need to add a track that lasts the entire length of the recording. Maybe you just want to add a guitar solo during the bridge, or a tambourine shake during the chorus, or background vocals during the out-chorus. In any case, there's no reason for the musicians to sit there in the studio while the entire song plays in the background. Cubase lets you go directly to a specific section of the original recording, and start recording from there.

The key to this type of limited-length recording is to set the starting point for where you want the new recording to commence. This is done by using the project cursor in the project window's ruler. The new recording will start from the cursor's current position, not from the very beginning of the recording.

To set the cursor and start your recording, follow these steps:

1. Disable recording for those tracks you've previously recorded by clicking the red **Record Enable** button off for those channels in the mixer.
2. Enable recording for your new tracks by clicking on the **Record Enable** button for those channels in the mixer.
3. Set the input levels for the new tracks you'll be adding.
4. Activate monitoring for those channels you want to hear in the monitor mix for your new recording pass.
5. Turn on the click track by clicking on the **Click** control in the transport panel.
6. Turn off the click track precount by clicking the **Precount** control in the transport panel to deactivate it.
7. Go to the project window and position the cursor a few measures before where you want the new recording to start, as shown in Figure 4.13.
8. Click in the ruler at the point you want the recording to start.
9. Ready your musicians for recording.
10. Click the **Record** button in the transport panel.
11. Playback begins at the point you selected.
12. The musicians should start playing when their parts come up in the play-back.
13. When the musicians have finished recording their parts, click the **Stop** button. (You don't have to wait for the entire recording to play back before stopping the new recording.)

Figure 4.13 *Setting a starting point for recording in the ruler.*

As you can see in Figure 4.14, the new recording event starts in the middle of the original recording, where you set the cursor in the ruler. You can play back the new recording by setting a new position in the ruler, or by clicking the **Go to Previous Marker** button to return to the beginning of the original recording.

Figure 4.14 *A new track recorded from a specific start point.*

> **Note**
>
> Displaying lanes takes a little work. Learn how to do it in the "Changing the Order of Events in a Stack" section in Chapter 6.

Overdubbing an Existing Track

It happens. You get a perfect recording that isn't quite perfect. The guitarist flubs a note, or the vocalist hits a clam, or the drummer totally screws up a fill. What do you do?

Fortunately, Cubase makes it easy to record new events onto an existing track. The new recording event is placed over the previous event—which still exists, by the way. So if you end up liking the original track better than the rerecording, you can revert to the original. Nothing you record is ever lost, unless you deliberately delete it.

> **Caution**
>
> Be careful about punching in instruments that have a long sustain or resonance, such as a cymbal crash or trumpet blast. If you punch out before the sound dissipates, the edit will be quite noticeable to astute listeners.

Rerecording the Entire Track

If you simply don't like a track as recorded, you can replace it by recording an entire new track on top of it. Here's how you rerecord a single track:

1. Disable recording for all tracks except for the one you want to rerecord.
2. Enable recording for the track you want to rerecord by clicking on the **Record Enable** button for that channel in the mixer.
3. Activate monitoring for those channels you want to hear in the monitor mix for your new recording pass.
4. Optionally, turn on the click track by clicking on the **Click** control in the transport panel. (Depending on the other tracks you've recorded, you may not need to use the click track when overdubbing like this.)
5. Ready your musician(s) for recording.
6. Click the **Record** button in the transport panel.
7. The click track counts off the two-measure precount, then recording starts.
8. When the recording is over (and make sure you've recorded over the *entire* original track), click the **Stop** button.

Recording Multiple Takes

Some musicians like to record multiple takes of various instrumental and vocal parts, and then use the take that sounded the best. This is particularly useful when recording instrumental solos. Just have the soloist make several passes through the chord changes, recording each new pass in turn. You can then audit each of the passes, and keep the one you like best for your final recording.

Normally, newly recorded events are stacked on top of previously recorded events in the event display, which makes it difficult to see and play back older takes. To view all the different takes of a given track, you want to display each take as a separate "lane" in the event display, as shown in Figure 4.15. You can then select which take to play back by moving it to the front of the stack; just right-click on the event and select **Move To > Front** from the pop-up menu.

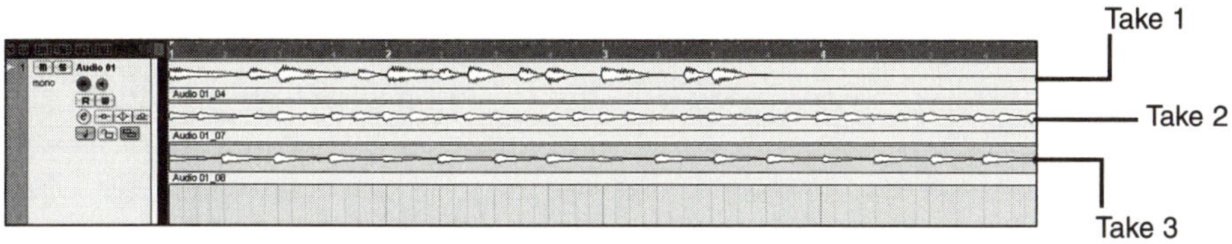

Figure 4.15 *Displaying multiple takes as separate lanes in the event display.*

Punching In to Rerecord Selected Segments

When you need only to replace a short section of the original recording, you use a technique called punch in/punch out. With this technique, the playback of the original recorded event proceeds until a specific replacement point is reached; at that point, the new recording is "punched in." When the specified end point is reached, the new recording is "punched out"; recording is turned off and playback of the original event resumes. You can punch in and punch out to overdub segments of any length—including a fraction of a beat.

When you use punch-in recording, you also want to activate Cubase's *pre-roll* function. This tells Cubase to start playback a set amount of time before the punch-in recording begins, so that the musicians can hear what they'll be playing to, in context.

Finally, to perform this type of punch-in operation, you need to split your previous event into three individual events—pre-mistake, mistake, and post-mistake—and delete that event for which you want to punch-in an overdub. Now, assuming that you're reading this book in order, you haven't learned how to split events yet. So to perform a punch-in overdub, you'll first need to read ahead to Chapter 6 and learn all about event editing. (Sorry about that; this is one of those operations where it's hard to tell what comes first, the cart or the horse.)

Here's how it works:

1. Using the techniques presented in Chapter 6, split the event you want to overdub into three parts. Place one split point just before the area you want to overdub, and a second split point just after that area. This creates three separate events, as shown in Figure 4.16.

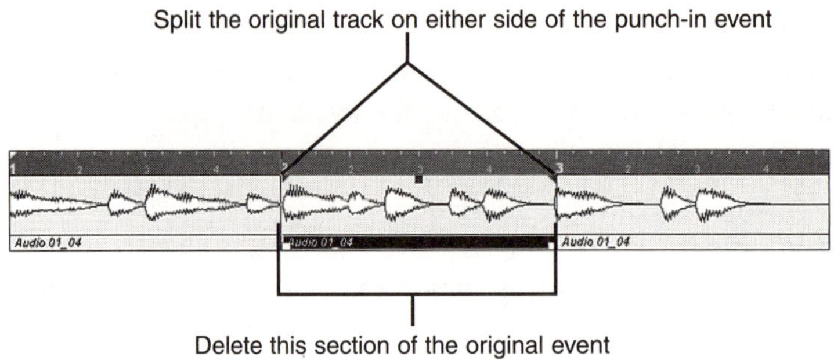

Figure 4.16 *Deleting that portion of the event that contained the mistake.*

> **Note**
>
> Learn all about splitting and deleting events in Chapter 6.

2. Delete the event that corresponds to the section you want to overdub. This should leave a recorded event before the mistake, then a blank area (where the mistake was), then a recorded event after the mistake.
3. Set the point where you want to start recording (the punch-in point) by positioning the cursor in the ruler at the beginning of the blank area—in other words, at the start of the event that you deleted—and then Ctrl-clicking your mouse.
4. Set the point where you want to stop recording (the punch-out point) by positioning the cursor in the ruler at the end of the blank area—in other words, at the end of the event that you deleted—and then Alt-clicking your mouse. The section to record is now highlighted in the ruler, as shown in Figure 4.17.

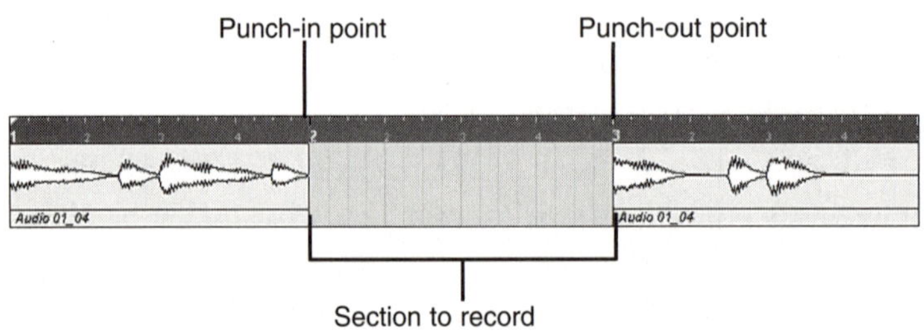

Figure 4.17 *Setting the punch-in and punch-out points in the ruler.*

> **Tip**
>
> To extend playback past the punch-out point, you can activate Cubase's post-roll function. It works pretty much the same as pre-roll, except it controls the playback past the punch-out point.

5. In the transport panel, click on the **Punch In** control, as shown in Figure 4.18.
6. Click the **Punch Out** control to activate it.
7. Click the **Use Pre-Roll** control to activate it.
8. Click the **Pre-Roll Amount** control and enter the amount of pre-roll you want, in minutes and seconds.

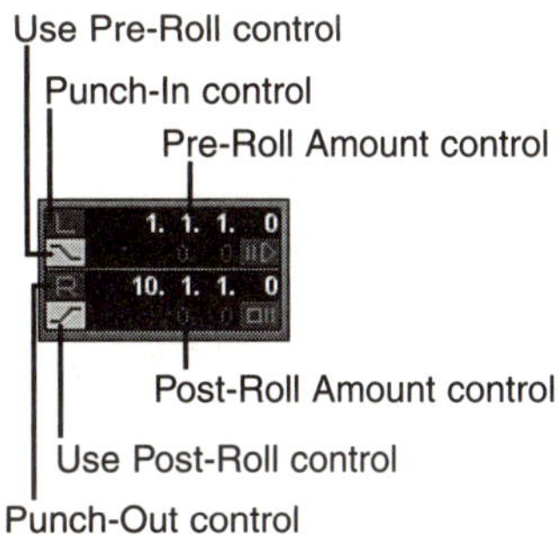

Figure 4.18 *Activating punch-in, punch-out, pre-roll, and post-roll in the transport panel.*

9. When you're ready to record, select the track to record and click the **Record** button.

When you click **Record,** playback will start as determined by the pre-roll settings. The new recording will start when the punch-in point is reached, and stop when the punch-out point occurs.

> **Note**
>
> You can also create new tracks using the punch-in technique.

The Least You Need to Know

- Evaluate your recording project ahead of time so you know how many and what kinds of tracks to create.
- For easier management, organize and color-code your tracks by function.
- Before you record, select the best recording quality settings, set proper input levels, and activate and create the monitor mix.
- For most types of popular music, you'll want to use a click track when recording.
- After the initial recording has been made, you can record additional tracks, or overdub sections of existing tracks.
- Punch-in recording lets you start and stop recording at specific points.

Chapter 5

Recording MIDI Tracks

In This Chapter

- Understanding how MIDI differs from audio recording
- Configuring Cubase for MIDI recording
- Making a MIDI recording
- Overdubbing MIDI tracks
- Quantizing MIDI recordings

Cubase can perform two different yet related types of recording. As you learned in Chapter 4, you can use Cubase for traditional audio recording, using microphones or direct-injected instruments (such as electric guitars and basses). Cubase also lets you record via MIDI, which doesn't require any microphones at all. MIDI is a much different type of recording, one that has more in common with computers than it does with reel-to-reel tape decks.

Differences Between Audio and MIDI Recording

Just what is this MIDI thing, anyway? Well, let's start with the word itself; MIDI is an acronym for Musical Instrument Digital Interface. If that sounds like a bunch of technical gobbledygook, that's because it is—which tells you just how different MIDI is from traditional audio recording.

With traditional audio recording, you're recording actual sounds—those waveforms that travel through the air and are captured by the microphone. (Or, in the case of direct-injected instruments, the waveforms generated by the instrument's electrical impulses.) MIDI, in contrast, doesn't record sounds. Instead, MIDI records computerized instructions. These instructions tell any computer what sounds to generate, in terms of frequency (musical pitch), velocity (volume level), and duration (note length).

Notice that the MIDI instructions don't say anything about what instrument plays those sounds. That's because MIDI instructions can be sent to any MIDI instrument. They're just instructions, after all. You can send the same instructions to a MIDI piano, a MIDI guitar, or a MIDI string section. It doesn't matter what the instrument is.

In fact, MIDI instruments are just computer-generated sounds designed to replicate the sounds of a real-world instrument. Some MIDI instruments use synthesized sounds, others use digitally sampled sounds from actual instruments; the realism of the sound depends on the accuracy of the synthesizer or digital sample.

> **Note**
>
> To be technically precise, when working with MIDI, Cubase functions as a MIDI *sequencer*. A sequencer is a device that records a stream of MIDI events and plays them back as instructed. Later, in the mixing/mastering process, Cubase converts these MIDI events into an audio recording. Learn more in Chapter 15.

And here we have the primary appeal of MIDI recordings. You can generate a musical part from any MIDI keyboard, and then send those instructions to any MIDI instrument. A single keyboard can generate a complete orchestral score, with different parts sent to different MIDI instruments—and recorded on different tracks within Cubase. Just play one part after another, sending each track to a different MIDI instrument. Before you know it, you've built up a recording using dozens of different instruments.

Cubase records MIDI tracks much the same way it records audio tracks. The big difference is that it doesn't record waveforms for the MIDI track; instead, as you can see in Figure 5.1, it records a series of note instructions. MIDI events can be split, cut, and copied just as you can with audio events; they can also be assigned to different MIDI instruments from within Cubase.

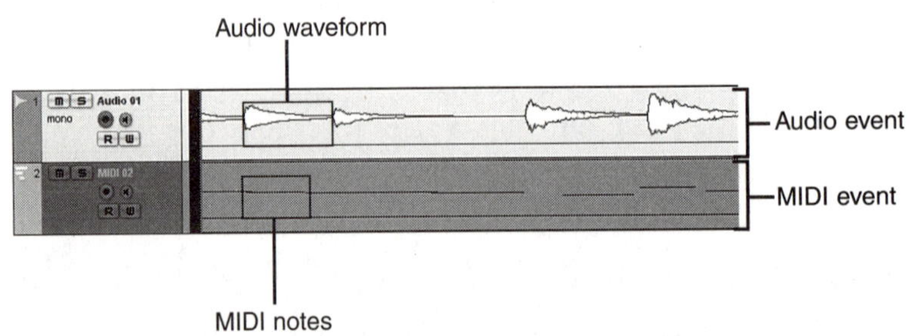

Figure 5.1 *Comparing a MIDI track with a traditional audio track.*

> **Note**
>
> Although you can edit MIDI events the same way you edit audio events, you can't edit MIDI instructions the same way you edit audio waveforms. Learn more about editing MIDI instructions in Chapter 8.

Because digital instructions take up a lot less space than a complex audio waveform, MIDI recordings take up much less file space than do audio recordings. This is another benefit of recording via MIDI; you can store a complete MIDI symphony in a fraction of the space a single audio instrument track would require. It's also somewhat easy to edit the MIDI instructions, thus changing pitch or volume or note length with a few clicks of the mouse. (And MIDI pitch is always precise—MIDI instruments never play off-key!)

Fortunately, you're not limited to using exclusively either MIDI or audio tracks. Cubase lets you combine audio and MIDI tracks in the same project. You can use both types of instruments as your needs dictate.

Setting Up Your MIDI Equipment

Most computers and sound cards don't have direct MIDI inputs. To connect a MIDI instrument to your computer, you need to go through a MIDI interface box, as we discussed in Chapter 2. The interface box connects to your computer via USB or FireWire, and to your MIDI instrument via two MIDI cables.

The interface box should have both MIDI In and MIDI Out connections. Your MIDI keyboard also has MIDI In and MIDI Out connections, as well as a MIDI Thru connection. (More on that last one in a moment.) As shown in Figure 5.2, you connect the MIDI Out jack on your MIDI keyboard to the MIDI In port on the interface box, then connect the MIDI In jack on your MIDI keyboard to the MIDI Out port on the interface box. Don't get confused; you always connect in to out and out to in.

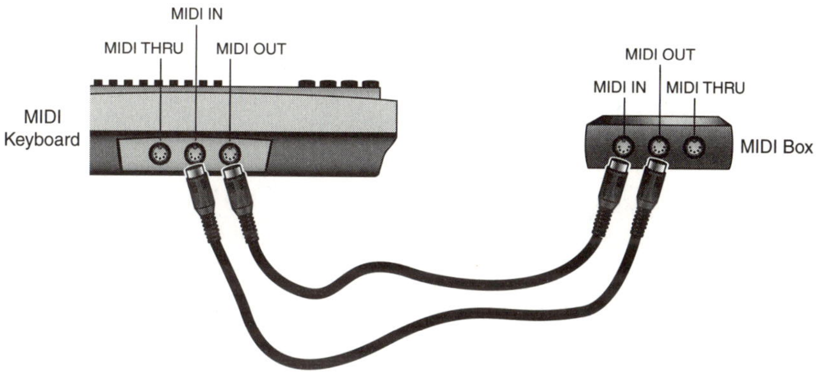

Figure 5.2 *A typical MIDI installation.*

The MIDI Thru connection on your MIDI keyboard is used to connect to an optional external MIDI sound module. You probably don't need one of these sound modules; they're used for playback only, typically in live performance situations, where they provide a broader selection of MIDI instrument sounds.

> **Note**
>
> Space doesn't permit the discussion of all of Cubase's MIDI configuration options, or the topic of troubleshooting problem setups. If you have questions or problems connecting and configuring any specific piece of equipment, direct your attention to the Cubase operation manual or to Steinberg's website and online knowledgebase (www.steinberg.net).

Configuring Cubase for MIDI Recording

If you plan on recording via MIDI, you have a bit of configuration to deal with. To be honest, MIDI configuration is somewhat less than intuitive and often problematic—but I'll try to give you the basics here.

Configuring Your MIDI Keyboard

When you're using an external MIDI keyboard, it's important that you actually receive a MIDI signal from that keyboard. You may also want to send the MIDI signal back from Cubase to the MIDI keyboard, so that you can hear the built-in instrument sounds from the keyboard itself (rather than through Cubase). Here's what you need to do:

1. Select **File > Preferences** to display the Preferences dialog box, shown in Figure 5.3.
2. In the left-hand pane, scroll down to and select **MIDI.**
3. In the right-hand pane, check the **MIDI Thru Active** option.
4. Click the **Apply** button, then click the **OK** button.

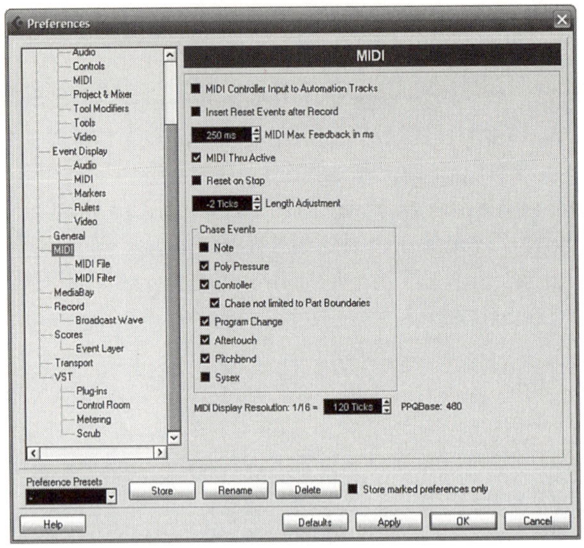

Figure 5.3 *Activating MIDI Thru in Cubase.*

That's what you need to do from within Cubase; this configuration routes the MIDI signal through Cubase back through the MIDI Out connection back to your MIDI keyboard. But we're not done with this configuration just yet.

Now you have to set up the MIDI keyboard itself. (Most keyboards have an options or setup menu somewhere; read your instruction manual to find out where.) Look for an option called Local or Local Control, and turn this option to Off.

def•i•ni•tion

A **MIDI interface** is a synthesizer or sampler that holds a bank of MIDI instrument sounds. The MIDI interface can be computer-based (your computer probably has its own MIDI interface built-in) or included as part of an outboard MIDI keyboard or synthesizer.

With all these settings configured properly, the MIDI signal from your keyboard will be routed to Cubase, and then re-routed back to the keyboard so you can hear what you're playing.

Adding New MIDI Devices

Any time you connect a new MIDI device to your system, you have to install and configure it from within Cubase. You do this from the MIDI Device Manager, by following these steps:

1. Select **Devices > MIDI Device Manager.** This opens the MIDI Device Manager window, shown in Figure 5.4; any currently installed MIDI devices will be displayed in the Installed Devices list.
2. Click the **Install Device** button.

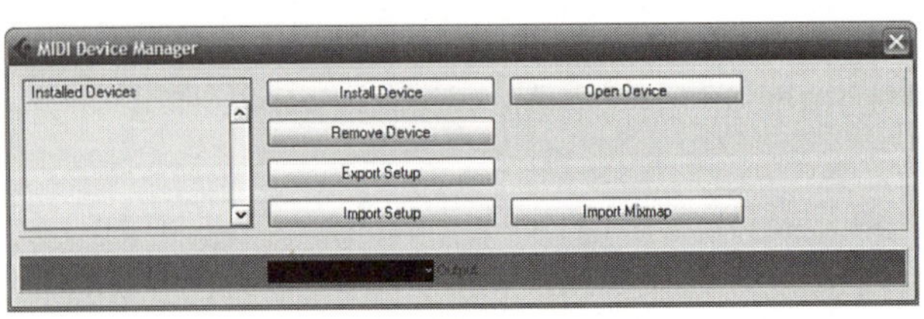

Figure 5.4 *Installing a new MIDI device via the MIDI Device Manager.*

3. When the Add MIDI Device dialog box appears, as shown in Figure 5.5, select the device you want to add and then click **OK.** (If your device isn't listed here but is compatible with the General MIDI or XG standards, select either GM Device or XG device, as appropriate.)

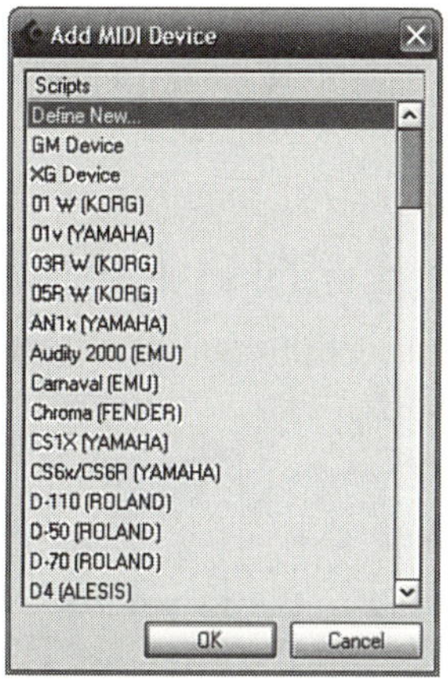

Figure 5.5 *Choosing the MIDI device to install.*

4. Select your newly added device in the Installed Devices list.
5. Pull down the Output list and select the MIDI output that is connected to the device.
6. Close the MIDI Device Manager window.

Before You Record: Planning Your MIDI Project

In Chapter 4, we discussed all the homework you need to do to plan an audio recording. Well, for better or for worse, planning a MIDI project is a lot easier. That's because you'll typically record only one track at a time, so you don't have to worry about activating multiple tracks and reconfiguring monitor mixes and all that. All you need to do is determine how many tracks you'll be recording—that is, how many different instruments you'll have on your MIDI recording. You can set up your project with all these tracks from the start, or just add them as you come to them. (And create any additional tracks you think you need as the project progresses.)

So there's no big pre-MIDI recording checklist you need to work through, no microphone setup to think through, no monitor mixes you need customize for the musicians you're recording. You'll still want to configure your own monitor mix, of course, and set the tempo for the click track. But that should be old hat by now; refer back to Chapter 4 to refresh your memory.

You also don't have to worry about the recording quality, because recording MIDI is merely recording a set of instructions. You set the recording quality later in the process, when it comes time to convert your MIDI tracks to true audio tracks for your final mixdown and mastering.

At this point, your entire prep work should consist of configuring Cubase to record your MIDI tracks—which we discuss next.

Preparing to Record a MIDI Track

Your system should now be properly set up for MIDI recording in general, but now you need to configure it for your specific MIDI project. Here's what you need to do:

1. Open a new project by selecting **File > New Project.**
2. When the New Project dialog box appears, select **Empty** and then click **OK.**
3. When the Select Directory dialog box appears, select where you want to save your project then click **OK.**
4. To create a new MIDI track, select **Project > Add Track > MIDI.** The new track appears in the track listing, as shown in Figure 5.6.
5. Route the desired MIDI device to this track by moving to the inspector, pulling down the In menu, and selecting the desired input from the list.
6. Record enable the MIDI track by clicking the red Record Enable button in the track list to turn on recording.
7. Select the MIDI output for this track by moving to the track inspector, pulling down the Out menu, and selecting the desired MIDI synthesizer.
8. Select the MIDI instrument sound for this track by moving to the track inspector and clicking through the Patch selector list until you find the sound you want.

Note

Most MIDI synthesizers have up to 128 different sounds, each in a different numbered program location. Consult your synthesizer's instruction manual to see which instruments are in which program locations.

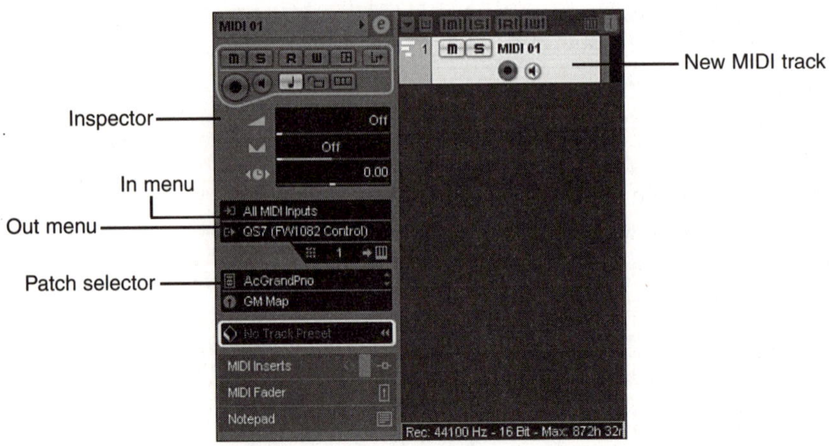

Figure 5.6 *Creating and configuring a new MIDI track.*

That's it. You might want to pick out a few notes on your MIDI keyboard to make sure you selected the correct instrument sound, but then you're ready to start recording.

Making a MIDI Recording

The process of making a MIDI recording is identical to making an audio recording. You'll want to program a monitor mix, of course, and set up a click track; see the appropriate sections in Chapter 4 for specific instructions for these operations.

When you have your monitor mix and click track all set up, follow these steps to make the recording:

1. Click the **Record** button in the transport panel.
2. Listen to the two measures of clicks in the precount.
3. Begin playing when the recording commences with the third full measure. A new MIDI event should be created in the event display, as shown in Figure 5.7.
4. When the performance is over, let the recording continue for a full measure after the last note.
5. Click the **Stop** button to end the recording.

> **Tip**
>
> You may want to turn on quantization for your MIDI recordings, which snaps the notes you play to pre-selected note values, for a more precise-sounding recording. Learn more in the "Quantizing Your MIDI Recording" section later in this chapter.

Unlike audio recording, when you record MIDI you don't have to bother with setting input levels. In fact, you really don't need to open the mixer at this point, unless you really want to. The MIDI instructions are recorded exactly as sent by the MIDI keyboard and laid down in the new MIDI event. For monitoring purposes, the output of the track is routed to a specific MIDI instrument sound, but you can change this at any time. You can also change the volume level for the MIDI track during the mixing process, using the level sliders in the mixer.

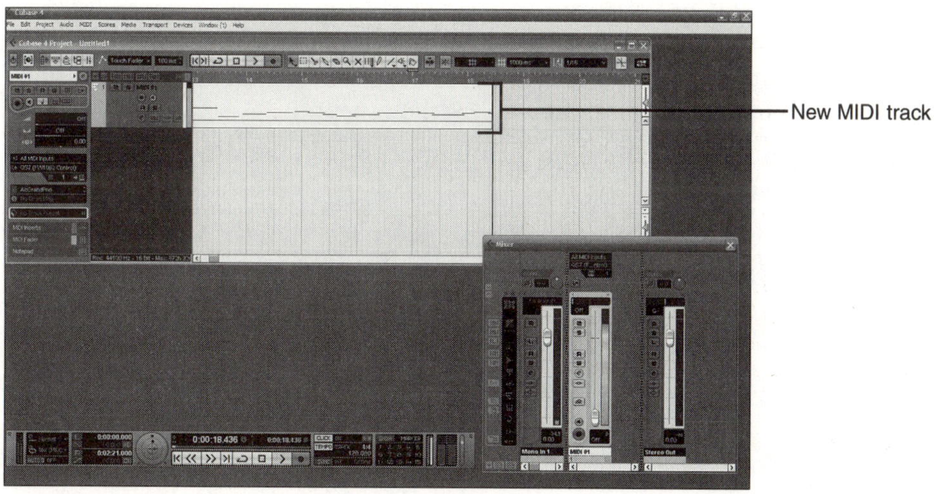

Figure 5.7 *Recording a new MIDI track.*

Importing MIDI Files

Another way to get MIDI tracks into your recording is to import an existing MIDI file created in another program. Any .MID file can be imported directly into a Cubase project.

To import a MIDI file, select **File > Import > MIDI File.** When prompted, you can choose to create a new project from this file, or import the file into the currently open project.

After an external MIDI file has been imported into Cubase, you can edit the individual MIDI tracks as you would with any other MIDI project, as well as record new tracks from within Cubase. You can also reassign the instrument sounds from what they were in the original file.

Many composers and arrangers prefer to create their scores in an advanced music notation program, such as Finale, Sibelius, or Notion. (Cubase has its own score editor, which we'll discuss in Chapter 8, but these other programs offer much more sophisticated score editing features.) However, these programs aren't recording programs, so the score has to be imported into Cubase for recording.

You start, within the music notation program, by exporting your score as a MIDI file. Then you switch to Cubase and import the MIDI file you just created from your score. After importing into Cubase, you can edit it as necessary, reassign MIDI instrument sounds, mix the volume levels, and master it into a final audio recording. Working with the two different programs like this provides the best of both worlds for serious composers and arrangers.

Playing Back the Recording

Listening to what you just recorded or imported is just as easy with MIDI as it is with audio tracks. Just make sure you've selected the proper instrument sound for that track in the inspector, then follow these steps:

1. Click the **Rewind** button on the transport panel to return to the start of the recording.
2. To listen to the playback without the click track, click the **Click** control off.
3. Click the **Play** button.
4. When the recording is over, click the **Stop** button.

Recording Additional Tracks

Of course, one of the reasons to record with MIDI is to layer multiple tracks into a master project, all recorded by little ol' you at your MIDI keyboard. As with audio recording, recording new MIDI tracks is as easy as creating a new track and making a new recording. It works like this:

1. Disable recording for those tracks you've previously recorded by clicking off the red **Record Enable** button for those tracks in the track list.
2. Enable recording for your new track for clicking the **Record Enable** button for that track in the track list to turn recording on.
3. Route the desired input to the new track by moving to the track inspector, pulling down the In menu, and selecting the desired input from the list.
4. Select the MIDI output for the new track by moving to the track inspector, pulling down the Out menu, and selecting the desired MIDI synthesizer.
5. Select the MIDI instrument sound for the new track by moving to the track inspector and clicking through the Program (prg) list until you find the sound you want.
6. Click the **Record** button in the transport panel.
7. The click track counts off the two-measure precount, then recording starts.
8. When you've finished playing, click the **Stop** button.

Overdubbing an Existing Track

Replacing all or part of an existing MIDI track is one operation that's a little different than when overdubbing audio tracks. That's because Cubase can treat overdubs in one of three ways:

- **Normal.** The new MIDI event supersedes the existing event—for as long as the new event lasts, that is. With MIDI tracks, overlapping events only overlap that specific section of the previous event. (With audio recording, an overlapped track is completely silenced.) If you re-record a short passage over a longer event, the original event will play until the new event starts, then will resume play when the new event ends.
- **Merge.** The new MIDI event is played *in addition to* the previous event. With this method, you can add extra notes to an existing event—for example, playing a left-hand piano part on top of an existing right-hand part. The new event doesn't replace or supersede the previous part, it plays along with it.
- **Replace.** The new MIDI event totally replaces any existing events on that area of the track. The existing event, during the section of the new event, is totally wiped from the track, not just overlapped as with a Normal overdub.

You set the MIDI overdub mode by clicking the **Linear Record Mode** control in the transport panel, shown in Figure 5.8. When the pull-down list appears, select the desired overdub mode. (The default mode is Normal.)

Figure 5.8 *Configuring the MIDI overdub mode.*

> **Tip**
>
> You can also use punch-in and punch-out recording with MIDI tracks, just as you did with audio recording. See the "Punching In to Rerecord Selected Segments" section in Chapter 4 for instructions.

To overdub a track or section of a track, follow these steps:

1. Click the **Linear Record Mode** button on the transport panel and select the desired MIDI overdub mode—Normal, Merge, or Replace.
2. Enable recording for this track by clicking on the **Record Enable** button in the track list.
3. Click in the ruler at the point you want the recording to start.
4. Click the **Record** button in the transport panel.
5. Playback and recording begins at the point you selected; start playing now.
6. When you've finished overdubbing this section, click the **Stop** button.

Quantizing Your MIDI Recording

One of the nice things about MIDI recording is that it can be extremely precise. You're not recording actual waveforms; you're recording instructions. Obviously, the pitch information will be perfect (unless you edit it otherwise), but it's possible that your rhythm might be a bit off. After all, if you press a key slightly before or after the beat, MIDI will interpret this literally, and send an instruction that places the note slightly before or after the beat—not directly on the beat, where you intended to put it.

> **Tip**
>
> In most instances, you'll want to quantize to sixteenth notes. Anything more precise sounds robotic; anything less precise runs the risk of misinterpreting the music.

If you want your MIDI recordings to be more rhythmically precise, you can configure Cubase to *quantize* your recordings. When you quantize a MIDI recording, the notes you play are automatically snapped to the nearest note value. You can select the note value to snap to.

You should configure and activate quantization before you make your MIDI recording. All you have to do is pull down the Quantize Type list in the project window toolbar and select a note value, as shown in Figure 5.9.

The available settings on the Quantize Type list range from 1/1 (whole note) to 1/64 (sixty-fourth notes), and also includes settings to quantize to triplets and dotted notes. Activate quantization before recording by clicking the Auto Q control in the transport panel, shown in Figure 5.10.

If you need more precise quantization, select **MIDI > Quantize Setup;** this displays the Quantize Setup dialog box, shown in Figure 5.11.

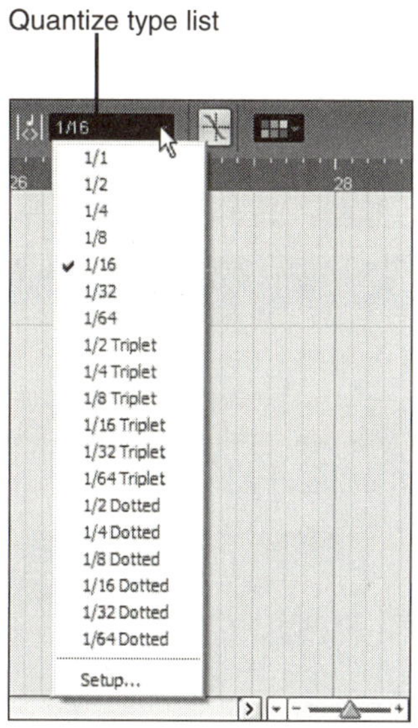

Figure 5.9 *Setting a quantization value for MIDI recording.*

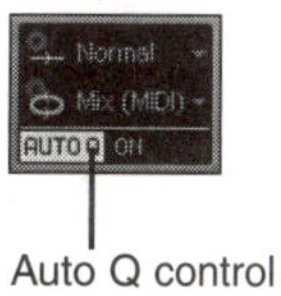

Figure 5.10 *Activate auto quantization from the transport panel.*

From here you can configure several different quantization settings. Most useful, if you're laying down jazz tracks, is the Swing control; this determines how "loose" or "tight" you want your eighth notes to play. A 0% Swing level plays straight eighth notes; a Swing setting in the 65% range plays eighth notes with a triplet feel, just like jazz musicians play a swing beat.

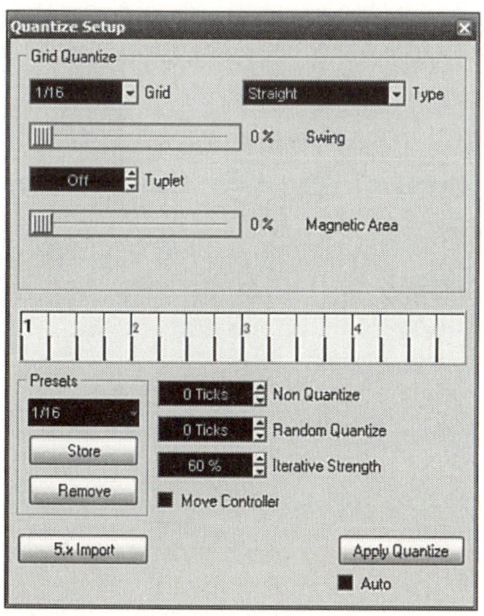

Figure 5.11 *Configuring quantization settings in the Quantize Setup dialog box.*

Tip

You can also apply quantization to a previously recorded MIDI track by opening the Quantize Setup dialog box and clicking the **Apply** button.

Also useful is the Magnetic Area control. This determines how close a note has to be to the selected grid to be snapped to that note value. Increase the Magnetic Area percentage to snap more notes to the grid; you can see the effect by the shaded blue areas in the dialog box's grid display.

Choosing MIDI Instruments

When we were discussing setting up Cubase for recording a MIDI track, we passed by one key setting fairly quickly. I'm talking about choosing MIDI instrument sounds for your tracks, which you'll agree is somewhat important.

As you recall, you assign MIDI instruments to tracks from the inspector. Just select the MIDI track in the track list, then use the Programs (prg) control to cycle through all the available sounds on your selected MIDI output device. You assign a virtual instrument to a MIDI track as that track's output. That is, the MIDI instructions you record are outputted to the MIDI interface and instrument you select.

It's important to remember that a MIDI instrument is a virtual instrument. When you assign a trumpet sound to a MIDI track, for example, you're not really tracking a real trumpet; you're tracking either a synthesized sound that resembles a trumpet, or a digital sample of a trumpet.

Where you do get MIDI instruments? Well, there almost certainly is a MIDI synthesizer included as part of your computer's operating system; you may also have additional MIDI synthesizers installed from other devices, as well as a MIDI interface built into your MIDI keyboard. Each of these MIDI devices will have different instruments included in their program banks.

Many manufacturers offer software-based MIDI instruments that you can install on your system. A so-called *soft synth* (short for *software synthesizer*) can then be installed into your Cubase program, so that the new virtual instrument is available for your recording projects. You can find a comprehensive list of soft synths at zZounds' Synth Zone website (www.synthzone.com/softsyn.htm).

Cubase also offers an alternative to traditional MIDI instruments, in the form of VST instruments. After installed, a VST instrument can be assigned to any MIDI track just as you would a MIDI instrument, or played in real time like a real instrument. Steinberg sells a variety of high-quality VST instruments; learn more in Chapter 9.

Of course, the quality of the virtual instrument sounds will differ from interface to interface. The best sounds, in my opinion, come from third-party soft synths and VST instruments that are created from high-quality digital samples of popular instruments. The least appealing sounds, again in my opinion, come from the MIDI synthesizer built into Microsoft Windows. In any case, you should audition the available sounds before you make your final choice.

And that final choice can come anywhere in the recording/mixing/mastering process. Remember, Cubase doesn't capture waveforms when you make a MIDI recording; it records instructions which can be applied to any MIDI instrument. It's a quick and easy thing to switch instruments for any MIDI track at any point in time, up to the mastering of the final recording. If you don't like a particular sound you've selected—change it!

The Least You Need to Know

- Audio recording captures sounds via waveforms; MIDI recording captures computer instructions on how to play specific notes.
- MIDI recordings are not tied into any specific instrument; MIDI tracks can be output to any MIDI instrument sounds.
- Before recording MIDI tracks, Cubase must be configured to work with your MIDI keyboards and devices.
- Recording a MIDI track is similar to recording an audio track, although the actual sound you hear is determined by which devices and instruments you select for MIDI output.
- When you overdub a MIDI track, you can choose to have the new event supersede that section of the original event, merge with the original event, or replace the existing event.
- For more rhythmically precise MIDI recordings, activate Cubase's quantization feature.

Part 3

Editing

Don't like what you've recorded? Somebody play a few clams in the middle of an otherwise great-sounding track? Then discover how to edit your Cubase recordings. Now a perfect recording is as easy as clicking your mouse!

Chapter 6

Editing Audio and MIDI Events

In This Chapter

- Zooming in on an event
- Splitting and joining events
- Deleting and muting events
- Selecting events from a stack
- Moving and copying events

Back in the pre-digital recording days, a perfect recording required a perfect performance by all the musicians in the studio. Any musician hitting a wrong note or playing out of tune would ruin the recording, and force yet another take. (This is why experienced studio musicians earned big bucks back in the day; producers paid for professional results.) Oftentimes the final recording was simply the best of all available takes, even if a few mistakes remained.

The advent of digital recording changed all that. With Cubase, you don't have to settle for an imperfect recording. The program includes all types of editing functions that let you remove mistakes, insert replacement notes, rearrange complete sections, and even change pitch and tempo. It's all done digitally, and—if done right—the edited result sounds just as if it were recorded that way.

The most basic form of editing in Cubase, for both audio and MIDI files, involves the editing of recorded events. As you know, each instance of recording in Cubase is known as an event. What you might not know is that you can work with these audio events to edit your recording in any number of ways. That's because events can be split, muted, moved, copied, and deleted—which, in turn, lets you revisit, re-imagine, and rearrange the recordings you make.

Zooming In on an Event

When you want to edit an event, it often helps to zoom in on the event so that all the details are larger, making them easier to locate and edit. You can zoom events both vertically and horizontally. A horizontal zoom expands the ruler to make the event longer in the event display; a vertical zoom expands the height of the event so that you more easily view the details of the event's waveform. (Figures 6.1, 6.2, and 6.3 show an event at normal resolution, then zoomed in the horizontal and vertical directions.)

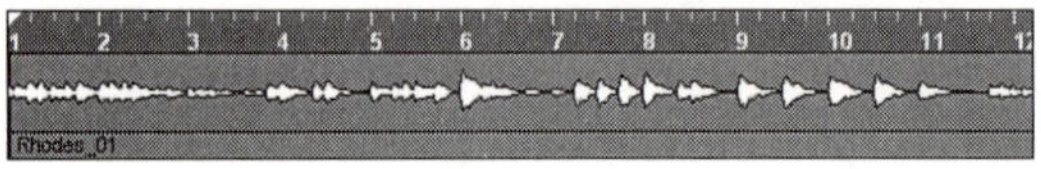

Figure 6.1 *An audio event shown at its original size.*

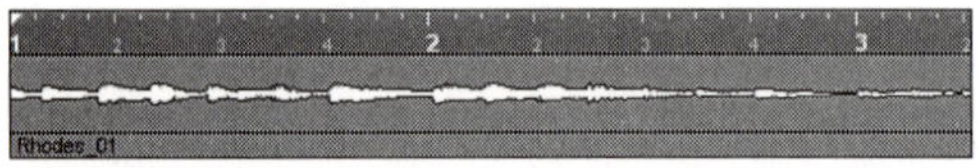

Figure 6.2 *The event zoomed horizontally; it's easier to see specific hits within the event.*

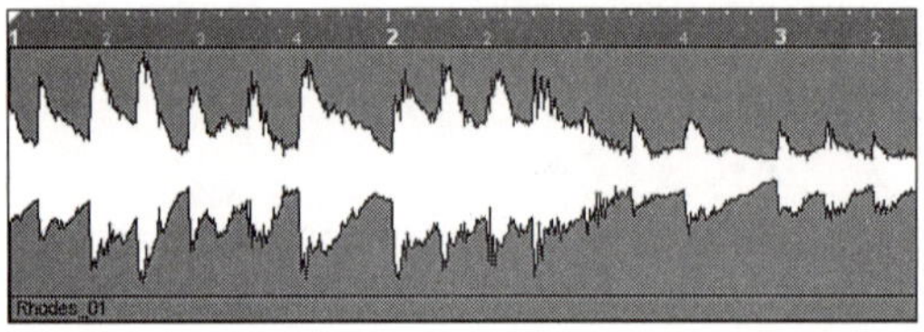

Figure 6.3 *The event zoomed vertically; it's easier to see the pitches in the waveform.*

To zoom in horizontally, you want to expand the ruler in the project window's event display. To do this, move the horizontal zoom control to the right, as shown in Figure 6.4.

To zoom in vertically, you want to expand the height of the tracks in the event display. To do this, move the vertical zoom control down.

Of course, another way to zoom into an event is to use the zoom control, located in the project window's toolbar. (As you can see in Figure 6.5, this is the button that looks like a little magnifying glass.) Just click the Zoom tool, and then click your cursor on the event or point that you want to zoom into. Click multiple times to zoom in even closer.

Finally, when you're examining audio waveforms, it sometimes helps to expand the waveform itself vertically—to make it taller—to better see all the parts of the signal. (Figure 6.6 shows what an expanded waveform looks like.) To increase the height of a waveform, adjust the vertical zoom control at the top right of the project window.

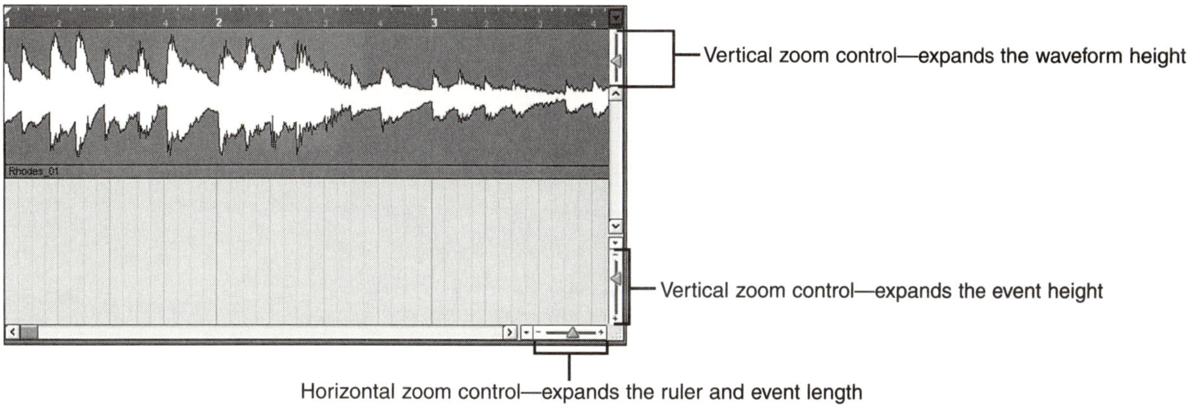

Figure 6.4 *The various zoom controls in the project window.*

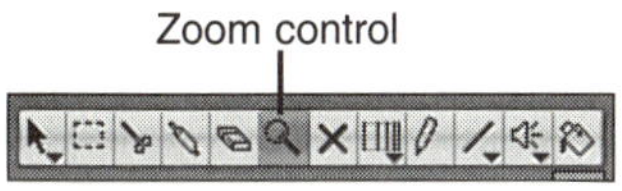

Figure 6.5 *Use the zoom control to zoom into any selected area.*

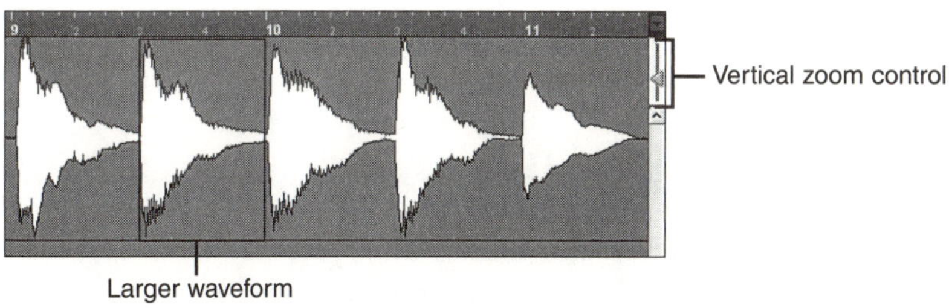

Figure 6.6 *Expanding the waveform vertically.*

Splitting One Event into Multiple Events

If you record a track in one complete pass, you create a very long audio event—one that lasts for the entire length of the overall recording. This is all well and good, but what do you do if you need to edit just a portion of this event? Well, the first step in event editing is learning how to split a single long event into multiple shorter ones, which you can more easily edit individually.

For example, let's say you have a four-minute-long event of a keyboard track—but it's not perfect. Somewhere in the middle of the second verse, the keyboardist hit a few clunkers that you'd like to get rid of or replace. Rather than recording the entire track all over again, you can simply split the original event into sections, and then delete the section with the clunkers. (Alternately, you can use punch-in recording, which we discussed in Chapter 4, to record a new section to replace the clunker section, which you still need to split off and delete.)

> **Tip**
>
> You can split an event any number of times, and in any place you like. Splits don't have to occur at measure lines or on a beat; they can be inserted anywhere within the event. To split an event exactly at a measure point, make sure the Snap button on the toolbar is clicked on. Click the Snap control off to split events between bar lines.

To split an event, follow these steps:

1. Click the **Scissors** tool in the project window toolbar.
2. Click at the point on the event where you want the split to occur, as shown in Figure 6.7.

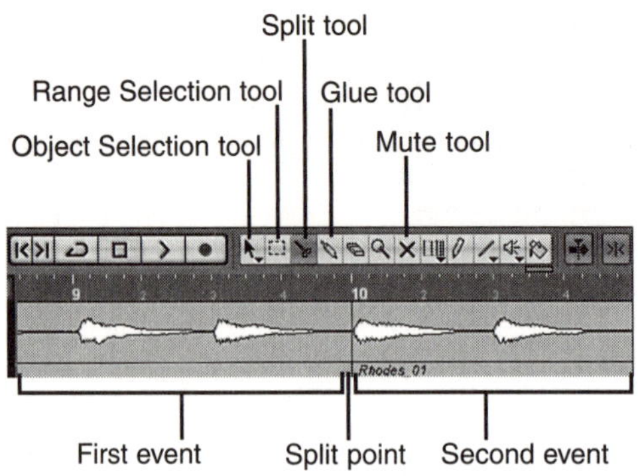

Figure 6.7 *Splitting an event in two.*

A blue line now appears at the split point, and the original event has been split in two—one event to the left of the blue line, another to the right. Each of the new events can now be edited separately.

Joining Two Events into One

Sometimes, after you're done editing individual events, you may want to rejoin them into a single event again. (In the mixing process, it's often easier to manipulate one long event rather than several shorter and disconnected ones.) This is easy enough to do; just follow these steps:

1. Click the **Glue** tool in the project window toolbar.
2. Click the first event.

The Glue tool works by gluing the first event you select to the next event. Therefore, two adjoining events become one.

> **Note**
>
> If you join two events that had a space between them, the space is included as part of the new, longer event.

Deleting an Event

Not everything you record is a keeper. Maybe it's a bad note, maybe it's a bad note choice; in any case, it's something you recorded that you wish you hadn't.

Fortunately, Cubase lets you excise just about any part of any recorded event. If you split your events carefully, you can isolate those areas of a recording that you want to delete.

Here's how to do it:

1. Click the **Erase** tool in the project window toolbar.
2. Click the event you want to delete.

One click, and the offending passage is gone. It's that easy!

> **Tip**
>
> To undo any action you've just applied, select **Edit > Undo** (or press **Ctrl+Z** on your computer keyboard).

Muting an Event

Maybe you don't really want to delete a section of your recording. Maybe you just want not to hear it, but still keep it around—in the off chance you might change your mind later. This scenario calls for Cubase's Mute tool, which silences any selected event.

Here's how it works:

1. Click the **Mute** tool in the project window toolbar.
2. Click the event you want to silence.

The muted event is no longer included in your recording's mix. You can unmute an event at any time by clicking it a second time with the Mute tool.

Fading an Event In or Out

Here's a common problem. You insert a new track or event into an existing recording, but the start of the new event sounds somewhat jarring in the mix. What you want is to fade in the new event, so that it doesn't hit listeners in the face full-volume.

Cubase lets you fade in or fade out individual events. It's as easy as dragging a handle. Just follow these steps to create a fade-in effect:

1. Select the **Object Selection** tool in the project window toolbar.
2. Select the audio event and locate the blue handle in the upper-left corner of the event.
3. Use your mouse to drag the blue handle to the right, to where you want the event to attain full volume.

As you can see in Figure 6.8, when you reposition the blue handle, a diagonal line appears. This line represents the fade-in effect. Notice how the waveforms get larger as the line progresses; this indicates that the volume is gradually increasing.

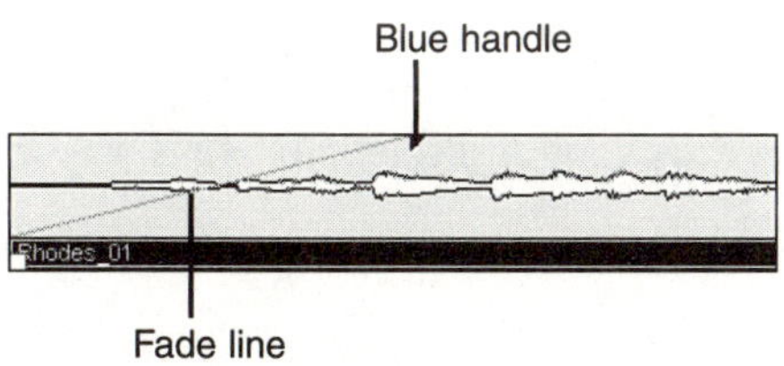

Figure 6.8 *Fading in an event.*

To create a fade-out effect, follow these same steps, except move the blue selection handle at the upper-right corner of the event to the left.

Changing the Order of Events in a Stack

> **Note**
>
> The front-most event is always the one that's active, even if the front event is shorter than events behind it. When events overlap, the rear events are always muted, start to finish.

When you record multiple passes in a single track, you create multiple audio events. These events are arranged in a stack, with the earliest events at the back and the latest ones at the front. When you initiate playback, only the front-most (most recent) event is played.

If you want to use an event deeper in the stack, you have two ways to proceed. The first method is to move the front event to the rear of the stack, which then makes the second event the new front event. To do this, right-click on the front event and select **Move To > Back** from the pop-up menu. You can continue doing this until you reach the event you want in front.

The second method is to show each event as a separate "lane" within the track, as shown in Figure 6.9. Here's how to do it:

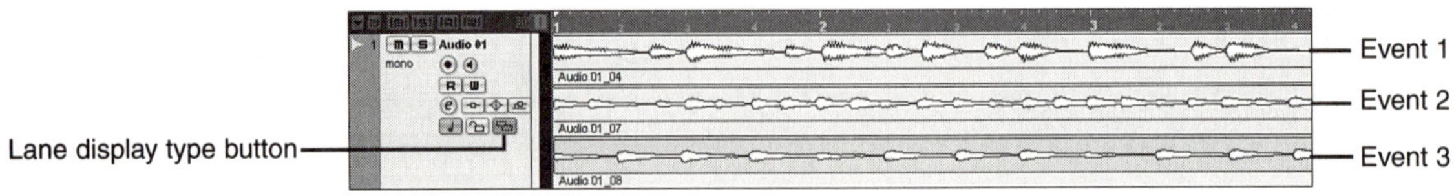

Figure 6.9 *Displaying multiple events as separate lanes in a track.*

1. Right click on the track in the track list and select Track Controls Settings from the pop-up menu.
2. When the Track Controls Settings dialog box appears, select Lane Display Type in the Available Controls list.
3. Click the **Add** button.
4. Click **OK** to close the dialog box.
5. Return to the track list and position your cursor at the bottom of the selected track, then click and drag your cursor to expand the track downward.
6. Click the **Lane Display Type** button for the selected track.
7. From the pop-up menu, select **Lanes Fixed.**

You'll now see all the events you've recorded for that track. To move a specific track to the front of the stack, right-click on the event and select **Move To > Front** from the pop-up menu.

Moving an Event

Events may have been recorded in a specific order on specific tracks, but they don't have to remain where they started. Cubase's event display is a visual environment that lets you drag and drop events from any one place to any other place, using your mouse. You can move an event earlier or later in time, or from one track to another.

To move an event, simply grab it with your cursor and drag it to a new position. It's no harder than that.

You can also move an event to another track. Again, just grab the event and move it to the other track. Even cooler, you can move an event and create a new track; just drag the event to a position under the bottom-most track in the event display. When you drop the event in place, a new track will automatically be created.

Building-Block Recording

The ability to move events lets you essentially rearrange the sections of your recording. Used properly, you can turn verse one into verse two, move a guitar solo from the chorus to the bridge, and even turn the intro into an out-chorus. It's just like playing with building blocks.

This sort of musical rearrangement is done all the time. A band goes into the studio, lays down a song as originally conceived, but then changes their mind about the order of the lyrics. No problem; the engineer simply swaps vocal sections by moving events. Or maybe the band decides that the chorus should come after the bridge, not before it. Again, the engineer moves events to put the song in the new order.

This process becomes even more useful when you use event copying. Maybe you really like the lick the guitarist played at the end of verse one, and want to hear it at the end of every verse. That's easy enough to do, by copying the first lick and pasting it into the end of all subsequent verses. Or maybe the band had trouble locking into a groove, but you found one perfect measure where the drummer, bassist, and rhythm guitarist were all in synch. Just copy that measure and paste it multiple times throughout the song. Voilà—a perfect song-length groove, created from a single measure.

Some purists might find the idea of constructing songs from a series of recorded building blocks to be "unnatural." Maybe it is. But it's how a lot of music gets made these days, as the compositional process merges with the recording process; the final composition is created in the engineering booth, not in the recording studio itself.

Of course, the ultimate form of building-block composition is so-called loop-based music. This is how many rap, hip-hop, and dance recordings are made. To learn more about loop-based recording, turn to Chapter 11.

Copying an Event

Just as you can move an event, you can also create a copy of any event and paste it anywhere in your recording. This is a great way to replicate sections of your recording; you can copy events as short as a cymbal crash or as long as a verse or chorus.

To copy an event, follow these steps:

1. Select the **Object Selection** tool in the project window toolbar.
2. Click the event you wish to copy.
3. Select **Edit > Copy.**

4. Select the track where you want to add the copied event.
5. Click within the ruler where you want to add the copied event.
6. Select **Edit > Paste.**

You can paste an event multiple times—just repeat steps 4 through 6.

Aligning Events

After you move an event, you might find that it doesn't quite align properly with the rest of the recording. Effective moving requires accurate positioning. You can improve your accuracy by activating Cubase's snap function. With snap turned on, the start of any event you move is automatically snapped to the nearest measure or second, as indicated by the ruler. This is a quick and easy way to align events in the project window.

You turn on snap mode by clicking the **Snap** button in the toolbar.

The Least You Need to Know

- It's often easier to work with an event when you zoom into it—either vertically or horizontally (or both).
- Events can be deleted, muted, moved, or copied.
- To edit a specific passage, you can split a single long event into multiple shorter ones.
- Multiple events can then be rejoined into a single event by using the Glue tool.
- Multiple takes within a track are represented by multiple events in a stack; the front-most event is the one that takes precedence.

Chapter 7

Editing and Processing Audio Samples

In This Chapter

- Using the sample editor
- Editing individual notes and waveforms
- Applying digital signal processing to individual events
- Using audio processing to increase gain, reduce noise, fade in and out, and change pitch and tempo

The raw audio you record with Cubase is contained in a series of audio events. Each event is actually a digital waveform that represents the analog waveform of the original instrument or vocal. To trained eyes, that waveform maps out everything you need to know about the recorded sound—pitch, amplitude, and duration.

In Chapter 6 you learned how to perform large-scale editing on your recordings, by cutting and pasting whole events. But Cubase also lets you edit the waveforms within events, by using a tool called the sample editor. Careful use of the sample editor lets you tweak the waveforms you've recorded, deleting individual notes, rearranging notes in the passage, and so forth. It's editing at the smallest possible level, of the finest details.

In addition, Cubase provides a number of digital signal processing (DSP) effects that you can apply directly to any audio event. When you apply audio processing, you change the waveforms you recorded—and therefore the sounds you hear. This processing can be subtle (increasing the gain or adding reverb) or dramatic (reversing the event or changing its pitch).

Using the Sample Editor

> **Note**
>
> The sample editor edits only audio events, not MIDI events. Because MIDI events are actually sets of digital instructions, they have no waveforms to edit.

When you want to directly edit the audio waveforms you've recorded, you use Cubase's sample editor. The sample editor edits the contents of one audio event at a time. You open the sample editor by double-clicking on the selected event.

As you can see in Figure 7.1, the sample editor has a toolbar along the top that mirrors most of the functions of the project editor's toolbar. The main part of the sample editor displays the waveform for the selected event. You can scroll up and down or right and left through the entire waveform by using the vertical and horizontal scroll bars.

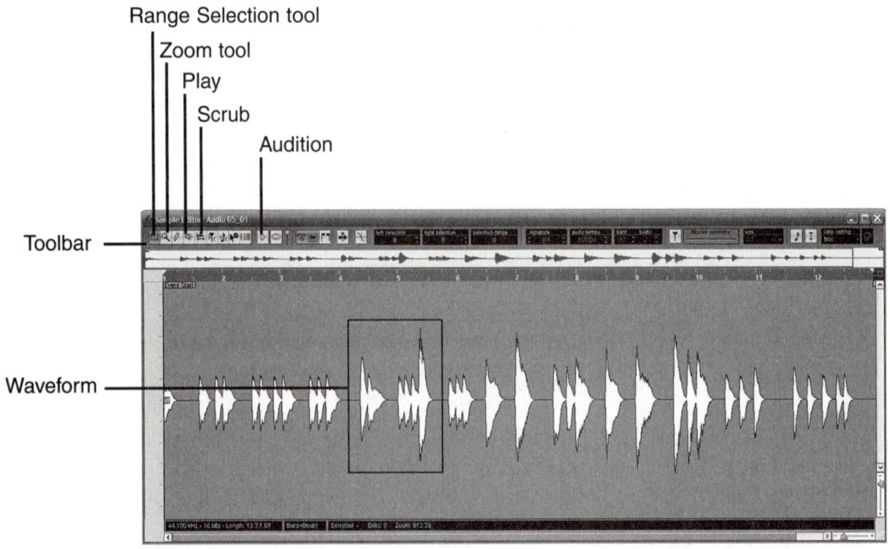

Figure 7.1 *The sample editor window.*

Zooming Into the Waveform

When you're making fine edits to sections of the waveform, it really helps to zoom into the area you're editing. You can zoom the waveform larger by using the vertical and horizontal scroll bars at the bottom right corner of the window, or by using the Zoom tool on the toolbar.

Figure 7.2 shows a section of previous waveform, zoomed larger both vertically and horizontally. As you can see, each individual note (including the note's attack and decay) is clearly distinguished in the zoomed waveform; at this level of detail, you can easily isolate and delete or edit individual notes.

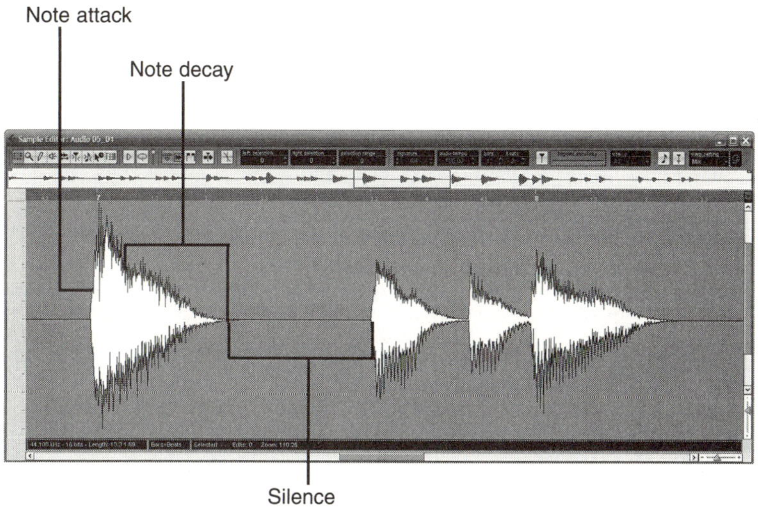

Figure 7.2 *A small section of the larger waveform, zoomed in to view more detail.*

> **Tip**
>
> If you zoom in all the way on a waveform, you'll see the individual points that make up the wave. If you want, you can use Cubase's Draw tool to alter the shape of the waveform, therefore changing the sound of the recorded note or pitch. (Beware—this is a very powerful way to edit. Small changes can have a big effect!)

Selecting a Range to Edit

Most of your editing in the sample editor will use the Range Selection tool. With this tool selected you can drag your cursor over the area you want to edit (typically a note or two), thus selecting that area. As you can see in Figure 7.3, the selected area shows a lighter color in the sample editor workspace. You can then right-click this area to select various editing options.

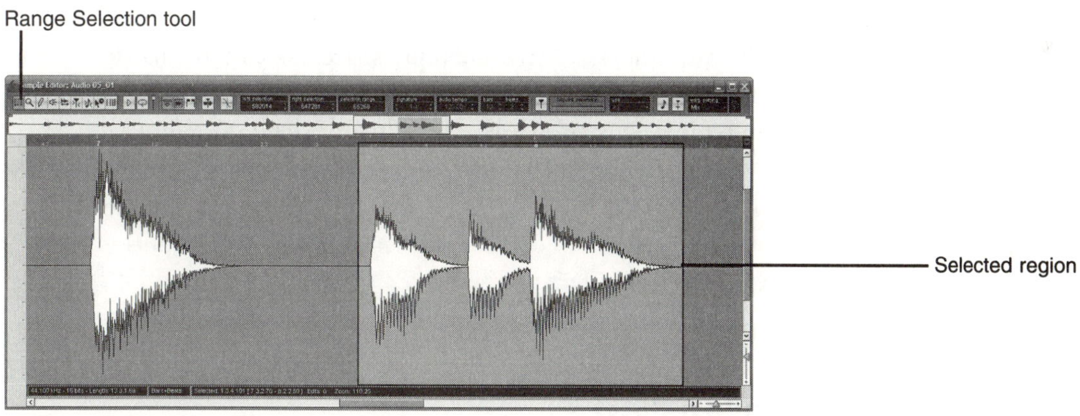

Figure 7.3 *Selecting a region to edit.*

Hearing Your Edits

To play back any selected region, either before or after you make your edits, click the **Audition** button on the toolbar. To play back the entire waveform in the sample editor, click the **Play** button in the toolbar and then click the **Play** button in the transport panel. You can also manually play areas of the waveform if you click the **Scrub** button in the toolbar, and then move your cursor across the waveform.

Don't Get Too Perfect

It's great that Cubase lets you edit virtually all aspects of a recording. It's not great when you take editing to the illogical extreme.

Although it's possible to edit out every imperfection, no matter how slight, you can sometimes create a recording that's too perfect. When the tempo is impeccably locked in place, the intonation is pitch perfect, and the instruments are playing flawlessly in synch with each other, the resulting sound loses a little of its humanity. It may be perfect, but it doesn't sound quite right.

A human-sounding recording is, by nature, a little imperfect. Great musicians sometimes push and pull the tempo, bend notes just a little above or below the pitch, and play a millisecond or two out of step with their fellow performers. These "imperfections" make a recording breathe, and give it life and energy. This is why an unedited recording of a live performance sounds almost imperceptibly different—and better—than a meticulous studio recording augmented by all the latest digital technology. All the digital recording functions you have at your fingertips, as useful as they are, can drain all the life out of a recording.

Personally, I prefer a recording with a few wrong notes left in, compared to one that has been digitally scrubbed of all its humanity. Although it's great to be able to fix the most egregious recorded mistakes, digital editing and processing should be used judiciously. Energy and inspiration are always preferable to precision and perfection!

Editing in the Project Window

As useful as the sample editor is, it has its drawbacks. One of those drawbacks is the way editing takes place. For example, when you delete a section of an event in the sample window, it doesn't leave an empty space; instead, the balance of the event scoots to the left to fill up the space. This can cause you to inadvertently erase entire beats from a song, which is generally not what you want to do.

When you want to delete and move notes, a better approach is to edit audio events directly in the project window. You can use the techniques you learned in Chapter 6 to zoom into an audio event, and then use the editing tools in the project window's toolbar to affect your edits.

Let's look at a few of the most useful types of edits you can perform.

Erasing Individual Notes

Want to delete a bad note or two—and insert a range of silence, instead? It's easy when you edit directly in the project window. Here's all you need to do:

1. Zoom into and select the audio event you want to edit.
2. Select the **Range Selection** tool in the toolbar.
3. Click and drag the cursor across the area you want to delete, as shown in Figure 7.4.
4. Right-click your mouse and select **Edit > Delete** from the pop-up menu. (Alternately, you can select **Edit > Delete** from the project window's menu.)

The area you selected is now deleted, as shown in Figure 7.5. All that's left is silence—and the rest of the audio event remains in place.

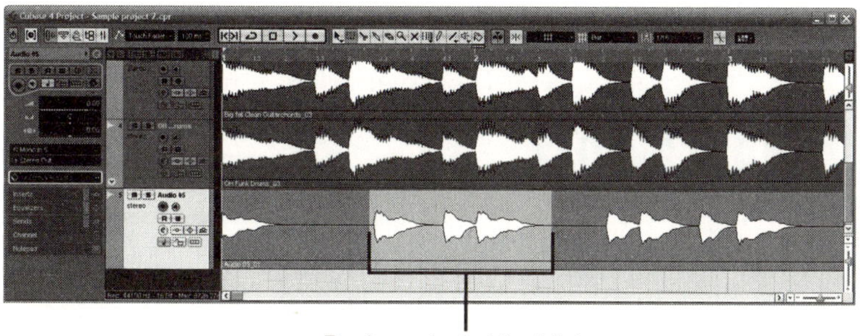

Figure 7.4 *Selecting a section of an audio event to delete.*

Figure 7.5 *The selected area deleted—and silence inserted.*

Moving and Copying Notes

You can also use the sample editor to copy and move individual notes from one place to another within an event. If you work carefully, you can completely alter whatever it was the musician played—up to and including rewriting a guitar solo, or inverting a drum beat!

To move a portion of the waveform to another position, follow these steps:

1. Zoom into and select the audio event you want to edit.
2. Select the **Range Selection** tool in the toolbar.
3. Click and drag the cursor across the area you want to move.
4. Right-click your mouse and select **Edit > Cut** from the pop-up menu.
5. Click the cursor within the waveform where you want to paste the area you just cut.
6. Right-click your mouse and select **Edit > Paste** from the pop-up menu.

Two things have just happened. First, the area you cut is removed from the audio event, with silence inserted. Second, the area you cut is pasted on top of the new portion of the event; anything that was there previously is now replaced by the pasted region.

Alternately, you can use a similar process to copy notes from one place to another. Just repeat this process, but in step 4 select **Edit > Copy** instead of **Edit > Cut.** This copies the selected region, rather than cutting it from its original position—which lets you hear the same note(s) in two different places of your song.

Processing Audio Events

In addition to fine-editing waveforms via the sample editor, Cubase also lets you apply larger-scale audio processing to any audio events you've recorded. You can apply this processing to any single event, group of events, or region within an event. The processing alters the waveform directly; after applying the processing, the processed waveform appears in the event display.

How Audio Processing Works

Audio processing occurs offline, before you initiate playback or mixing. The processing is applied directly to a selected event, therefore altering the event itself. When you play back or mix the project, no real time processing is needed, because the event itself has already been processed; this reduces your computer's CPU load, which makes for faster, more accurate system performance.

In addition, there are some audio processes that simply can't be applied to all the events in the signal path. For example, Cubase lets you reverse an event—that is, play it backward. You can't reverse an entire track in real time, because Cubase can't know what to start with until it comes to the end. Cubase can, however, reverse a selected event by processing it offline, before initiating playback.

Applying Processing to an Event

You can apply any of Cubase's audio processes or plug-ins to any audio event or region. Naturally, you can select more than one event at a time and apply processing to all the events you selected. You're still working on an event level, you're not applying processing to an entire track or project.

Processing an event is a fairly easy and fairly standardized process. In general terms, it goes like this:

1. Select the event or events you want to process.
2. Select **Audio > Process** or **Audio > Plug-ins,** then select the effect you want to apply.
3. The dialog box for that effect now opens.
4. Each effect has its own particular controls and settings. You set the controls as necessary for the effect you want to achieve.
5. To hear what the effect sounds like before you apply the final processing, click the **Preview** button.
6. If you like what you hear, click the **Process** button to apply the processing.

Tip

To select multiple events, hold down the shift key while you click each event. You can select and apply processing to multiple events within the same track, or in different tracks.

It's really that easy. Select the event, select the effect, configure the effect, preview the effect, and then process the audio.

Offline vs. Online Processing

Audio processing differs from using insert and send effects, which you learn about in Chapter 14. Inserts and sends are applied to the signal path in real time, and require vast amounts of processing power from your computer. Audio processing, on the other hand, takes place offline, outside of the signal path, and thus doesn't affect your computer's CPU load. To reduce the load on your PC, then, you should choose offline processing over online effects whenever practical.

Cubase lets you apply both audio processing and plug-in effects offline to individual events. So you can choose any process from the **Audio > Process** menu, or any plug-in from the **Audio > Plug-ins** menu and apply it directly to an event or selected region. Plug-in effects can also be applied as online insert and send effects; audio processes can't be used as inserts or sends.

When should you use offline processing? There are three scenarios where this type of processing should be chosen over insert or send effects. First, any time you want to apply an audio process (from the **Audio > Process** menu), you have to apply it offline to an event; applying it as an insert or send effect simply isn't a choice. Second, you should use offline processing when you want the effect to apply to only part of a track—that is, to an individual event within a larger track. Finally, offline processing makes sense if you have a slow or underpowered computer, and don't have the horsepower necessary to apply the same effect via online inserts and sends.

Undoing Event Processing

Any event processing you apply can be just as easily unapplied. This is because Cubase creates a new audio clip for any processed event. You only see the processed event in the project window, of course, but the original, unprocessed audio event still exists—and can be returned to.

To undo any audio processing or effect applied to an event, follow these steps:

1. Select the event for which you want to remove the audio processing.
2. Select **Audio > Offline Process History.**
3. When the Offline Process History dialog box appears, as shown in Figure 7.6, all the applied effects are listed in the Action column. Click the processing you want to remove.
4. Click the **Remove** button.
5. Click the **Close** button to close the dialog box.

As you can see, every single processing action you take for an event is clearly listed. (Cubase remembers what you've done, even if you don't!) You can step back through all the processing you've applied to return to any previous state, all the way back to the original unprocessed event.

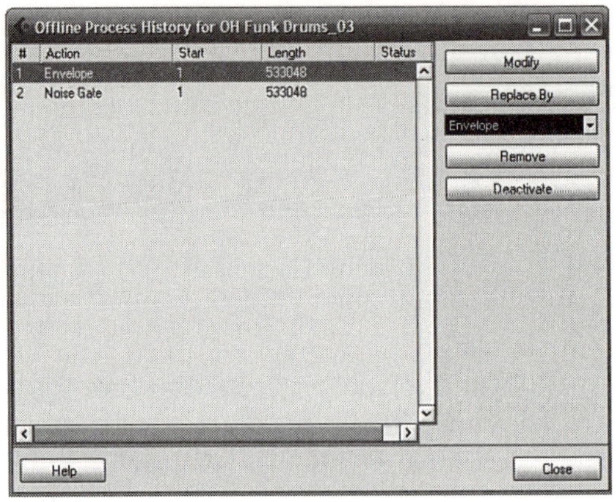

Figure 7.6 *Removing processing from an audio clip in the Offline Process History dialog box.*

Increasing the Gain

Cubase 4 offers a number of popular audio processing effects in the **Audio > Process** menu. There isn't space here to explore every available effect, but I will take a quick look at some of the more popular effects.

The first process to consider is one that many novice engineers find themselves using with frequency. It's a process that increases the gain, or volume level, of a recorded signal.

> **Tip**
>
> A recording made at too low a level doesn't get the recorded audio far enough above the level of background noise. That's one reason you want to record at as high a level as practical; you increase the distance between the useful audio and the unwanted noise floor.

Why, you ask, would you need to increase the gain in this fashion? Don't you just slide the level slider up to increase the volume?

Well, the problem comes when you record a voice or instrument at too low a level. After all, you can only increase the volume to the highest level you recorded; unlike what you saw in *This Is Spinal Tap*, there's no "11" on Cubase's mixing board.

Low recording levels typically result from using a microphone that requires a pre-amplifier without a pre-amp, or from plugging a guitar or keyboard directly into your system with the instrument's internal volume control turned down too low. In either situation, the result is a track that doesn't come anywhere near the 0 dB mark.

To make this track sound similar to the other tracks you've recorded, you need to normalize the volume levels between tracks. You could lower the volume of the other tracks, but then you get an entire recording that's at too low a level. The better approach is to increase the level of the low-volume track, which Cubase lets you do via digital signal processing.

> **Caution**
>
> When you increase the gain for an event, you also increase the noise level. For this reason, use the gain control sparingly, and be prepared to live with an increased level of background noise.

To increase the gain of an event, you use Cubase's Gain process. The more you increase the gain, the louder the track becomes. Here's how it works:

1. Select the event(s) or region that was recorded at too low a level.
2. Select **Audio > Process > Gain.**
3. When the gain control launches, as shown in Figure 7.7, move the slider to the right to increase the gain.

4. Click the **Preview** button to hear your changes.
5. If you increased the level too much, you'll see a "Clip Detected" message below the slider. Move the slider to the left and click the **Preview** button again; repeat this process until you apply just enough gain without clipping.
6. Click the **Process** button to apply the audio processing.

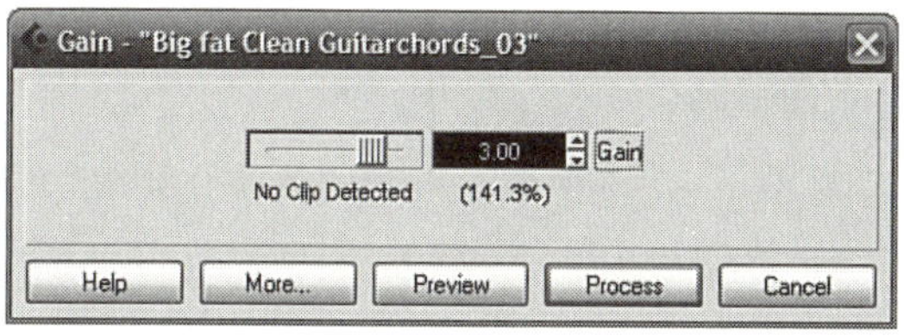

Figure 7.7 *Increasing the gain of an event.*

Silencing Noisy Passages

When you make a noisy recording, much of the noise is hidden by the recorded sound itself. That is, when an instrument is playing, the listener hears the instrument, not the background noise.

However, when the instrument stops playing (or the vocalist stops singing), that background noise is no longer masked. The listener hears the noise clearly and distinctly, and that isn't good.

This is why audio engineers invented *noise gates*. A noise gate is a device or process that identifies passages that should be silent, and automatically erases all noise and hiss from those passages. The process works by setting a volume threshold; all signals below that threshold are deleted.

Cubase includes a Noise Gate process that you can apply to any selected event or region in your recording. Here's how it works:

1. Select the event(s) or region you want to process.
2. Select **Audio > Process > Noise Gate.**
3. When the noise gate control launches, as shown in Figure 7.8, adjust the **Threshold** control to set the level below which you want the audio silenced. (This may take some trial and error.) In most instances, this level can be set fairly low.
4. Adjust the **Attack Time** control to specify how fast the gate will open after the threshold has been exceeded. In most instances, you want a fairly low attack time; setting a longer attack time softens the attack of the instrument, adding a "swell" type of effect to the sound.
5. Adjust the **Min. Opening Time** control to specify how long the gate should remain open. If you find the noise gate switching on and off during an instrument's normal decay, set a longer duration.

> **Tip**
>
> You can also use a noise gate to cut off the ring from sustained drum sounds (cymbals and toms), remove unwanted room ambience, shorten reverb decay times, and reduce leakage from one microphone to another.

> **Tip**
> You can also use the Range Selection tool to select a region across multiple events. This is useful when you want to apply a fade across all recorded tracks.

6. Adjust the **Release Time** control to specify how quickly the gate closes. Short release times can sometimes sound a bit abrupt; choose a longer duration for a smoother effect.
7. Click the **Preview** button to hear your changes; make further adjustments as necessary.
8. Click the **Process** button to apply the audio processing.

Figure 7.8 *Using a noise gate to reduce background noise.*

Fade In and Out

When you want to add a soft attack to a new event, use Cubase's Fade In process. Likewise, you can create smooth fade outs by using the Fade Out process. They both work in similar fashion.

Know, however, that Fade In/Out applies to the entire area selected. So if you select an event, the fade in (for example) will start at the beginning of the event and reach full volume at the end of the event. For this reason, you want to select a region within an event for the fade to take place.

Here's how it works:

1. Click the **Range Selection** button in the project window toolbar.
2. Select the region where you want the fade to take place, as shown in Figure 7.9. (For a fade in, the region should start at the beginning of an event and end sometime after; for a fade out, the region should stop at the end of the event and start sometime before that.)

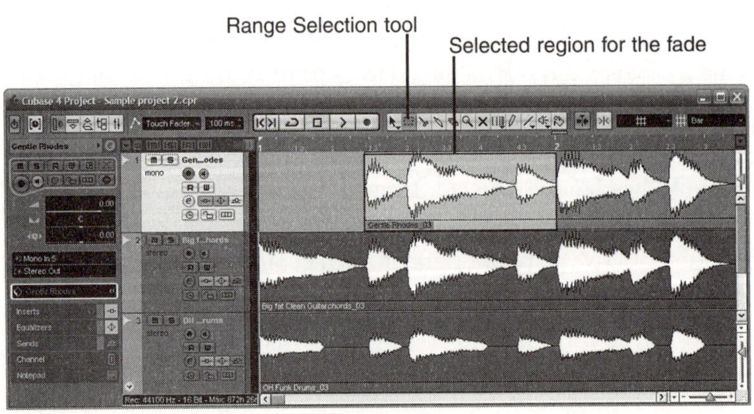

Figure 7.9 *Selecting a region for the fade effect.*

3. Select **Audio > Process > Fade In** or **Audio > Process > Fade Out.**
4. When the Fade In or Fade Out dialog box (shown in Figure 7.10) appears, select the kind of curve you want. (For most instances, the middle button—damped spline interpolation—works fine.)
5. Select the desired shape of the fade curve; the curve will be displayed in the fade display.
6. Click the **Preview** button to hear the fade, then make any necessary changes.
7. Click the **Process** button to apply the fade.

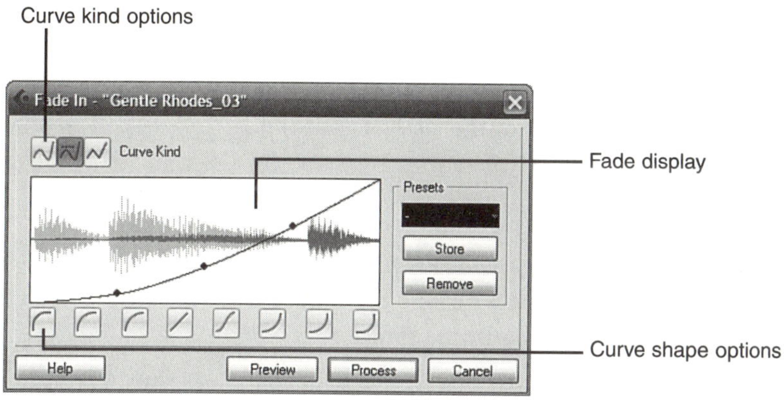

Figure 7.10 *Processing a fade out effect.*

As you can see in Figure 7.11, the waveform in the selected area now grows from the zero point to the regular level.

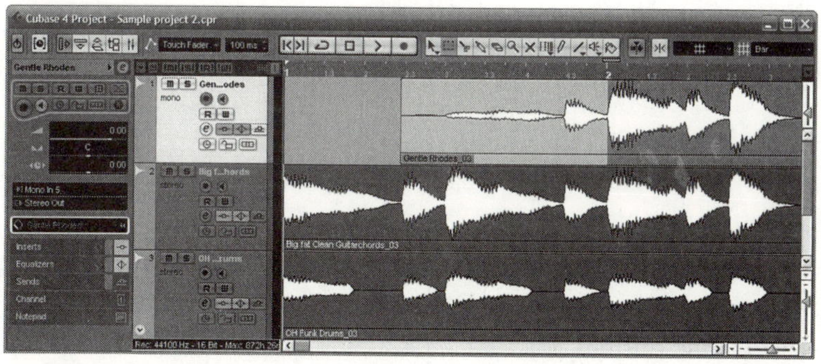

Figure 7.11 *A waveform fading into normal volume after a fade effect is applied.*

Playing an Event Backward

Remember when people thought if you played "I'm So Tired" from The Beatles' *White Album* backward, you'd hear the hidden message, "Paul is dead"? (If you're too young to remember this, ask your parents about it.) Well, Paul

McCartney is still alive, but backward masking is still a fun little trick you can add to your own recordings.

Back in The Beatles' heyday, backward sounds were inserted into recordings by the simple method of playing a tape backward. Aside from leaving subliminal messages to fans, this technique also lets you play instruments backward, which can often create a cool-sounding effect. (For fun, try adding backward cymbal crashes—you hear the decay first, leading up to the big attack.)

In Cubase, you can reverse the playback of any event or region by using the Reverse process. It's one of the easiest effects to add; here's how it works:

1. Select the event(s) or region you want to reverse.
2. Select **Audio > Process > Reverse.**

That's it. The waveform is now reversed in the event, so when you play it back, it plays from finish to start, instead of the right way around.

Changing Pitch

Imagine that you've recorded a backing track for a vocalist to sing to. The singer arrives, but says "This is a little outside my range. Can you lower the key a half-step?" Don't laugh; it happens all the time.

In the old days, the only way to change pitch was to speed up or slow down the tape, which also affected tempo. Fortunately, computer technology enables more sophisticated changes, which in this case means changing the pitch without changing the tempo.

You can change the pitch of any individual event, or for all the events in a recording. (To change an individual event, just select that event then start with step 2, below.) We'll examine how to change the pitch of an entire recording; follow these steps:

1. From the project window, select **Edit > Select > All.** This selects all the events in your project.
2. Select **Audio > Process > Pitch Shift.**
3. When the Pitch Shift dialog box appears, as shown in Figure 7.12, select the **Transpose** tab.
4. Click the **Transpose** control up or down the number of semitones (half-steps) you want to change the pitch. For example, to transpose down a half-step, select -1 semitones.
5. Make sure the **Time Correction** option is checked. (If this is unchecked, changing the pitch will affect the length of the recording.)
6. Click the **Preview** button to listen to how the recording will sound in the new key.
7. Click the **Process** button to finalize the pitch change.

Tip

The virtual keyboard in the Pitch Shift dialog box shows middle C in red. That note, transposed, is shown in blue. You can view the transposed value of other pitches by changing the **Root Note/Pitch** control in the Pitch Shift Base section of the dialog box.

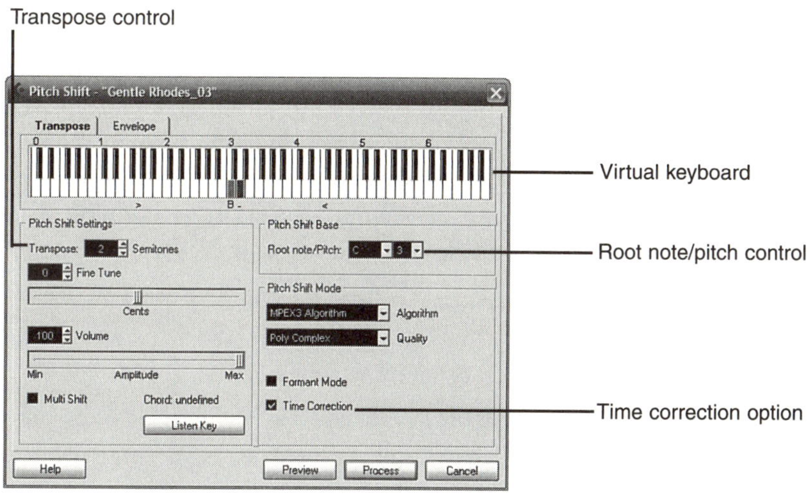

Figure 7.12 *Changing the pitch of a recording.*

Stretching and Shrinking Your Recording

When you're doing television or movie work, you often have to work within rigid time constraints. Imagine that you've recorded a theme song for a movie or television show. The song clocks in at exactly 63 seconds in length, but the producer comes to you and says that the closing credits are only 60 seconds long. Somehow, you have to make that 63-second recording fit into a 60-second slot—without affecting the pitch.

Once again, this is the sort of previously impossible problem for which Cubase offers a fairly elegant and effective solution. In the old days, your only option would be to speed up the tape, which would also raise the pitch of the recording. But now, thanks to Cubase's digital audio processing features, it's a simple matter of clicking a few buttons and letting Cubase do the work for you.

Unlike the pitch-changing operation, time stretching requires a little bit of preparation up front. (That's right—this operation involves math!) Start by writing down the desired length of the recording. Next, write down the actual length of your existing recording. Now divide the desired length by the current length. The number you get from this calculation, expressed as a percentage, is what you'll need to use in Cubase's Time Stretch dialog box.

Note

You've probably noticed that the Time Stretch dialog box has settings for Length in Seconds—so why can't you just enter the current and desired length and skip the math? The problem is that the dialog box measures only the length of one event at a time, not the total length of the track. If an event starts after the zero point, or ends before the events in another track, the total length of the recording won't be shown in the dialog box—which is why you need to work with percentages.

For example, if the desired length is 60 seconds and the current length is 63 seconds, you divide 60 by 63 and get 95.238 percent. Write that number down.

One last bit of preparation. As part of the time-stretching process, you need to glue all the events in each track together. If you stretch individual events separately, you only stretch the events—not the space between the events. (This really screws up the rhythm!) So our step-by-step process starts with gluing all the events in a track together, so you can stretch the entire track—including the former spaces between events.

Here's how to do it all:

1. In the project window's track listing, click the first track.
2. Select **Edit > Select > All on Selected Tracks** to select all the events on the current track.
3. Click the **Glue** button in the toolbar.
4. Click on any event in the selected track. This glues all the events on that track together into one long track.
5. Repeat steps 1 through 4 for every track in your project.
6. After all the events are glued together, select **Edit > Select All** to select all the events in your project.
7. Select **Audio > Process > Time Stretch.**
8. When the Time Stretch dialog box appears, as shown in Figure 7.13, uncheck the **Effect** option in the Time Stretch Ratio section.
9. Enter the percentage you calculated into the Time Stretch Ratio section.
10. Click the **Preview** button to listen to how the recording will sound at the new length.
11. Click the **Process** button to finalize the time stretch (or shrinkage).

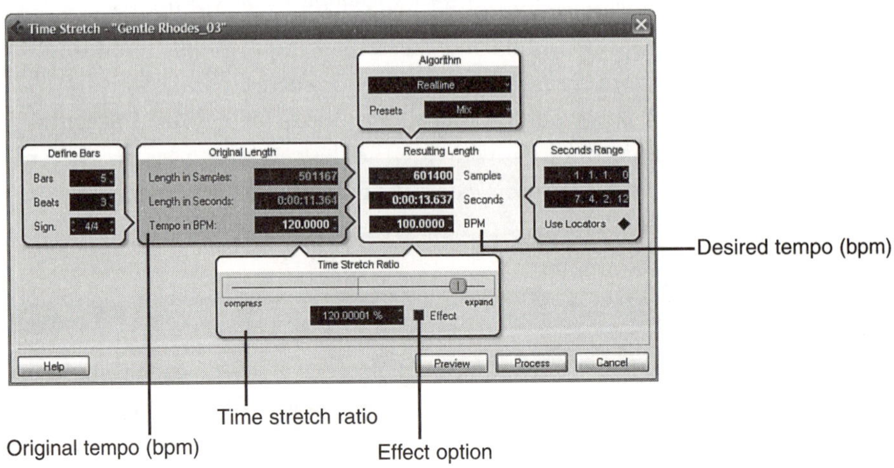

Figure 7.13 *Changing the length of a recording.*

Changing Tempo

Here's another fun situation. Imagine you've recorded a dance track at 120 beats per minute. But the track just before this one is at 110 bpm, and your producer wants the two tracks to merge seamlessly into another. That means slowing down the tempo of your song, without changing the pitch of the recording.

If you know the precise tempo of your recording, in beats per minute, you can use Cubase's Time Stretch feature to change to a new tempo. And this time, there's no math involved—although you still have to glue together all the events in each track. Just follow these steps:

1. In the project window's track listing, click the first track.
2. Select **Edit > Select > All on Selected Tracks** to select all the events on the current track.
3. Click the **Glue** button in the toolbar.
4. Click on any event in the selected track. This glues all the events on that track together into one long track.
5. Repeat steps 1 through 4 for every track in your project.
6. After all the events are glued together, select **Edit > Select All** to select all the events in your project.
7. Select **Audio > Process > Time Stretch.**
8. When the Time Stretch dialog box appears, uncheck the **Effect** option in the Time Stretch Ratio section.
9. Enter the current tempo into the Tempo in BPM control of the Original Length section.
10. Enter the desired new tempo into the BPM control of the Resulting Length section.
11. Click the **Preview** button to listen to how the recording will sound at the new tempo.
12. Click the **Process** button to finalize the tempo change.

Tip

As with pitch shifting, time stretching and tempo changing are done on each event individually. You can choose to stretch individual events, or—as presented here—select all the events in the project to stretch or shrink the entire recording.

Caution

Stretching or shrinking a recording by too large an amount can adversely affect the quality of the recording. It's best to make changes in small percentages, no more than 10 percent to 20 percent of the original recording.

The Least You Need to Know

- Detailed editing of audio waveforms can take place in either the project window or the sample editor.
- You can delete individual notes (and replace them with silence), or cut and paste any section of the waveform.
- Cubase lets you apply offline audio processing to any audio event or region.
- Audio processing takes place offline, and therefore doesn't use any real-time computer CPU resources.
- Popular audio processing effects include increasing gain, noise gating, fading in and out, changing pitch, altering the length of a recording, and changing tempo.

Chapter 8

Editing MIDI Tracks

In This Chapter

- Editing with the key editor
- Editing musical notes with the score editor
- Transposing pitch
- Changing volume levels

As you learned in Chapter 6, audio events and MIDI events can both be split, cut, copied, and otherwise edited to help you rearrange sections of your recording. Although you can't fine-edit MIDI events the same way you can edit audio waveforms, you can edit the MIDI instructions themselves, therefore changing pitch, duration, and other key note values.

Cubase offers a number of different ways to edit within your MIDI events—the key editor, list editor, and score editor. All these editors access and change the same MIDI instructions, they just do it in different ways, with different interfaces. That's because different users like to work different ways. For example, if you like to work with a visual representation of the MIDI notes, the key editor is a good choice for you. On the other hand, if you prefer to work with traditional music notation, then you want to use the score editor. Whichever editor you use, the same MIDI data gets changed.

The most useful of these editors are the key editor and the score editor, and I explain how to use both of them. (The list editor lists the details for each MIDI note in a text-based fashion rather than a visual fashion, and is therefore less intuitive for most users to use; I don't cover it in this book.)

Using the Key Editor

The most popular MIDI editor, especially among non-musicians, is the key editor. To open the key editor for a given MIDI event, select that event and then select **MIDI > Open Key Editor.**

As you can see in Figure 8.1, the key editor breaks the selected event into a giant grid. The horizontal axis of the grid corresponds to duration (as evidenced by the ruler running along the top of the grid); the vertical axis corresponds to pitch (as evidenced by the piano keyboard running along the left side). Notes are represented on the grid as a series of red boxes.

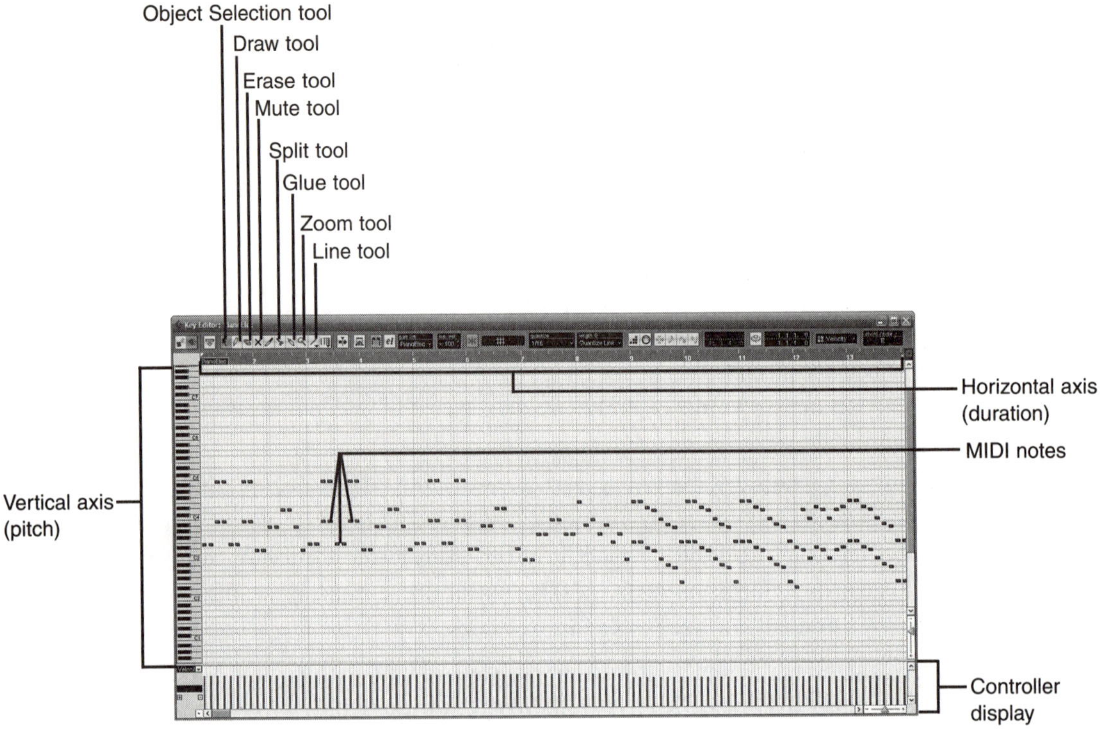

Figure 8.1 *The key editor.*

The position and size of a note on the grid determines its length and pitch. The wider a note box, the longer the note's duration. The higher a box on the grid, the higher the note's pitch. The effect is almost like that of an old-time piano scroll, the kind used in player pianos.

> **Note**
>
> The controller display can also be set to show various other MIDI instructions, such as pitch bend, aftertouch, program change, and so forth. Pull down the list at the left of the controller display to change what parameter is displayed.

Running along the very bottom of the key editor is yet another grid, called the controller display. By default, the controller display shows a series of vertical bars that correspond to the note boxes in the upper part of the grid. These bars represent the third dimension of our MIDI instructions, velocity or volume level. The higher the bar, the louder the note.

The toolbar at the top of the key editor window contains those tools you use to edit your MIDI notes. Read on to learn how to use these tools to perform various types of editing.

Deleting Notes

Ever play a note you wished you hadn't? You use the key editor to delete it. Here's all you need to do:

1. Select the **Erase** tool in the toolbar.
2. Click the note you want to erase.

Poof—it's gone!

> **Tip**
> It's important to select the right note to edit. This is where you want to use a combination of the ruler and the keyboard (along the top and left side of the grid) to locate individual notes. The ruler tells you in which measure (and where in that measure) the note is; the keyboard tells you the pitch of the note. Between these two guides, you should be able to figure out which note is which.

Muting Notes

Maybe you don't really want to delete a note. Maybe you want to hear what your piece sounds like without the note, while reserving the option of bringing the note back if you don't like what you hear. No problem; the key editor lets you mute the playback of notes, without actually deleting them. Follow these steps:

1. Select the **Mute** tool in the toolbar.
2. Click the note you want to silence.

Rearranging Notes

Deleting and muting are relatively easy operations. Moving notes from one place to another is a bit more difficult.

First, know that you can move any MIDI note either horizontally or vertically. When you move the note horizontally, you change where it appears in the track—that is, on which beat or in which measure. When you move the note vertically, you change the pitch assigned to that note.

Here's how to move things around:

1. Select the **Object Selection** tool in the toolbar.
2. Click the note you want to move.
3. Use your mouse to drag the note to a new position.

> **Tip**
> To move multiple notes at the same time, hold down the Shift key on your computer keyboard while you select the notes with the object selection tool. Alternately, you can click and drag the object selection tool to form a selection rectangle around a group of notes.

Shortening or Lengthening the Duration of a Note

So far, so good. Next up, let's see how you can shorten or lengthen the duration of a note—quite useful for when a note sustains longer or shorter than you intended. Here's what you need to do:

1. Select the **Object Selection** tool in the toolbar.
2. Position the cursor at the right edge of the note you wish to shorten or lengthen. The cursor should change to a double arrow, as shown in Figure 8.2.

3. Click and hold the mouse button to drag the right end of the note to the left to shorten, or to the right to lengthen.
4. Release the mouse button; the note should now be the new duration.

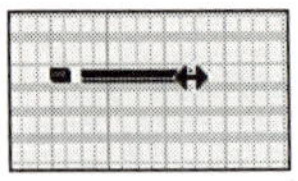

Figure 8.2 *Shorten or lengthen a note by stretching or shrinking the right edge.*

Adding New Notes

Okay, now let's do something that's a bit more difficult—adding new notes to your recording. To do this, use the Pencil tool to draw new notes on the key editor grid. Here's how it works:

1. Select the **Pencil** tool from the toolbar.
2. Locate the exact pitch and time position where you want to insert the new note.
3. Click this point in the grid and continue to hold down the left mouse button.
4. Drag the mouse to the right until the note is the desired duration, as shown in Figure 8.3.
5. Release the mouse button; the new note is now in place.

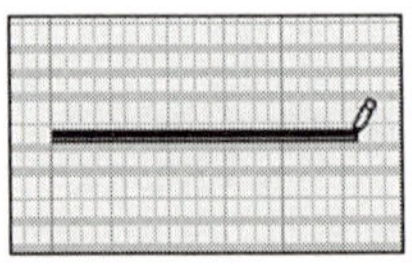

Figure 8.3 *Drawing a new note in the grid.*

Changing Volume Level

The last operation we'll use the key editor for is changing the volume level of one or more notes. In MIDI terms, the volume level of a note is called *velocity*, and you edit it in the controller display at the bottom of the key editor window.

Follow these steps:

1. Select the **Pencil** tool from the toolbar.
2. Locate the vertical bar in the controller display for the note you want to edit. (Each bar corresponds to a specific note on the upper grid.)
3. Click the vertical bar and continue to hold down the left mouse button.
4. Drag the bar up to increase the volume; drag it down to decrease the volume, as shown in Figure 8.4.
5. Release the mouse button.

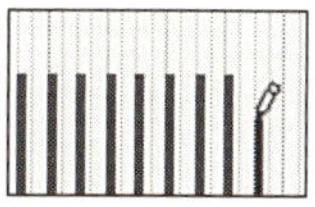

Figure 8.4 *Changing the velocity level for a note in the controller display.*

Using the Key Editor

The most popular MIDI editor, especially among non-musicians, is the key editor. To open the key editor for a given MIDI event, select that event and then select **MIDI > Open Key Editor.**

You open the score editor by selecting the track to edit and then selecting **MIDI > Open Score Editor.** As you can see in Figure 8.5, the score editor displays the contents of that MIDI track in standard music notation.

At the top of the score editor window is a toolbar that contains some familiar tools—and some new ones, too. We'll learn about these in short order.

Below the toolbar is an info line, which contains detailed information about any selected note. Below that is what Cubase calls the extended toolbar, which lets you select what types of notes to insert into the score. Then, below that, we have the display filter bar, which lets you choose which elements to display in the score editor window.

Tip

If you want to change the velocity of an entire track, there's an easier way to do it than using the key editor. See the "Changing Velocity" section at the end of this chapter to learn more.

Note

Complete operation of everything that the score editor has to offer would require a separate book. For our purposes, I assume that you're using the score editor to edit your previously recorded MIDI tracks, rather than to create your own musical compositions from scratch.

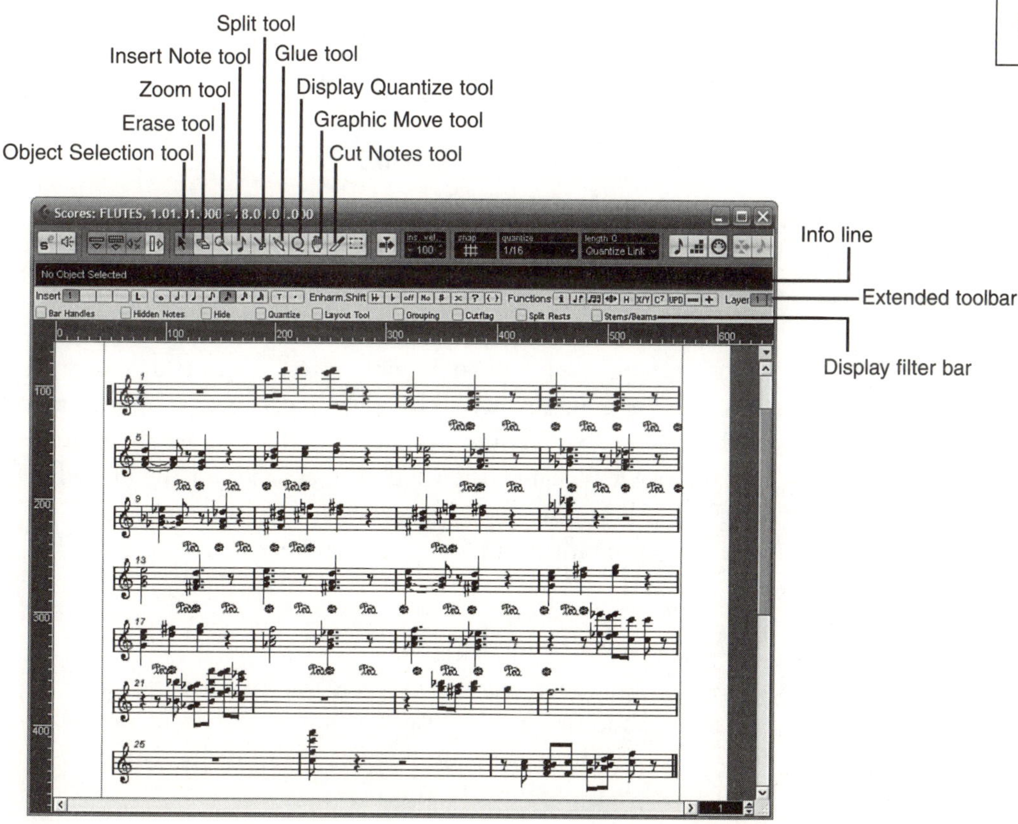

Figure 8.5 *The score editor.*

> **Tip**
> You can open a score with more than one track or part by holding down the Shift key and selecting multiple tracks in the track list, and then selecting **MIDI > Open Score Editor** (or **Scores > Open Selection**).

> **Note**
> Unfamiliar with music notation? Then you need to read my companion book, *The Complete Idiot's Guide to Music Theory, Second Edition* (Michael Miller, Alpha Books, 2005). It teaches you everything you need to know about reading and writing music—from the ground up.

Deleting Notes

Deleting notes within the score editor is deceptively simple; click a note with the Eraser tool and it's deleted. However, when you delete a note, what happens to that space in the musical score? Fortunately, the score editor is somewhat intelligent; when it removes a note, it inserts a rest. Here's how it works:

1. Click the **Eraser** tool on the toolbar.
2. Click the note you want to delete.

What happens next depends on what type of note you deleted. Here are the rules that Cubase follows:

- If you deleted a solo note, Cubase inserts a rest in its place.
- If you deleted one note in a multiple-note chord, the rest of the notes remain in place; only the note you selected is deleted.
- If you deleted a note that was tied to another note, both notes are deleted.

Moving Notes

The score editor lets you move any note to any other position in your score. If you move the note directly up or down, you move it to a different pitch. If you move the note sideways, you change the placement of the note within the measure (or in another measure), which completely changes the rhythm of the piece—which makes this entire note-moving business a trifle tricky.

The process itself is easy enough:

1. Click the **Object Selection** tool on the toolbar.
2. Left-click your mouse and then hold the note you want to move.
3. Drag the note to a new position.
4. Release the mouse button.

> **Tip**
> If you move a note somewhere you didn't intend to, press Ctrl-Z on your computer keyboard to undo the move.

My advice to you is to be very careful when moving notes. When you change pitch, be sure to position the note directly above or below its original position; any sideways movement will also affect the rhythm. And if you move the note sideways, know that Cubase will change the rhythm to account for the moved note, both in its original position (by inserting a rest) and in its new position (by altering the note lengths of adjacent notes). As I said, it's tricky!

Adding New Notes

One of the real strengths of the score editor is the capability of writing your own music, note by note. Although you can use this functionality to compose music from scratch, you can also use it to add notes to your previously recorded MIDI track. It is not a simple procedure, however.

To add a new note to your score, follow these steps:

1. Select the **Insert Note** tool from the toolbar.
2. From the extended toolbar, select the note value (whole note, half note, quarter note, and so on) for the note you want to add.
3. If the note you're adding needs to be flatted or sharped, select the appropriate accidental from the extended toolbar.
4. Click the cursor at the exact position and pitch where you want to add the new note.

If you added the new note into an empty measure, the new note is inserted into the position you selected, with rests added before and after to complete the rest of the measure. If you added the new note into an already existing measure, one of two things could happen. If you added a note of the same value on top of or below an existing note, you create a chord and none of the rhythms are changed. If you inserted the note rhythmically between two existing notes or rests, the values of the surrounding notes or rests are rewritten to make room for the inserted note. It can, admittedly, be a tad tricky.

Lengthening or Shortening a Note

The same technique you used to add a new note is also used to change the duration of an existing note—sort of. Essentially, you sit a new note of a new duration directly on top of an existing note while you hold down the Alt key on your computer keyboard; this changes the duration of the original note. Here's how it works:

1. Select the **Insert Note** tool from the toolbar.
2. From the extended toolbar, select the new note value.
3. Hold down the Alt key and click the cursor exactly on top of the note you want to change.

When you Alt-click a note like this, Cubase replaces the existing note with the new note. If you replaced a longer note with a shorter one, Cubase inserts a rest to compensate for the leftover space.

Flatting or Sharping a Note

As you learned previously, one way to change the pitch of a note is to drag it up or down to a new pitch. This only changes pitch within the current key, however. If you need to move in adjacent half-steps, you can simply flat or sharp the note. Follow these steps:

1. Select the **Object Selection** tool from the toolbar.
2. Click the note you want to change.
3. Click the flat or sharp button on the extended toolbar.

Pretty easy!

Tip

You can also use this technique to add double flats, double sharps, or natural signs to a note.

Composing Music with the Score Editor

Steinberg has designed the score editor to be more than just a simple MIDI editor. It's powerful enough to function as a free-standing music notation program, so that composers and arrangers can create their music, start to finish, from within the Cubase program.

Although I've discussed only basic editing, you can use the score editor to create a new blank score with any number of staves, and then fill those staves with notes and chords and rhythms to create your own compositions. The score you create can be played back and recorded within the main Cubase program, or printed out for other musicians to read or play.

The question, then, is whether the Cubase score editor is as good a music notation program as freestanding notation programs, such as Finale, Sibelius, or Notion. The answer is a definite maybe.

Both Finale and Sibelius are long-established notation programs, while Notion is more of a newcomer to the game; all are quite popular among professionals, academics, students, and others in the music field. These programs (Notion excepted) have been around for a long time, and have benefited from years and years of listening to user needs and fine-tuning the programs' features and functionality. None of these programs are particularly easy to use (although Notion has an arguably easier-to-learn user interface), but all are extremely powerful. Just about anything you need to notate can be done from within these three programs.

The Cubase score editor, on the other hand, isn't quite as mature a program as Sibelius or Finale. It can do a lot—as much as many musicians will need—but it doesn't offer many of the advanced notation options that are standard in the dedicated programs. The score editor is also a little harder to use for individual note entry; it just takes a little more work to do what you want to do than it does with the other programs. (Although, to be fair, it's easy enough to use when you want to enter your music via MIDI keyboard.)

All this said, there is no reason why you can't use the score editor to compose and arrange your music—many professional musicians do. But it's just as easy to score your music in Finale, Sibelius, or Notion, and then import your work into Cubase as a MIDI file. The point is, if you're interested in composing for recording, you shouldn't feel limited to using the score editor; you can use any music notation program you like, and then import your files into Cubase for recording.

And, of course, the score editor is a great tool for musicians who want to fine-tune their MIDI recordings. For composers and arrangers, it's easier to change their music by changing the notation than it is by moving blocks around the grid in the key editor. The end goal of the process, after all, is to create music; the score editor is a useful tool to help you do just that.

Simple MIDI Track Editing

There are two common types of MIDI editing that don't require the use of any special editors. When you want to change pitch or volume level for an entire track, you can do so directly from the track parameters panel in the track inspector—which makes the whole process extremely easy.

Transposing Pitch

When you record a part in one key but later find you need to play it back in another key (because of requests from singers, or trying to match one part with another), it's very easy to transpose that part when it was recorded on a MIDI track. After all, the pitch that's played is just a MIDI instruction; change the instruction and you change the pitch.

Changing the pitch of an individual note is best done in either the key editor or score editor, but changing the pitch of an entire track can be done within the project window—which is, quite frankly, a lot easier. Just follow these steps:

1. From the track list, select the MIDI track(s) you want to transpose.
2. Select **MIDI > Transpose.**
3. When the Transpose dialog box appears, as shown in Figure 8.6, there are two ways to change pitch. You can use the arrow buttons of the Semitone control to nudge the pitch up or down, a half-step at a time. Or you can enter a new key in the New Scale control.
4. Click **OK** when done.

That's it. (I told you it was easy!)

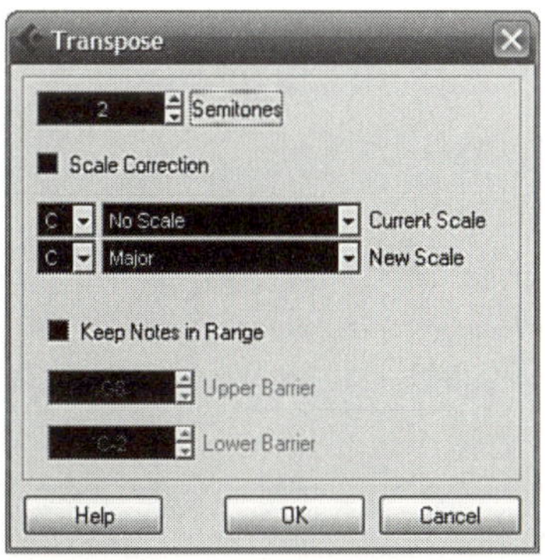

Figure 8.6 *Changing the pitch of a MIDI track with the Transpose dialog box.*

Changing Volume

Earlier in this chapter you learned how to use the key editor to change volume, or velocity, for individual notes within a MIDI event. If you want to change the volume for an entire event, you can use the Volume control in the track inspector, instead.

Here's how it works:

1. From the track list, select the track for which you want to change the volume.
2. In the inspector, go to the Volume control, as shown in Figure 8.7.
3. Use your mouse to drag the volume slider to the right (to increase the volume) or to the left (to decrease the volume).

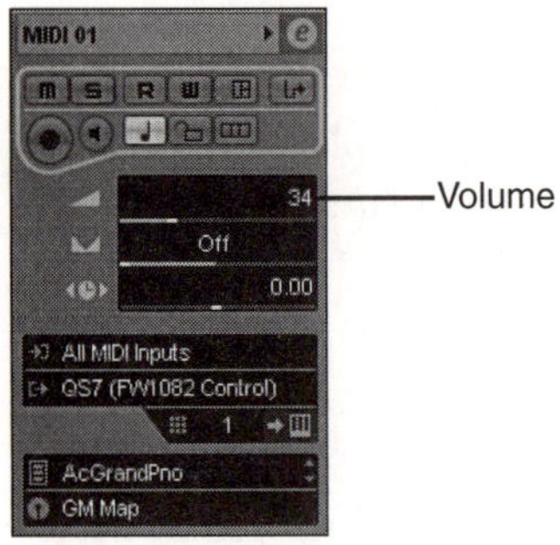

Figure 8.7 *Changing the volume for a MIDI track.*

The Least You Need to Know

- MIDI notes can be edited with Cubase's key editor; double-click on any MIDI event to edit it.
- The key editor lets you edit pitch, note duration, and velocity (volume level), by moving blocks around on a grid.
- To edit musical notes in a MIDI event, use the score editor, which presents your MIDI track in musical notation.
- Changing the pitch or velocity for an entire MIDI event can be done from within the project window.

Part 4

Special Techniques

There's lots of fun stuff you can do with Cubase. Here is where you learn how to use VST instruments, create loop-based recordings, and put together funky drum parts!

Chapter 9

Using VST Instruments

In This Chapter

- Discovering Cubase's built-in VST instruments
- Activating VST instruments in Cubase
- Assigning VST instruments to MIDI tracks
- Freezing VST tracks
- Creating VST instrument tracks

In Chapter 5 you learned about MIDI instruments. Cubase is configured to work with both general MIDI instruments and with its own specific type of virtual instruments, which it calls *VST instruments*. Like a MIDI instrument, a VST instrument is a type of software synthesizer or sound device that is played within Cubase via MIDI, and treated like any other MIDI instrument. The great thing about VST instruments is their versatility. Most VST instruments function like real-world instruments in that they offer dozens if not hundreds of different variations on a basic sound. Choose a VST piano, for example, and you can choose between different models of piano, different room sizes, different ambiance and delay settings, different sound settings (sustain, string/hammer release, hardness/softness), and on and on.

In addition, equipping your system with a number of VST instruments is much less expensive than buying the physical instruments themselves. Most VST instruments offer the same sounds and functionality as real-world synthesizers and samplers, but are much less expensive than the originals. They're also quite easy to configure; all the settings, sounds, and effects are saved within the Cubase song file. Plus, being software-based, they don't take up valuable physical space in your home studio!

For many recording musicians, VST instruments are the key to recording a broad variety of natural-sounding instruments without having to play and record the actual instruments themselves. One guy with a MIDI keyboard and a collection of VST instruments can sound like an entire orchestra, and most listeners will never know the difference.

Caution

The only drawback to using VST instruments is the computer processing power they require. Although adding one or two VST instruments to a project probably won't overtax your system, using a large number of these virtual instruments might be too much of a burden for your computer, resulting in increased latency rates. If you plan on doing a lot of recording with VST instruments, make sure you have a fast computer with lots of memory—at least one gigabyte, if not two.

Cubase's VST Instruments

The key to using *VST* instruments lies in the instruments themselves. Between Steinberg and a small army of third-party developers, you can find just about any type of VST instrument you can think of. From acoustic guitar to symphonic strings to polyphonic synthesizer, there's a VST instrument that will definitely suit your needs.

def•i•ni•tion

VST stands for Virtual Studio Technology, a standard developed by Steinberg for virtual instruments and plug-in devices. A *VST instrument* (sometimes abbreviated *VSTi*) is a virtual instrument used to play back MIDI tracks, using the VST standard.

Built-In VST Instruments

To get you started, Cubase 4 comes with six built-in VST instruments. Here's what you get:

- **Embracer**—a polyphonic synthesizer designed for pads and accompaniment sounds, shown in Figure 9.1. Can output mono, stereo, and full 360-degree surround sound.
- **HALionOne**—a powerful sample-based instrument, shown in Figure 9.2. This sampler comes with more than 650 ready-to-play sounds for dozens of acoustic and electronic instruments—including 58 different drum kits! It can play all samples created in the HALion Sound Bank (HSB) format.
- **Monologue**—a monophonic analog synthesizer, shown in Figure 9.3. Based on physical modeling technology, Monologue includes two oscillators, two filters, a white noise generator, and chorus, phaser, and flanger effects.
- **Mystic**—a synthesizer based on three parallel comb filters with feedback, shown in Figure 9.4. The sound source is an "impulse sound" based on physical modeling technology.
- **Prologue**—a virtual analog synthesizer, shown in Figure 9.5. Based on the popular D'cota synthesizer, Prologue offers 128-voice polyphony with hundreds of great-sounding presets.
- **Spector**—an integrated synthesizer based on two versatile spectrum filters, shown in Figure 9.6. Spector can utilize up to six different oscillators per voice, and comes with hundreds of VST presets.

def•i•ni•tion

A **polyphonic synthesizer** is an electronic synthesizer that can play multiple notes at one time.

Note

Cubase Studio 4 comes with the HALionOne and Prologue VST instruments.

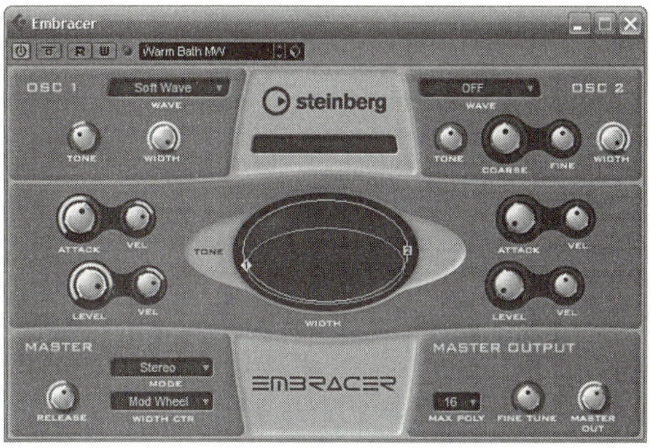

Figure 9.1 *Embracer polyphonic synthesizer.*

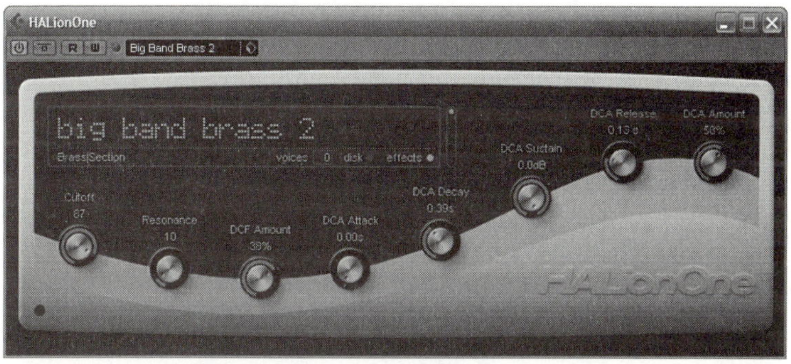

Figure 9.2 *HALionOne sample player.*

Figure 9.3 *Monologue monophonic synthesizer.*

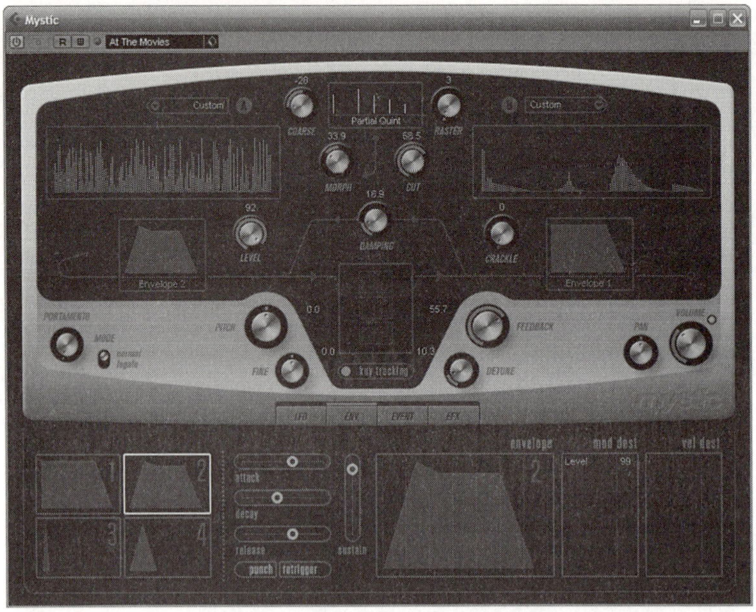

Figure 9.4 *Mystic comb filter-based synthesizer.*

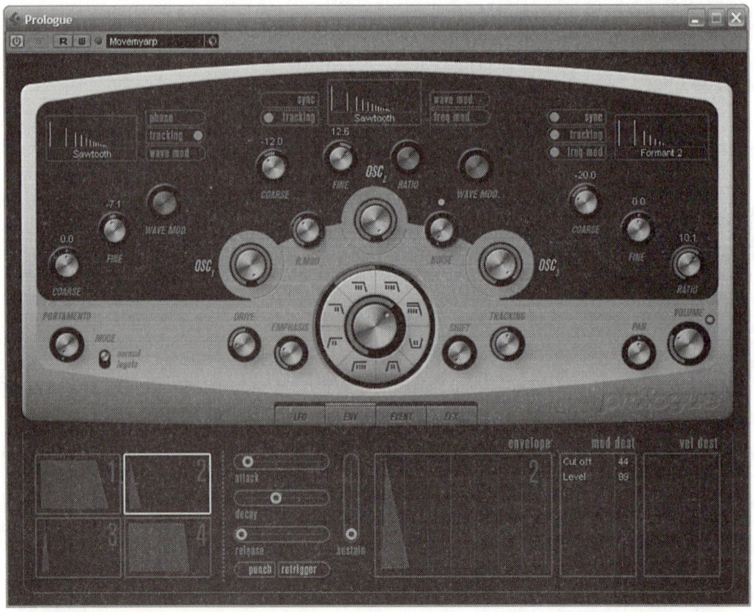

Figure 9.5 *Prologue virtual analog synthesizer.*

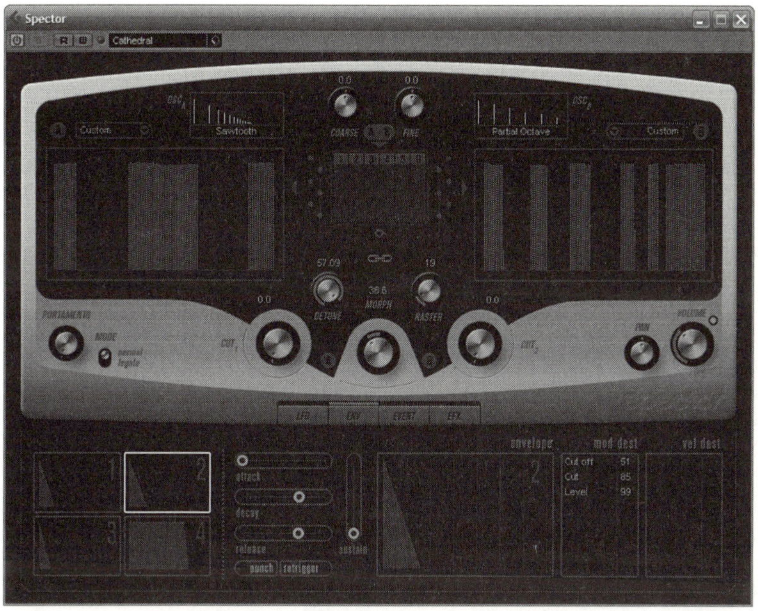

Figure 9.6 *Spector spectrum-filter synthesizer.*

Additional VST Instruments

Steinberg also sells a variety of add-on VST instruments, some of which are quite impressive sounding. In almost all cases, these add-on instruments are more natural-sounding and have more advanced options than the similar VST instruments included with the Cubase program. Pricing is typically in the $200–$300 range per instrument.

Steinberg's add-on VST instruments include:

- **Groove Agent 3**—Pro-level drum machine, complete with added percussion samples.
- **HALion 3**—Keyboard-based sampler/synthesizer.
- **HALion Player**—Affordable and easy-to-use sample player.
- **HALion String Edition 2**—Less-expensive orchestral string section sampler.
- **HALion Symphonic Orchestra**—Virtual symphonic instrument with high-quality orchestral samples.
- **Hypersonic 2**—Synthesizer workstation that includes samples, synths, and loops with a wide variety of sounds and internal effects.
- **The Grand 2**—Sampled acoustic grand piano.
- **Virtual Bassist**—Pro-level electric bass.
- **Virtual Guitarist 2**—Pro-level acoustic and electric guitar sounds.
- **Xphraze**—Polyphonic phrase synthesizer that includes a pool of 256 preset phrases and 256 user phrases.

I find several of these instruments essential for the serious recording musician. In particular, The Grand 2 (shown in Figure 9.7) is a source for very realistic acoustic piano sounds, and Virtual Guitarist (shown in Figure 9.8) is the perfect choice for adding rhythm guitar accompaniment to your recordings. What I really like about the Virtual Guitarist is that you can program it to play rhythm accompaniment in a variety of patterns and styles. This is particularly useful if you're a born keyboardist with no working knowledge of how guitar parts are put together.

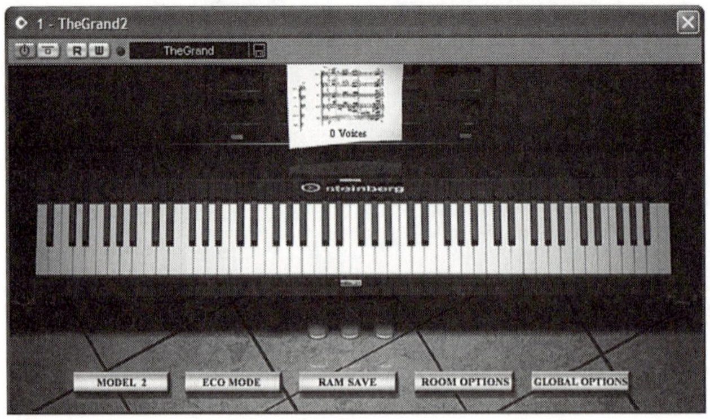

Figure 9.7 *The Grand 2 acoustic piano.*

Figure 9.8 *Virtual Guitarist, Electric Edition (SE version).*

Where to Find Even More VST Instruments

Steinberg isn't the only source of add-on VST instruments, of course. A number of different companies sell VST instruments of various types; the most popular of these companies include:

- Garritan Orchestral Libraries (www.garritan.com), offering the Garritan Personal Orchestra orchestral library, Jazz & Big Band Collection jazz instrument library, Stradivari Solo Violin virtual instrument, and more.

- LinPlug (www.linplug.com), offering Albino virtual synthesizer, SaxLab saxophone synthesizer, daOrgan drawbar organ, CronoX3 sample synthesizer, and more.
- MOTU (www.motu.com), offering the MOTU Symphonic Instrument orchestral library and other virtual instruments.
- MusicLab (www.musiclab.com), offering RealGuitar guitar synth, Rhythm'n'Chords rhythm guitar, and DrumTools drum machine.
- Native Instruments (www.native-instruments.net), offering Akoustik Piano, B4 Organ, Reaktor 5 synthesizer/sampler design studio, Electronic Instruments 2 XT collection, and more.
- SampleTank (www.sampletank.com), offering Miroslav Philharmonik orchestra and choir workstation, SampleTank sample workstation, and more.
- Synapse Audio Software (www.synapse-audio.com), offering Plucked String guitar/bass modeler, Hydra synthesizer, and more.
- Tweakbench (www.tweakbench.com), offering Carillon bell and chime synthesizer, Papaya mallet synthesizer, and other free VST instruments.
- UltimateSoundBank (www.usbsounds.com), offering the Charlie retro organ and the Plugsound line of virtual instruments (keyboards, fretted instruments, drums, and so on).

All these companies offer soft synths, virtual instruments, and instrument libraries that work within Cubase as VST plug-ins. Install the software as instructed by the manufacturer, and it will be available in Cubase for you to use in your recordings.

Activating VST Instruments in Cubase

When you buy a VST instrument, what you get is a piece of software, typically on CD-ROM. You install the VST instrument on your computer as you would any other piece of software; follow the manufacturer's instructions for best results.

After you've installed a VST instrument, you need to activate it within Cubase. This is actually a fairly simple process, as Cubase automatically recognizes all the VST instruments you install. All you have to do is add the instrument to Cubase's list of installed devices.

Follow these steps:

1. Select **Devices > VST Instruments** to open the VST Instruments panel, shown in Figure 9.9.
2. Click the first empty slot in the panel to display the pop-up menu.
3. Select the desired VST instrument from the menu.

> **Tip**
>
> If you want to use multiple sounds from the same VST instrument for different tracks in your recording, you'll need to load multiple instances of that VST instrument—one for each sound you want to use.

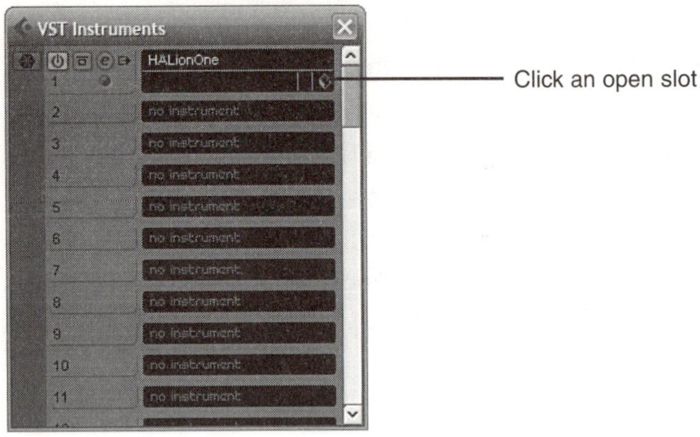

Figure 9.9 *Activating a VST instrument in the VST instruments panel.*

That's it; the VST instrument you selected is now automatically loaded into the Cubase program, and its control panel is opened on your desktop. Repeat these steps for each VST instrument you want to use in your current project.

Of course, loading the VST instrument isn't all you need to do. You'll also need to configure the settings for the instrument itself, which may involve choosing a particular sound and making other sound-related choices.

For example, when you activate the Virtual Bassist (shown in Figure 9.10), the Virtual Bassist control panel appears on your desktop. You can choose from dozens of different bass sounds, styles, and parts to play. You can even adjust the bass's "amplifier" and special effects, including tremolo, fuzz, and the like. It's actually a lot of fun playing around with these VST instruments, trying to get the exact sound that you want.

Figure 9.10 *Configuring the Virtual Bassist from its control panel.*

Assigning VST Instruments to MIDI Tracks

There are two ways to work with VST instruments in Cubase 4. You can assign a VST instrument to an existing MIDI track, or you can create a new VST instrument track. We'll deal with the first method first.

When you assign a VST instrument to an existing MIDI track, the VST instrument is played by the MIDI track. The MIDI instructions are fed to the VST instrument, which responds by playing the notes as instructed.

When you activate a VST instrument in Cubase, that instrument now appears as one of the output choices in the MIDI track inspector. To assign the VST instrument to a specific MIDI track, follow these steps:

1. Select the MIDI track in the track list.
2. In the track inspector for that track, pull down the **Out** menu and select the VST instrument, as shown in Figure 9.11.
3. You now need to select a patch for the selected VST instrument. You do this by clicking the **Programs** control in the track inspector; this should open a new panel, like the one in Figure 9.12, from which you can select a patch from those available in the VST instrument.

def•i•ni•tion

A **patch** is a particular instrument sound produced by a synthesizer or sampler. For example, the VB1 virtual bass instrument includes patches for Bassic Bass, Sustain Bass, Round Bass, Fretless, Synth Bass, Clavinet, DX Bass, Hollow Bass, Sequenz Bass, Warm Bass, Slap Frets, Buzz Bass, Add Chorus, Synth Bass 2, Dark Click, and Synth Bass 3.

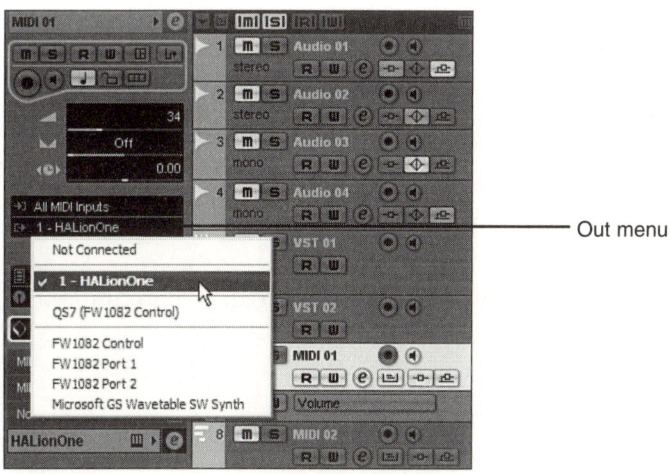

Figure 9.11 *Configuring a VST instrument as output for a MIDI track.*

You can make additional adjustments to the instrument sound by returning to the control panel for the VST instrument. When you play back the MIDI track, it will now play back through the selected VST instrument.

Tip

Because a VST track is nothing more than a MIDI track routed to a VST instrument, you can edit that track just as you would any other MIDI track, using either the key editor or score editor.

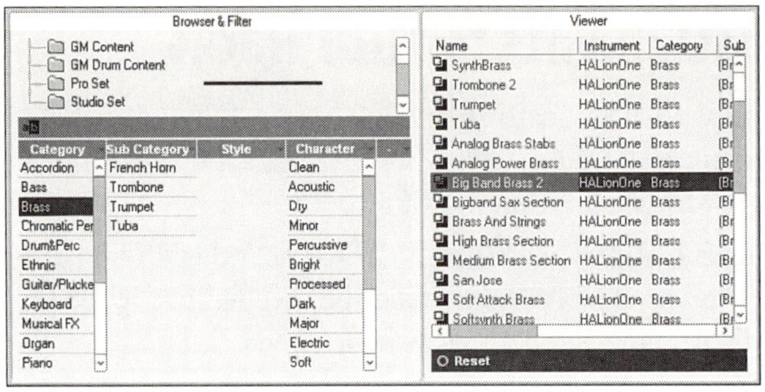

Figure 9.12 *Selecting a patch for the HALionOne VST instrument.*

Adding—and Playing—a VST Instrument Track

In previous versions of Cubase, the only way to add VST instruments to your project was by assigning them to MIDI tracks. That changes in Cubase 4, which offers the option of distinct VST instrument tracks in the project window. An instrument track is like a MIDI track, except that it's optimized for the selection and configuration of VST instruments. It's also the best way to add VST instruments that you play in real time when recording.

To add a VST instrument track, follow these steps:

1. In the project window, select **Project > Add Track > Instrument.**
2. This displays the Add Instrument Track dialog box. Click the Browse **Presets** option to expand the dialog box, as shown in Figure 9.13.
3. Select any desired options from the Category, Sub Category, Style, Character, or Instrument lists. (The Instrument list displays all the installed VST instruments.)
4. In the Viewer pane, select the VST instrument and patch you want to use.
5. Click **OK.**

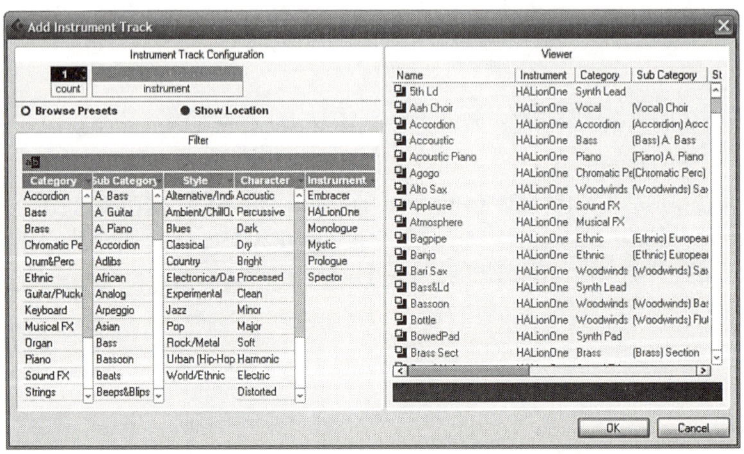

Figure 9.13 *Choosing a patch for the new VST instrument track.*

The new instrument track is now added to the track list, with the VST instrument and patch you selected activated. You can now edit any of the parameters for this track, and play the instrument "live," in real time, using your MIDI keyboard as input.

And, of course, you can also record the VST instrument you're playing. This process is no different from what you learned in Chapter 5. Once you've added the instrument track to your project, click the **Record** button in the transport panel and you're on!

> **Caution**
>
> If your system has too much latency, you'll find it difficult to play VST instruments in real time—there will be a noticeable lag between pressing a key and hearing the sound. You'll need to adjust your sound card's configuration settings to reduce the amount of latency, as much as possible without affecting your system's sound.

Freezing VST Tracks

As I noted earlier, one of the big drawbacks to using VST instruments is that they require a lot of computer processing power. If your project includes a large number of VST instruments, you could find an older or moderately powered computer slowing down past the point of usefulness. (As with all Cubase-related computer slowdowns, the first thing you notice is increased latency; what you play and what you hear get further and further out of synch.)

The way around this problem is to "freeze" those VST tracks that you've already finalized. This renders the VST track to an audio file, thus removing the VST processing from the project workload. (Audio tracks require much less processing power than do MIDI or VST instrument tracks.) The sound you hear is the same, but your computer no longer has to calculate the sound of the VST instrument in real time.

To freeze a VST instrument track, follow these steps:

1. Go to the inspector for the select VST instrument track and click the **Freeze** button, as shown in Figure 9.14.
2. When the Freeze Instrument Options dialog box appears, as shown in Figure 9.15, check the **Freeze Instrument Only** and **Unload Instrument When Frozen** options.
3. Click **OK** to close the dialog box and freeze the track.

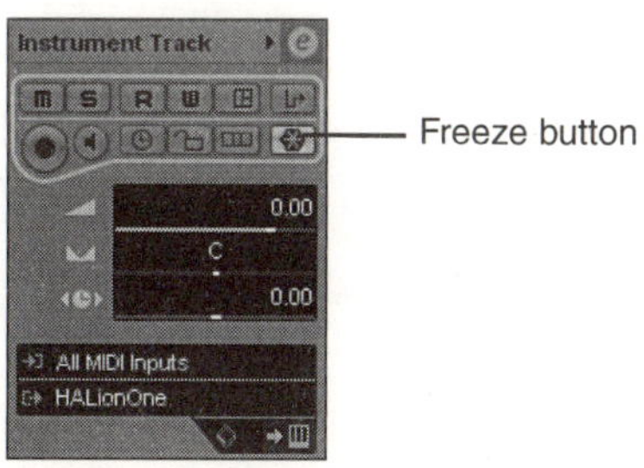

Figure 9.14 *Getting ready to freeze a VST track.*

The VST track will now be rendered to an audio track, and frozen to all editing. (Try it; when you double-click the event, nothing happens.)

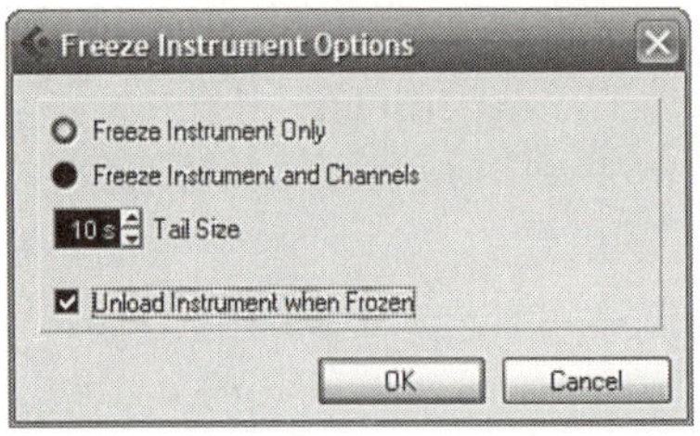

Figure 9.15 *Freezing a VST instrument.*

But what if you want to make changes to that frozen VST track? No problem—Cubase lets you unfreeze any track you've frozen. Just return to the VST instruments panel and click the Freeze button for the frozen channel. When you're asked if you really want to unfreeze the instrument, click the Unfreeze button, and you're back to where you were before you did the whole freeze thing.

The Least You Need to Know

- A VST instrument is a software synthesizer or sound device that is played via MIDI.
- Cubase 4 includes six built-in VST instruments.
- Other add-on VST instruments are available from Steinberg and other suppliers; among the available instruments are acoustic pianos, acoustic and electric guitars, electric basses, string sections, polyphonic synthesizers, and more.
- After it has been installed on your computer, you activate a VST instrument within Cubase by adding it to the VST instruments panel.
- To add a VST instrument to a MIDI track, select the VST instrument as the track's output.
- Cubase 4 also lets you add dedicated VST instrument tracks to your project—which you can play and record in real time.
- To free up system resources, you can freeze a VST track to an audio track—and then unfreeze it later if you need to edit it.

Chapter 10

Recording with Loops and Samples

In This Chapter

- Obtaining samples and loops
- Using Time Warp to match tempo and pitch
- Turning short loops into long recordings
- Rearranging your loops with the play order editor

In the heyday of studio recording, you rented a big studio, contracted a small army of seasoned session players, and let the tape run as the musicians played all together all the way through as many takes as it took to get it right. There were no overdubs, no replacing poorly played parts, no adding extra instruments after the fact. It was all done live in the studio, and while it may have given headaches to engineers at the time, you can't argue with the results. (Unless, that is, you really don't care for Phil Spector's Wall of Sound, Brian Wilson's *Pet Sounds*, or thousands of other classic recordings—in which case, I don't even want to talk to you.)

Today, however, you don't have to do it that way. Digital recording across an unlimited number of tracks means that you can add as many audio parts as you want, either live or after the fact. MIDI recording means that one person at a MIDI keyboard can reproduce a multi-track recording with the sounds of an entire orchestra. And then there's *loop* recording.

Understanding Loop Recording

A loop recording is in interesting beast. You start with a few measures of a drum beat, something hip and funky, and then repeat those measures over and over in a kind of loop. You build up the rest of the song by adding more loops

def•i•ni•tion

A **loop** is a short audio sample, typically repeated multiple times to create a longer track in a recording. A **loop-based recording** is a recording constructed primarily from repeated audio loops.

of other instruments; you put the bass on top of the drums, and then layer on keyboards, guitars, synths, strings, vocals, you name it. When you use audio loops in this fashion, you're composing as you record, one loop at time.

You can obtain audio loops from a number of different sources. Some loops are simply short audio samples ripped from existing recordings. Other loops are sold as part of loop libraries, created expressly for the purpose of creating *loop-based recordings*. Still more loops can be created on your own, via traditional audio recording, MIDI recording, or by programming a drum machine.

The key thing is that loops are short, they're repeatable, and they're capable of being fitted to a given recording in terms of tempo and pitch. Creating a composition/recording with loops is really like assembling a structure from a series of building blocks. Anyone can do it, and in many ways it's easier than creating a traditional composition. It's the way that many current recordings are made, especially in the hip hop, techno, electronica, and dance genres. Start with a funky beat, and loop your way from there!

Obtaining Audio Samples and Loops

When you're creating a loop-based recording, you have to get your loops and samples from somewhere. Fortunately, because we're working in the digital realm, there is a lot of digital music available for you to sample. You can sample audio from practically any compact disc, you can import samples from digital audio files you download from the Internet, and you can even purchase samples and loops from various companies. Whichever type of sample you go with, importing it into Cubase is a snap; Cubase lets you import all manner of digital audio files, as well as rip audio direct from CDs. And after you have your samples in your project, you can work with them as you would any other audio event.

Note

Cubase isn't the only program with which you can create loop-based recordings. (It is, however, one of the most sophisticated; most loop-based programs don't offer all the recording and editing features that you find in Cubase.) If you're looking for a simple loop-based music production program, check out ACID and ACID XMC and ACID Pro (www.sonymediasoftware.com/Products/), GarageBand (www.apple.com/ilife/garageband/), or ReCycle (www.propellerheads.se).

Sampling Audio from CDs

Many musicians build their loop-based recordings on samples ripped from other recordings. That's because it's relatively easy to sample portions of music available on commercial compact discs. Cubase lets you import entire songs from any CD, or just segments of a song (which are easier to work with if you only want a short sample). The CD tracks are imported as WAV-format audio events, which you can then work with as you would any other event in Cubase.

Caution

Many popular musicians use samples in their recordings. Before you sample another artist's music for your own recording, however, you need to obtain that artist's permission and (depending on what kind of deal you work out) pay a flat fee or royalty for use of the prior work. It is illegal to sample a copyrighted recording and then make money from the use of that sample without the owner's permission.

Here's how to do it:

1. With a project already open, select **Project > Add Track > Audio** to create a new empty audio track. Make sure you create a *stereo* track.
2. Select the newly created track in the track list.
3. Select **File > Import > Audio CD.**
4. When the Import from Audio CD dialog box appears, as shown in Figure 10.1, check the track that you want to import.
5. To import only part of the track, specify the start and the end of the section to grab by dragging the left and right handles in the grab selection ruler. (Use the Play button to confirm that you've selected the correct section of the track.)
6. Click the **Copy** button to convert the track or section to a WAV-format file.
7. Click the **OK** button to import the converted file to your project.

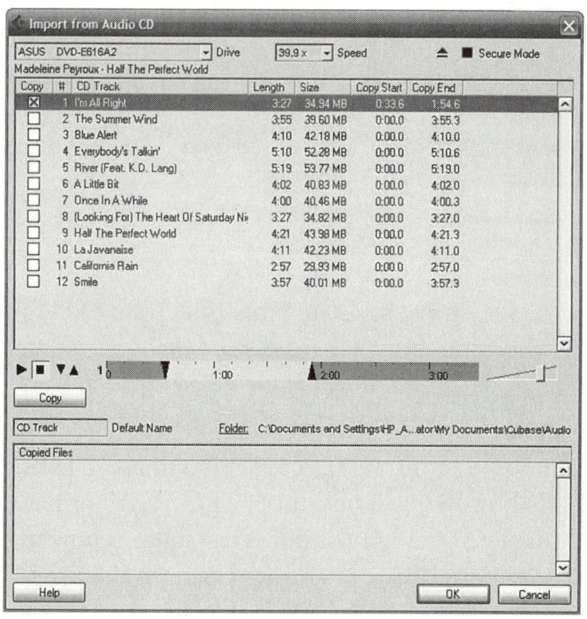

Figure 10.1 *Importing a CD track into a Cubase recording project.*

> **Note**
>
> To import any type of audio file, including files from a CD, you must have a project already open in the Cubase workspace. The audio file you import is inserted directly into your project as a new audio track.

The CD track (or portion thereof) is now presented as a new audio event in the selected audio track in your project. You can now work with the CD audio as you would any other audio event; you can split it, copy it, move it, process it, even change its pitch and tempo.

Importing Other Digital Audio Files

Sometimes the music you want to sample isn't on a CD, but is available as a digital music download. That's not a problem, since Cubase lets you import just about any type of digital audio file, including MP3 and WMA files. Just follow these steps:

> **Caution**
>
> At present, Cubase doesn't import files in the AAC format, which is the file format used for songs purchased from the iTunes Music Store.

1. With a project already open, select **Project > Add Track > Audio** to create a new empty audio track. Make sure you create a *stereo* track.
2. Select the newly created track in the track list.
3. Select **File > Import > Audio File.**
4. When the Import Audio dialog box appears, navigate to and select the file you want to import, then click the **Open** button.
5. When the Import Options dialog box appears, as shown in Figure 10.2, check the **Sample Rate** and **Sample Size** options, if these options are available. (This converts the sample rate/size of the imported file to the format currently used in your project.)

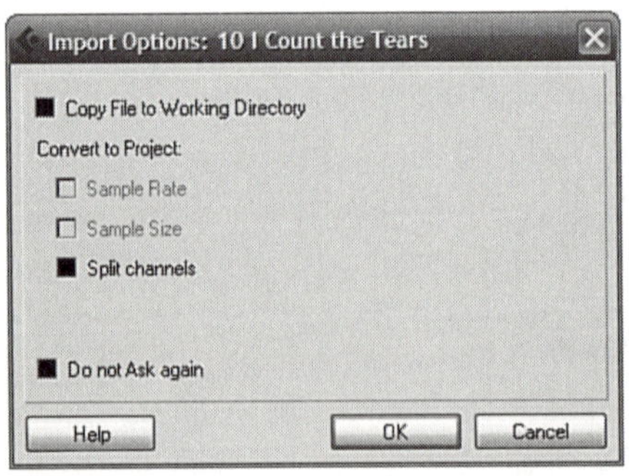

Figure 10.2 *Importing a digital audio file into a Cubase recording project.*

> **Caution**
>
> Although working with MP3, WMA, and other digital file formats might be convenient, you may not be satisfied with the sound quality. That's because these file formats compress the audio to make smaller sized files; compressed audio doesn't have the fidelity that you find on a CD or are used to working with in the recording studio.

6. If you want to import a stereo file as two separate mono files (one each for the left and right channels), check the **Split Channels** option.
7. Click the **OK** button.

The imported file is now a new audio event in the selected audio track. The file you import, regardless of its original format, will be converted to WAV format within Cubase. Know, however, that even though the imported audio is now in WAV format, the sound quality is no better than what was present in the original compressed file.

Finding Third-Party Loops and Samples

You don't have to sample your own loops. Many companies (and some professional musicians) offer pre-sampled or specially created loops and samples available for purchase or download. A *loop library* is likely to contain dozens, if not hundreds, of audio loops that you can use in your recordings. Using a loop library is a great place to start when you're creating loop-based recordings.

Most loop libraries are shipped on CD, although individual samples are more likely to be downloadable from the web. Some of the most popular suppliers of loops and samples include:

- ACIDplanet (www.acidplanet.com)
- AMG (www.amguk.co.uk)
- ccMixter (www.ccmixter.org)
- GuitarWavs.com (www.guitarwavs.com)
- Loopasonic (www.loopasonic.com)
- PowerFX (www.powerfx.com)
- Proloops (www.proloops.com)
- Smart Loops (www.smartloops.com)
- Sony Media Software (www.sonymediasoftware.com/loop_libraries/)
- Sounds Online (www.soundsonline.com)
- Sounddogs.com (www.sounddogs.com)

You can also find a great list of sites offering samples for download at the zZounds.com Synth Zone (www.synthzone.com/sampling.htm).

Almost all CD-based loop libraries offer their samples and loops in WAV format. As for downloadable samples, many are in WAV format, but some are offered as MP3 files. Although the file size (and download time) will be smaller with MP3 files, remember that MP3 has lower sound quality than the superior WAV format.

def•i•ni•tion

A **loop library** is a collection of audio loops or samples, typically distributed on compact disc.

Note

Cubase also imports loops created in the MP3, REX, and REX 2 file formats. (REX and REX 2 are file formats used by the ReCycle loop-production program.)

Importing Third-Party Loops

Using third-party loops within Cubase is easy, because all these loops are in WAV format, which is one of the digital audio formats that Cubase imports by default. Follow these steps to import a loop:

1. With a project already open, select **Project > Add Track > Audio** to create a new empty audio track. (If you're importing a stereo loop—which you probably are—you'll want to create a *stereo* track.)
2. Select the newly created track in the track list.
3. Select **File > Import > Audio File.**
4. When the Import Audio dialog box appears, navigate to and select the loop you want to import, then click the **Open** button.

> **Note**
>
> Many commercially available loops are offered in the ACID format. These loops are standard WAV files embedded with tempo and length information. Cubase imports an ACID loop as it would any WAV file, but uses the embedded information to activate Musical mode and adapt the loop's tempo to that already set in your recording project.

5. When the Import Options dialog box appears, check the **Sample Rate** and **Sample Size** options, if these options are available.
6. If you want to import a stereo loop as two separate mono events (one each for the left and right channels), check the Split Channels option.
7. Click the **OK** button.

The loop is now a new audio event in the selected track. Most loops are relatively short—typically, from one to four measures long—so the event probably won't fill up the entire track. You want to copy and paste the loop to fill up more space in your recording, which you learn how to do in the "Making Longer Loops" section later in this chapter.

Managing Loops with the MediaBay

Cubase 4 includes a new media management utility, called the MediaBay, that you can use to manage all the audio loops and media files stored on your PC. You can use the MediaBay to organize your loops and file, as well as search for files and filter the search results as appropriate.

You open the MediaBay, shown in Figure 10.3, by selecting **Media > Open MediaBay.** From here, you use the Browser pane to navigate to specific folders on your hard drive.

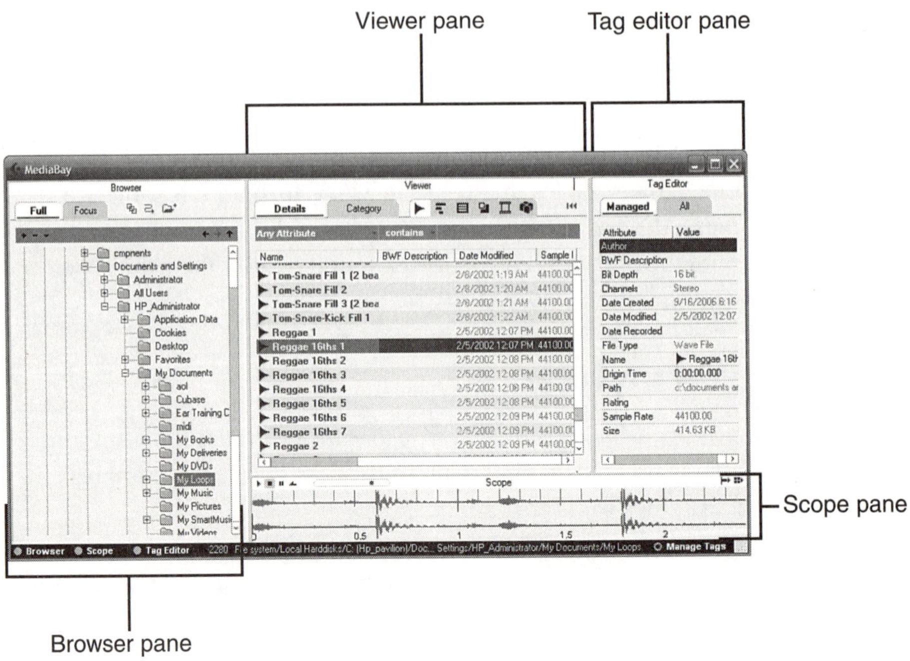

Figure 10.3 *Organizing audio loops with the MediaBay.*

Once you have a location selected, you select how you want to view your files in the Viewer pane. You can opt to view by Details (file name, description, and so on) or by Category (type of instrument or sound). You can also filter the results by selecting one or more media types—Audio Files, MIDI Files, or Track Presets.

When you select a file in the Viewer pane, details about that file are displayed in the Tag Editor pane. In addition, the file's waveform is displayed in the Scope pane in the bottom of the window; you can use the transport controls in the Scope pane to preview the selected file.

Any file you select in the MediaBay can be dragged and dropped onto a corresponding track in Cubase's project window. Using the MediaBay is, for many users, a fast and easy way to find and use loop files in their projects—especially when they have lots of loops stored on their systems.

Matching Tempo and Pitch via Time Warp

When you import a sample or loop into a Cubase project, it's imported just as it was on the original recording—at the original tempo, and in the original key. That isn't necessarily a good thing, as you need both the tempo and the pitch of the sample to match the tempo and pitch of the rest of your project. It wouldn't do, for example, to have a drum beat playing at 120 beats per minute (bpm) when the rest of your song is playing at 90 bpm.

Fortunately, Cubase provides useful Time Warp tools that let you change the tempo of a sample without affecting the pitch, or change the pitch without affecting the tempo.

Hitpoint Editing

Before adding Time Warp functions, Cubase used a method called *hitpoint detection* to divide loops into individual *slices*, which could then be manipulated to change the tempo. In essence, every hit on a drum track—every bass drum beat, every snare drum crack, every cymbal crash—is turned into a separate audio event. Sliced in this fashion, an event can be stretched by inserting space in between each event, or shrunk by moving the events closer together.

Although this hitpoint process worked well for tempo matching, it was quite cumbersome to use—which is why it's a very good thing that Cubase added time warp capabilities. Time warping is a lot more automatic than hitpoint detection, and the stretching/shrinking happens in real time. Given the choice of hitpoint detection or time warp editing, I choose the time warp every time.

By now, curious readers have no doubt noticed that Cubase 4 still retains all of the previous hitpoint features, right there in the sample editor. This is primarily for compatibility's sake; if you have an older project that used hitpoints, you can still work with that project in Cubase 4. That doesn't mean that you want to use hitpoints with a new project, however; my recommendation is to stick with time warp, and forget that hitpoints ever existed.

Of course, there are other uses for hitpoints. With great care, you can use hitpoint editing to rearrange the individual notes within a drum loop. There's even a "groove quantize" function, which lets you set different rhythmic feels for a drum loop. But these are advanced functions, not likely to be used by the average recordist, so I won't talk about them any more. Like I said, focus on time warp editing, and you'll be happy.

> **Note**
>
> You don't need to use time warp tempo matching with imported ACID loops, as these files have embedded beat and tempo information. Non-ACID WAV files, however (as well as audio sampled from CDs and MP3 files), do not contain this embedded information, and may require warping to get the tempo right.

Matching Tempo

To match the tempo of a sample with the rest of your project, you need to know how long the sample is, in terms of measures and/or beats. This is critical; if you enter the wrong amount, the tempo will be set incorrectly. The sample also needs to be cleanly cut, so that it ends with a precise duration. Sloppy samples are difficult for Cubase to work with.

All that said, tempo matching works fairly well, even if the process appears to be a little complex. The setup work happens in the sample editor, where you define the tempo and duration of the sample, and then activate what Cubase calls Musical mode. When Musical mode is activated, the audio sample will automatically adjust itself to your project's tempo—even if you change the tempo.

Here's how it works:

1. Double-click on the desired audio event to open the sample editor, shown in Figure 10.4.
2. Click the **Audio Tempo Definition** tool in the toolbar.
3. In the Signature field in the toolbar, enter the time signature of the loop. (In most cases, the time signature is 4/4.)
4. Next, you need to enter the duration of the sample, in either bars (measures) or beats. Enter the duration into the Bars or Beats field, as appropriate.

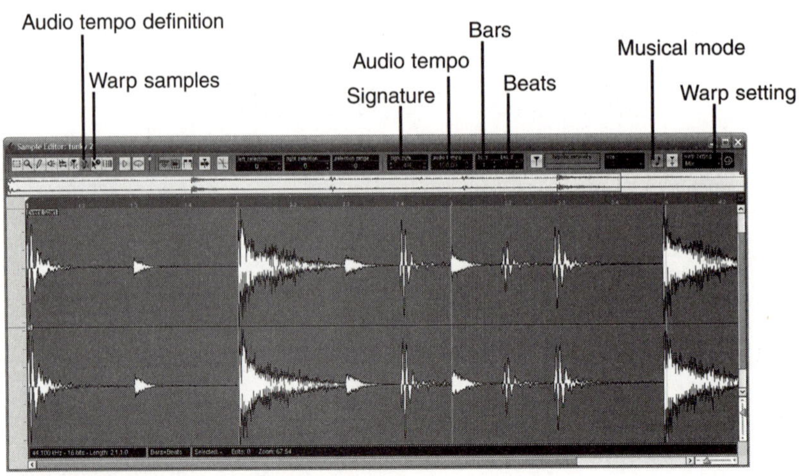

Figure 10.4 *Activating Musical mode for an audio sample.*

Let's stop for a moment before continuing to the next step. Assuming that you have a nice, clean sample, you should now see the ruler and grid bars adjust themselves into position, representing the major and minor beats of each measure. You should see the darkest, most dense waveforms (which represent the snare drum backbeat) positioned on the second and fourth beat of each measure. Lighter waveforms (representing the bass drum kicks) will be positioned as they occur throughout the sample. To hear what you're seeing—that is, to confirm that the backbeats are on two and four, and so on—click the **Audition** button in the toolbar.

> **Caution**
>
> If you don't click the Warp Samples button, your sample will be truncated instead of stretched or shrunk—which is not the effect you want.

Now, on to the next steps:

1. Cubase now automatically calculates the tempo of the sample, and displays it in the Audio Tempo field.
2. Click the **Warp Samples** button on the toolbar.
3. Click the **Musical Mode** button on the toolbar.
4. Click the **Warp Setting** control and select the setting from the list that best matches the type of sample you're working with. For example, if you're working with a drum loop, select Drums; if you're working with a guitar sample, select Plucked; if you're working with most other instruments, select Mixed.
5. Close the sample editor.

When you return to the project window, the event is now sized to the measure/beat duration you selected, as shown in Figure 10.5—and a little musical note appears at the bottom left of the event, signifying Musical mode. If you change the tempo of your project (in the transport panel), the sample will automatically adjust its tempo to match.

Figure 10.5 *The sample returned to the project window with Musical mode activated.*

Fine-Tuning the Beat

Here's another problem that time warp can fix. Not all musicians always play exactly on the beat. Suppose you have a sample where the drummer hits the snare drum slightly after the beat, and you want a tighter track. Short of choosing another sample (or having the drummer rerecord his part), what do you do?

It's time to do the time warp again.

When you're working in the sample editor, Cubase lets you create *warp tabs* that correspond to major attacks in the audio sample. (For example, on a drum track you could create warp tabs for each hit of the bass drum and snare drum.) Then, using time warp technology, you can scoot around the warp tabs, placing them (if you want) precisely on the beat, no variation. This can make any drummer sound rock solid, and fix a slew of different timing- and rhythm-related problems.

Tip

You can change the overall tempo for your project by going to the transport panel and clicking the Tempo control to turn it off, so that it reads Fixed. Enter a new tempo in the Tempo field, and all the audio tracks in Musical mode will automatically adjust to the new tempo.

Note

Obviously, Cubase's various Time Warp tools can be used to fine-tune any audio recordings, not just loop-based projects. (Although, to be fair, it's a lot quicker to fix a sloppy two-measure loop than it is to fix an entire song that has questionable timing.)

To change the beat timing of any audio sample, follow these steps:

1. Double-click on the desired audio event to open the sample editor.
2. Click the **Audio Tempo Definition** tool in the toolbar.
3. In the Signature field in the toolbar, enter the time signature of the loop.
4. Next, enter the duration of the sample, in either bars (measures) or beats, into the Bars or Beats field.
5. Click the **Warp Samples** button in the toolbar.
6. Click the **Musical Mode** button in the toolbar to activate it. This locks the sample into the correct measure/beat length.
7. Locate the start of the waveform that doesn't line up precisely with the beat, then click the cursor at that point. This creates a warp tab, as shown in Figure 10.6.
8. Grab the warp tab with your mouse and drag it into a new position on the beat, as shown in Figure 10.7.

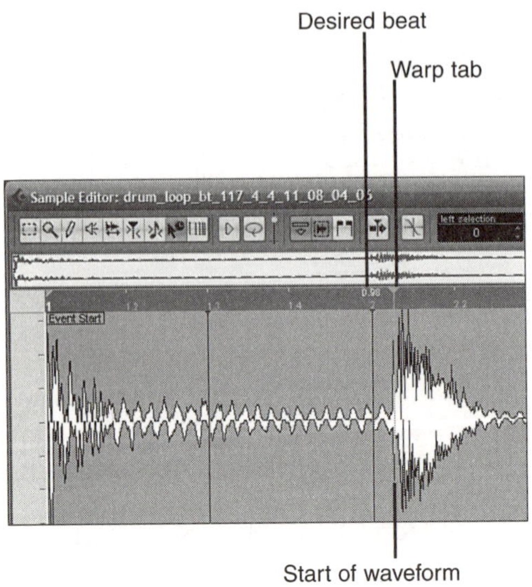

Figure 10.6 *Creating a warp tab for an off-beat note.*

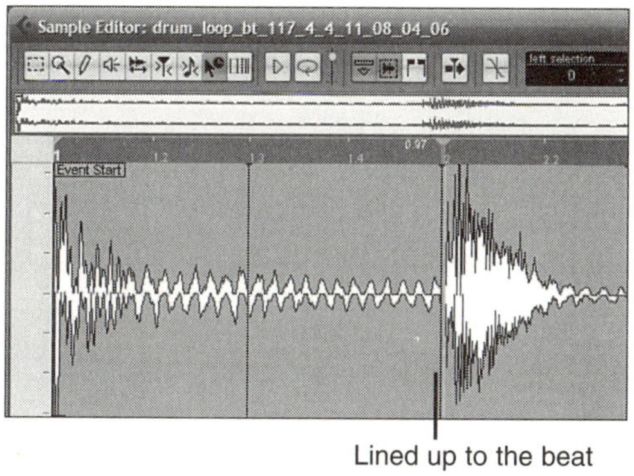

Figure 10.7 *The same waveform, moved to be perfectly on-beat.*

That's all there is to it. You can set any number of warp tabs in a sample, and move them around as necessary to place all the hits precisely on-beat. Not only can you imbue your loops with machine-like precision, you can give any musician the appearance of rock-solid timing!

> **Caution**
>
> Sometimes moving one waveform will nudge another waveform out of position. If this happens, create a warp tab for the second waveform and move it back onto its proper beat. Repeat this procedure for any other waveforms that are likewise nudged.

Changing Pitch

Matching tempo and fixing sloppy beats is good, but what do you do when the sample you import is in a different key than the rest of your project? Well, time warp can help here, too, although the process isn't quite as automatic.

Cubase lets you adjust the pitch of an event in real time, but there's no way to magically identify the key and match it to the key of the other events in your project. So we're left with simple transposition—which, of course, occurs without affecting the tempo of the sample.

Here's how to change the pitch of a sample in real time:

1. In the project window, select the event you want to adjust.
2. Enter a value in the Transpose field in the info bar, as shown in Figure 10.8. Each whole number you enter transposes the pitch up or down a half-step; enter a "-" before the number to move down.
3. Press the **Enter** key on your computer keyboard to lock in the transposition.

For example, entering **2** in the Transpose field transposes the event *up* two half-steps. Entering **-2** transposes the event *down* two half-steps.

> **Tip**
>
> You can even use warp tabs for the opposite purpose—to make computer-created rhythms sound more human. Just nudge a few notes off the beat here and there, and you'll create a more human-like feel. (Few human musicians always play precisely on the beat!)

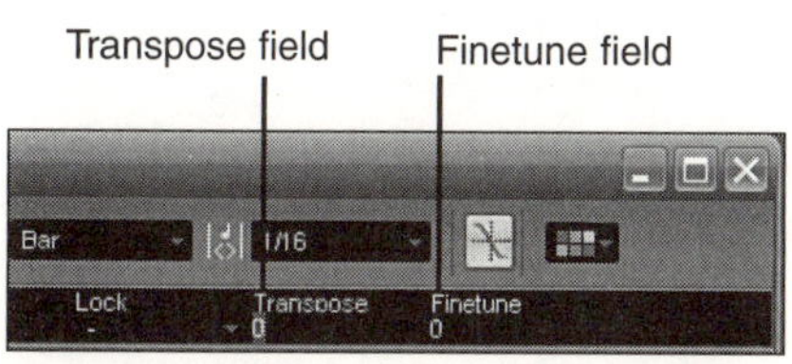

Figure 10.8 *Transposing the pitch of an audio sample.*

Tip

If the pitch of an event is less than a half-step off—that is, if it's just *slightly* out of tune—then you should use the Finetune field instead of the Transpose field. When you use the Finetune control, you can change the pitch in intervals of 1/100th of a semitone.

Extending Your Loops

So far we've worked with relatively short loops—anywhere from one to four measures long. But four measures do not a song make, which means we need to extend those loops to fill the entire length of the recording.

There are four ways to turn a short loop into a longer one—or, more precisely, a series of shorter loops. We look at each in turn.

Tip

You can audition a loop over a longer period of time before you copy it across multiple measures. In the project window, set a start and end point in the ruler. (Ctrl-click at the start point; Alt-click at the end point.) Then position the cursor at the start point, click the **Cycle** button in the transport panel (the button to the left of the Play button), then click **Play**; Cubase will now cycle through the selected measures until you click Stop. And if you want to audition a loop in the sample editor, just click the Audition Loop button to activate it before you click the Audition button.

Copy and Paste

The first way to extend a loop uses the same cut-and-paste method you're already familiar with. Follow these steps:

1. Select the event you want to copy.
2. Select **Edit > Copy.**
3. Move your cursor to the end of the first event (the start of the next measure).
4. Select **Edit > Paste.**

The drawback to this approach is twofold. First, it requires four individual steps. Second, it only lets you add one event at a time. But still, it's easy.

Duplicate

The next approach requires fewer steps than the cut-and-paste approach. It uses Cubase's Duplicate tool, like this:

1. Select the event you want to copy.
2. Select **Edit > Duplicate.**

Cubase now makes a copy of the first event and pastes the copy immediately after the first event, as shown in Figure 10.9. Easier than using copy and paste, but you're still working with just one event at a time.

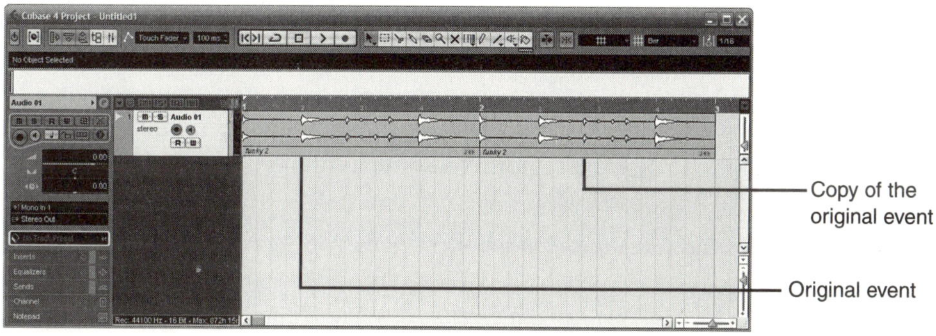

Figure 10.9 *Duplicating an event one time.*

Repeat

If you want to copy more than one instance of an event, use Cubase's Repeat tool. This tool lets you specify how many copies of the event you want to paste back into your project, like this:

1. Select the event you want to copy.
2. Select **Edit > Repeat.**
3. When the Repeat dialog box appears, as shown in Figure 10.10, use the Count control to specify how many copies you want to make.
4. Click **OK.**

Figure 10.10 *Specifying the number of copies in the Repeat dialog box.*

As you can see in Figure 10.11, if you specify 2 copies, Cubase places two copies of the event all in a row following the original event.

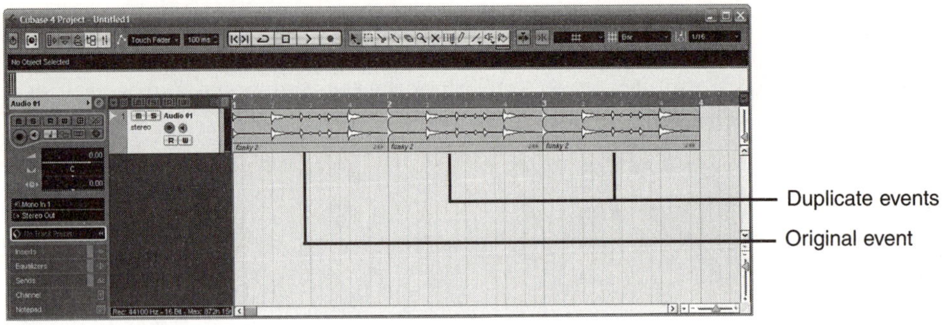

Figure 10.11 *Duplicating an event a specified number of times.*

Fill Loop

If you're not sure how many copies you need to make of your original event, you can let Cubase do the calculation for you with the Fill Loop tool. This tool lets you specify in the ruler the region you want to fill, and then it does the filling for you. Here's how it works:

1. Ctrl-click in the ruler at the start of the area you want to fill. This sets the start point.
2. Alt-click in the ruler at the end of the area you want to fill. This sets the end point, as shown in Figure 10.12.
3. Select the event you want to copy.
4. Select **Edit > Fill Loop.**

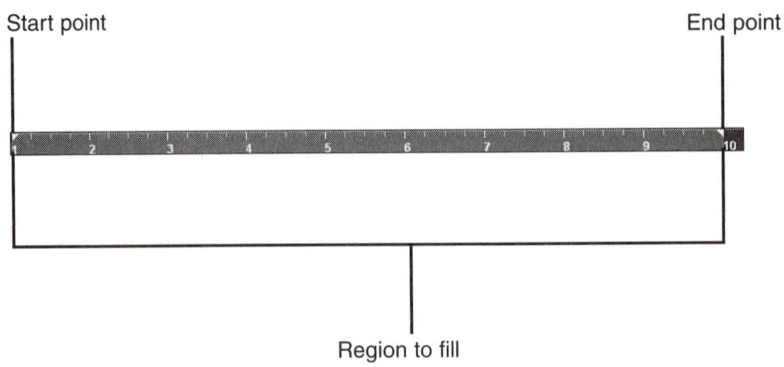

Figure 10.12 *Setting the region to fill.*

As you can see in Figure 10.13, the original event is now copied as many times as possible to fill the area specified. This is the easy way to make your loop fill an entire section of your song.

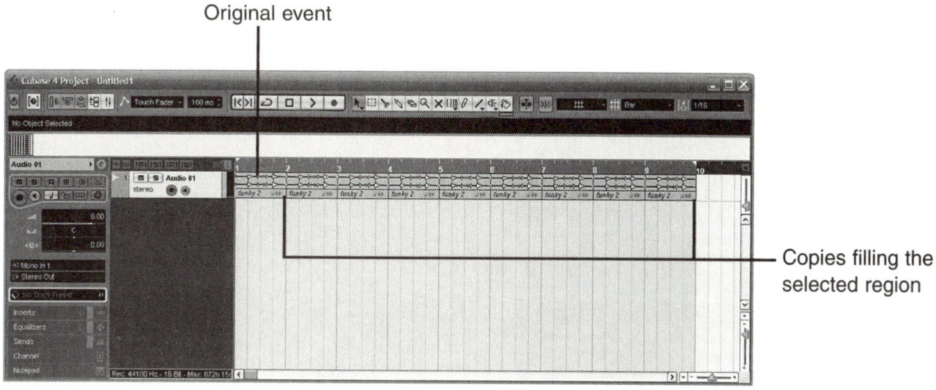

Figure 10.13 *An event filled with the necessary number of loops.*

Rearranging the Parts of Your Recording with the Play Order Editor

When you're creating a loop-based recording, you don't have to work in a linear fashion. That is, you don't have to start with measure 1 and end with measure 128, with each measure in between following in consecutive order. You can work this way if you want, but it's not very efficient—especially if you repeat certain sections exactly throughout the recording.

> **def•i•ni•tion**
>
> The **play order** is the order in which various sections of a recording are played back. Play order is determined by the play order editor.

For this reason, Cubase lets you divide your project into sections, and then set a *play order* for the sections. You can opt to play section B before section A, or repeat section C five times, or skip section D entirely. It's like working with Lego blocks; you can construct your recording, start to finish, in whatever order you like.

Using play order parts lets you compose and record in a non-linear fashion. You arrange your loops and larger sections in one order or another, experimenting with what sounds best where. After you decide on the final order, you can create a traditional linear recording according to the play order you select.

Creating a Play Order Track

The first step in this type of non-linear recording is to create what Cubase calls a play order track. This track is what you use to determine which parts are played in which order.

Creating a play order track is as simple as selecting **Project > Add Track > Play Order.** The currently empty play order track is added at the bottom of the list, as shown in Figure 10.14.

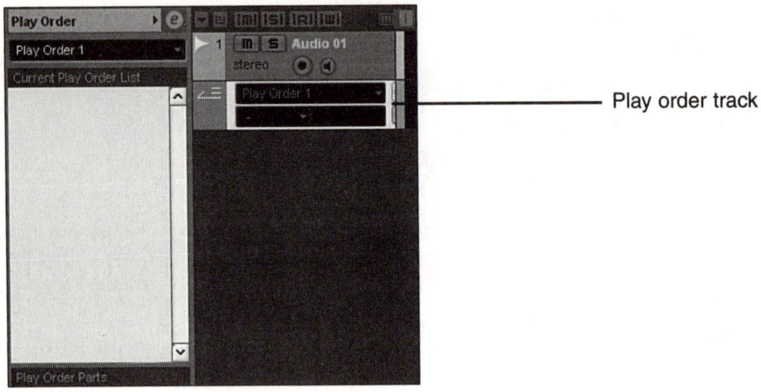

Figure 10.14 *Adding a play order track to your project.*

Creating Play Order Parts

Next, you need to identify the parts of your recording, and define them as play order parts. It's as easy as drawing regions in the play order track. Follow these steps:

1. Click the **Pencil** tool on the toolbar.
2. Identify the segment of your project that you want to be the first play order part.
3. In the play order part, click and draw the area corresponding to the first play order part. As shown in Figure 10.15, that area is now identified as part A.
4. Repeat steps 2 and 3 for each additional part you want to add.

> **Note**
>
> To properly use the play order track, make sure the Snap button in the toolbar is on, and that the Grid Type control is set to Bar.

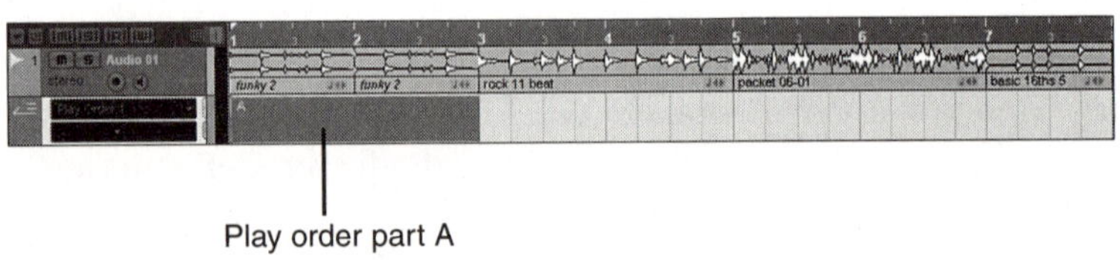

Figure 10.15 *Creating a play order part.*

A few things to note. First, you can start and end a play order part anywhere in the project; you don't have to start with part A in measure 1. Second, the play order parts are automatically lettered in the order in which they're created; the first part you create is labeled A, the second part is labeled B, and so on. Third, the play order parts do not have to be in a linear order; that is, part B can come before part A, as shown in Figure 10.16. Finally, not every measure of your project has to be assigned to a play order part; any measure that is not part of a part will not be included in the final recording.

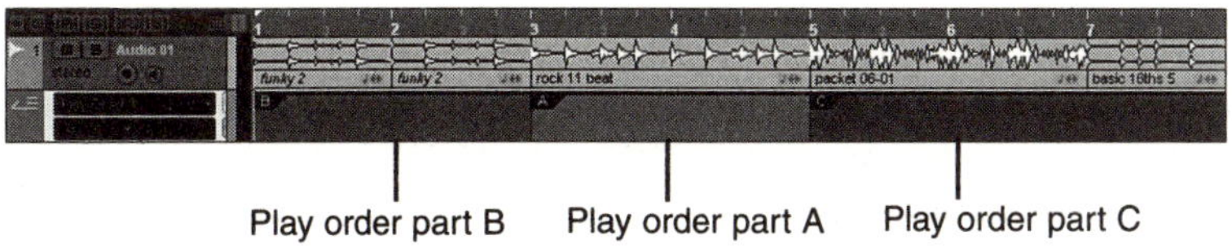

Figure 10.16 *Play order parts do not have to flow in linear order.*

> **Tip**
>
> By default, play order parts are created in exact measure lengths. To create a play order part less than a measure long, change the Grid Type control in the info bar from Bar to Beat.

By the way, if you don't like the parts you've created, you can move them around—without affecting the other tracks in your project. Just select the Object Selection tool and use your mouse to drag any play order part to a new position. In addition, you can stretch or shrink a part by dragging the left or right border of a part one direction or another. You can even stack parts on top of each other, as shown in Figure 10.17.

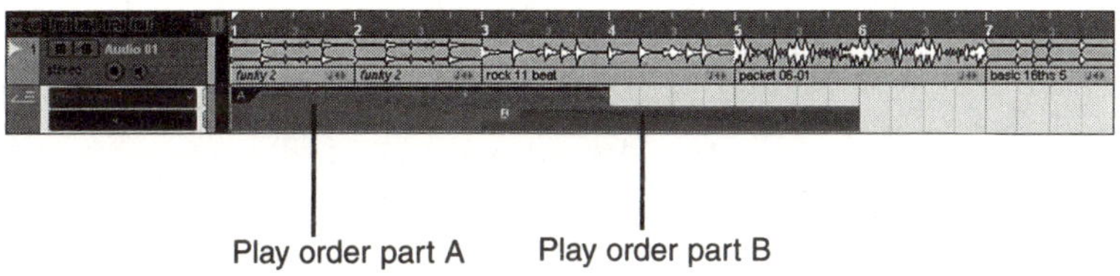

Figure 10.17 *Overlapping play order parts.*

Creating a Play Order List

After you've identified all the sections of your project in terms of play order parts, you can start rearranging your project. You do this by using the play order editor to create a play order list; the list tells Cubase what parts to play and in which order.

Here's what you need to do:

1. In the track list, select the play order track.
2. In the track inspector, click the **Edit** button.
3. This opens the play order editor, as shown in Figure 10.18. All the play order parts you created are shown in the play order parts window, in the order in which they were created.
4. Assemble your play order list by dragging parts from the play order parts window (on the right) to the Current Play Order List window (on the left). You can drag parts more than one time, to occupy multiple positions in the play order list.
5. Rearrange the parts in the play order list by dragging them up or down in the list.
6. When you have the play order determined, click the **Rename Current Play Order** button.
7. When the Enter New Name dialog box appears, enter a name for this play order list, then click **OK.**
8. Close the play order editor when you're done.

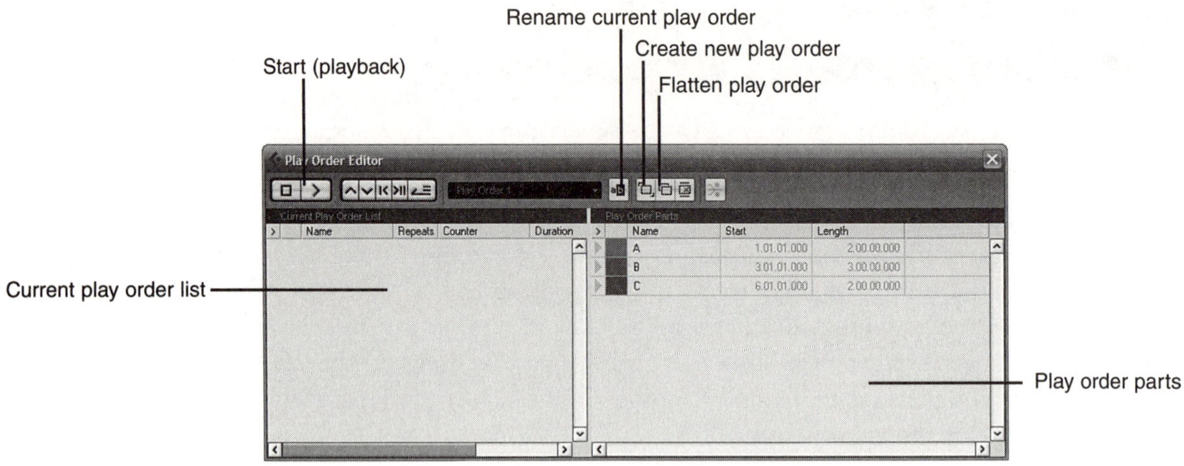

Figure 10.18 *Creating a play order list in the play order editor.*

As you can see in Figure 10.19, your play order list can be as simple or as complex as you want. To audition how this play order list sounds, make sure the Activate Play Order Mode button is selected, then click the **Start** button.

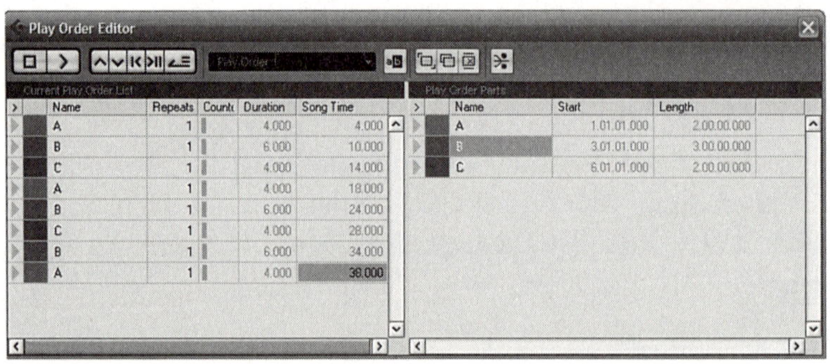

Figure 10.19 *A completed play order list.*

You can create as many play order lists as you want for any given project. To create an additional play order list, re-open the play order editor, click the **Create New Play Order** button, and get back to work.

Turning Your Play Order List into a Final Recording

Once you've finalized a play order list, you need to turn it into a real recording. You do that by "flattening" the list of parts into a traditional linear project. This is the easiest part of the whole project; just follow these steps:

1. In the track list, select the play order track.
2. In the track inspector, pull down the Play Order list and select which list you want to use.
3. Click the **Edit** button in the track inspector.
4. When the play order editor opens, click the **Flatten Play Order** button.

Cubase now takes all the different parts you've created and rearranges them in the event display, as specified in the play order list. What you have is a very traditional linear project—assembled from all the individual play order parts. From here you can continue editing the project, or proceed directly to mixing and mastering.

The Least You Need to Know

- Loop-based recording uses a series of short audio samples and drum loops to construct a complete composition.
- Samples and loops can be taken from audio CDs and digital audio files, or purchased as part of commercial loop libraries.
- To match the tempo of a loop or sample with that of your recording project, use Cubase's Time Warp function.
- Time warp also lets you fine-tune sloppy beats and transpose samples from one key to another.
- To assemble your loop-based recording, divide your project into play order parts and then arrange them in the play order editor.

Chapter 11

Creating Drum Tracks

In This Chapter

- Constructing the perfect drum track
- Enhancing drum loops
- Designing drum grooves with Groove Agent
- Using the drum editor

At the heart of most loop-based recordings is the drum track. Whether you use a sampled drum loop, create a drum track with a MIDI drum machine, or record a live drummer, it's important to get that drum beat *just right*.

Cubase offers lots of different ways to create and fine-tune your drum tracks. You can use the Time Warp functions, discussed in Chapter 10, to tempo match drum loops and adjust individual hits on or off the beat. You can use event editing, discussed in Chapter 6, to copy and rearrange different drum loops within your recording. Even better, you can use VST instruments, discussed in Chapter 9, to create your own MIDI drum tracks. Which approach you use depends on the sound you want to achieve and your own temperament. And, of course, you're not limited to just one approach; the most creative producers/recordists mix and match the various techniques to create interesting and unique rhythm tracks.

Constructing the Perfect Drum Track

Recording drum tracks is fairly easy—if you're a drummer. You hear the beat in your head, you play it on the drum kit. It's as easy as that.

Most recordists, however, are not drummers. (And this is probably a good thing ….) When you're not a drummer, the task of creating a smokin' drum track is slightly more difficult. You might know what kind of beat sounds good, but you don't necessarily know how to lay it down.

def•i•ni•tion

A **drum machine** is a synthesizer or soft synth that creates drum sounds and patterns.

Of course, even non-drummers can tap out simple beats with their hands. You do it all the time, pounding away on tabletops and car dashboards. Well, if you can tap out a rhythm on a tabletop, you can tap it out on a *drum machine*. Physical drum machines feature hard rubber pads made just for this purpose; software-based drum machines have virtual on-screen pads, or let you do your tapping on the keys of a MIDI keyboard. What you tap is converted into a MIDI drum track in Cubase, which you can then use as-is or fine-tune via various MIDI editing techniques.

Both hardware- and software-based drum machines create their sounds from real-world drum samples, recorded by real drummers using real drums. These sampled drum sounds are applied to the rhythms you create with the drum machine. When you tap a snare drum pad, it plays a sampled snare drum sound. The result is very life-like—which it should be, because you're playing actual drum sounds.

If even tapping is beyond you, you can always turn to pre-recorded drum loops. As you learned in Chapter 10, there are many commercial loop libraries out there, available in a variety of styles and sounds. Plug in a two-measure loop, repeat it across your entire song, and you have a great rhythm track. Want a different groove? All you have to do is choose a different loop. What could be easier?

Of course, you can also create drum tracks using live drummers. This is my preference, being a drummer, although I realize the challenges this presents. Mic'ing a drum set is a real challenge, requiring a large number of mics and lots of fine-tuning on the engineering front. Most engineers use at least four mics to record a drum set: one on the snare drum, one on the bass drum, and two overheads to capture the rest of the kit. More sophisticated recordings put a separate mic on every drum and cymbal; given a big drum kit, you see the challenge. (Do you have a big enough mixing board to handle 16 drum mic inputs—plus all the other instruments?)

What are the relative advantages and disadvantages of working with either MIDI or audio drum tracks? Well, working with MIDI offers easier editing; it's a snap to use the drum editor (which we'll discuss later in this chapter) to move drum hits around, or even add or subtract notes as you like. Audio editing isn't quite as easy, although Cubase's Time Warp feature does let you snap notes to a beat—or move them slightly off-beat, if you like.

Sound-wise, to my ears nothing beats the sound of live drums—either recorded by you or in the form of prerecorded drum loops. The big problem with using short loops or simple MIDI tracks is that you're dealing with a drum track created from the repetition of a two- or four-measure phrase, so you don't get the effect of a complete performance. Most drummers do not play the exact same two-measure pattern throughout an entire song; to make loops and MIDI tracks sound more realistic, you should piece together multiple loops to create a project-long drum part.

Drum loops and MIDI tracks are also right on when it comes to tempo, where many live drummers aren't quite as perfect, tempo-wise. A little give and take in terms of tempo is a good thing; a drummer who rushes or drags the beat can ruin an otherwise-great recording. Although you can do some tempo changing with Cubase's Time Warp feature, it's easier to do on a two-measure loop than it is on a four-minute song.

So which approach should you use? That's a choice you have to make—and you may make different choices on different projects. Read on to learn more.

> **Tip**
>
> If you have a live drummer handy, you can create your own personal library of drum loops. Just record the drummer playing a particular groove, and take the best two or four measures to create your loop. Two measures here, two measures there, you have your own personal loops that are sonically distinct from overused commercial loops.

Enhancing Drum Loops

Perhaps the easiest way to get a perfect drum track is to use a commercially available drum loop, like the kinds we discussed in the previous chapter. When you go this route you typically get anywhere from one to four measures of drums, which you can then loop throughout your entire recording.

The problem with using a commercial drum loop is that you're not the only person in the world using it. Hundreds, if not thousands, of other musicians are using that exact same loop, which means that their recordings will sound similar to yours, at least from the rhythm perspective. Of course, there's probably no such thing as a truly unique drum track these days, but still.

There are ways, however, to add more personality to widely used drum loops. It all comes down to how much work you want to put into it.

Editing the Loop

The most obvious way to personalize a commercial drum loop is to edit it. Add a hit there, take out a hit there, maybe even alter the feel by moving the snare drum slightly before or after the beat. Any little change you make, no matter how subtle, helps to make that beat your own.

You do all this within the sample editor, of course. You can then use the cut and paste functions to move snare and bass drum hits from one part of the measure to another, or you can remove individual hits by inserting silence, instead.

For example, Figure 11.1 shows a drum loop with standard two and four snare drum backbeats. If we cut the snare hit from the second beat and paste it into the "and" after two, we get a much different feel, as shown in Figure 11.2. And it's all done by working with an existing loop; no new recording necessary.

Stacking Loops

If you're working with a simple drum loop, you can make it sound more sophisticated by stacking a second loop on top of it. Just create two tracks in the project list, and import different audio loops to each track, as shown in Figure 11.3. Make sure the two drum loops sound good together, of course, and that they don't get in each other's way. This will require a little trial and error, but the results can be very interesting.

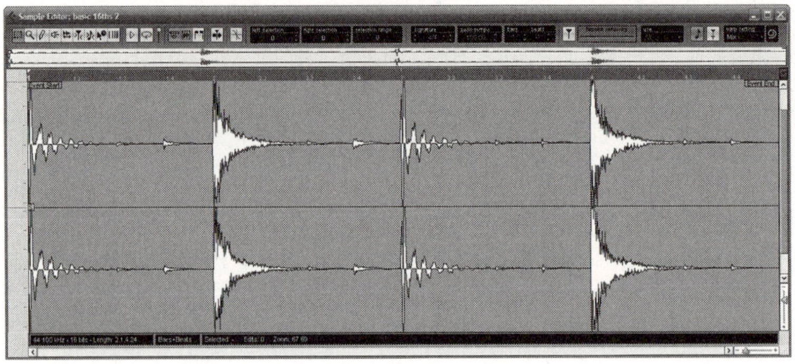

Figure 11.1 *A drum loop with traditional two and four snare drum hits.*

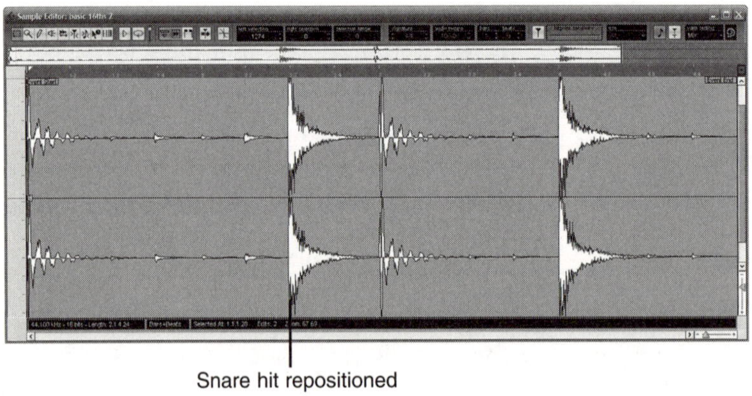

Figure 11.2 *The same loop, with the snare hit on two moved to the "and" after two.*

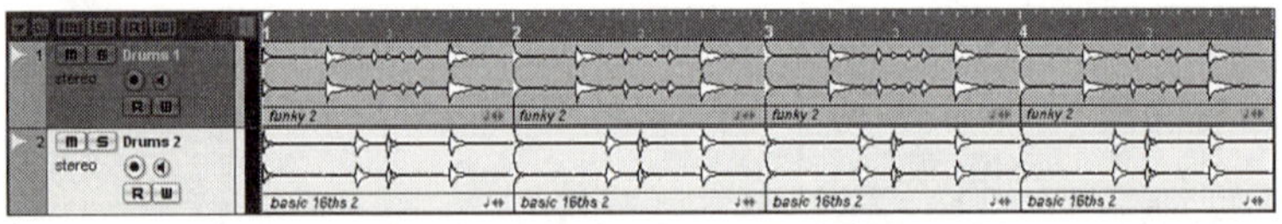

Figure 11.3 *Two drum loops stacked on top of one another can create a dense and interesting groove.*

> **Note**
>
> Lest you think the concept of stacking multiple drum parts is a new technique, know that many of the hippest Motown grooves of the 1960s were created by two drummers playing two separate parts at the same time. If you don't believe me, get a copy of the *Standing in the Shadows of Motown: Deluxe Edition* CD and listen for yourself; the second disc of this two-disc set includes several famous Motown recordings with the vocal tracks removed, so you can better hear how the Funk Brothers created those famous grooves.

Using Multiple Loops

Even easier is the technique of creating a long drum groove out of two or more shorter loops. All you have to do is insert one loop after another, and you end up with a more complex linear groove.

For example, Figure 11.4 shows a 4-bar groove created from four 1-bar loops. The first loop (let's call it "A") is repeated in the middle of the groove, like this: A B A C. Use your imagination to create multiple-loop grooves of any length in the same fashion.

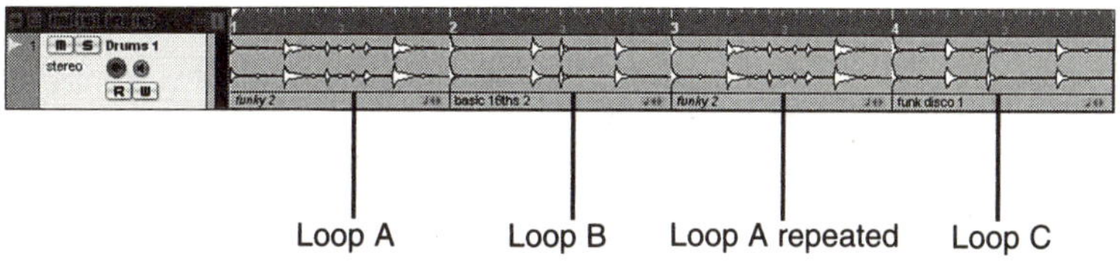

Figure 11.4 *A 4-measure groove created from four 1-measure drum loops.*

Adding Fills

Most human drummers don't play a static groove over the entire length of a song. Drummers typically break up a groove at the end of a phrase by playing some sort of fill, typically using different accents or different drums. (Many fills go around the toms, rather than staying on the snare and hi-hat.)

You can emulate this by inserting a different drum loop at the end of a 4- or 8- or 16-bar phrase. Many loop libraries include "fill" loops, just for this purpose. Or, if you like, you can program your own fills by using a MIDI drum machine, or even insert a live fill recorded by a real drummer. Just remember, the goal is to break up the groove and set up the next musical phrase.

Adding Live Drums to a Loop

Adding live drums at the end of phrases is one cool effect; adding live drums throughout the groove is another. Here is where you start thinking about combining sampled and live sounds.

For example, you might want to take a sampled drum loop and have a real drummer play along with it. The drummer can play the entire set, or he may want to emphasize only part of the kit. You can get an interesting effect by doubling the real drummer on the snare drum backbeats, or by having him play a live hi-hat over the sampled beat. The goal is to insert a bit of the human element over an otherwise machine-like groove. As with all these techniques, the best approach is to experiment.

Note

If you want to learn more about playing different drum beats, check out my companion book, *The Complete Idiot's Guide to Playing Drums, Second Edition* (Michael Miller, Alpha, 2004). It's a good way to learn how drummers think and work, even if you're not a drummer yourself.

In Defense of Live Drums (and Live Drummers)

A confession. Even though I play keyboards and guitar and certainly know my way around a mixing board, I am, first and foremost, a drummer. As such, I've observed the advent of drum machines and loop libraries with a bit of trepidation. Not only do I hate seeing computers put deserving musicians out of work, I'm also not convinced that these digital drummers can ever sound quite as good as the real thing.

Yes, I know that many loops are actually recordings of live drummers. But most loops are only 1–4 measures long. Listening to a drummer play for 4 bars isn't the same as hearing him play an entire song. Human drummers vary what they play according to the rest of the music, and seldom play the exact same 4-measure groove throughout an entire song. That's why, to my ears, most loop-based recordings never sound quite right; they're too machine-like, without the human variable.

In addition, tempo-matched loops and MIDI tracks are too precise. Human drummers add a bit of imprecision to everything they play. That might sound like a bad thing, having a drummer play a little before or a little after the beat. But that looseness with a groove is what gives a recording the human feel; humans are not 100% precise. To many ears—including mine—these rhythmically perfect recordings sound more than a little artificial. Humans just don't sound that good. Our human ears listen for and expect those little imperfections.

More important, slight rhythmic imperfections add life to a recording. A precise 120 bpm beat throughout an entire song may look good on paper, but it doesn't ebb and flow like a human performance would. Live musicians make a performance breathe; they push the beat a little here, pull it back a little there, maybe even speed up a tad in the chorus and slow down again in the verse. In this way, deliberate rhythmic imperfection can turn a good recording into a great one.

I recognize that many would argue this point. When you're recording dance tracks, for example, you need a steady beat to keep the dancers' feet on the floor. Yet most of the great dance tracks of the disco era were recorded by real live musicians, with the tempo varying a bit here and there, and nobody complains that you can't dance to them. Of course, there's a difference between speeding up 10 bpm over the course of a few measures and varying the tempo 1 or 2 bpm over the entire song. To my ear, small differences are not only acceptable, they're necessary to give life to a track.

These are all reasons why I'll always prefer live drummers over prerecorded loops and machine-generated MIDI tracks. But that's just me; a talented producer/recordist can certainly create good-sounding tracks using these methods. It requires more than rote cutting and pasting, however. To make a loop-based or MIDI drum track sound great, you have to fine-tune it to add back in some of that random human element that the machines otherwise take out. That's why Cubase lets you perform all the drum-related editing that we talk about in this chapter and throughout the book—to make computer-generated music sound more human. It's worth the effort.

Using Pre-Programmed Grooves with Groove Agent

Another option for creating a drum track is to use Steinberg's Groove Agent, a VST instrument that not only provides a wealth of drum sounds but also creates the beats for you—in MIDI format.

As you can see in Figure 11.5, Groove Agent is a very sophisticated virtual drum machine. Instead of selecting a specific set of drum set sounds, you instead select a specific kind of groove. You can then fine-tune that groove, as well as fine-tune the drum sounds used in that groove. We'll walk through a brief example.

> **Note**
>
> Groove Agent is an add-on VST instrument not included with Cubase 4. We'll talk about Groove Agent 2 here; the latest version, Groove Agent 3, should be available by the time you read this.

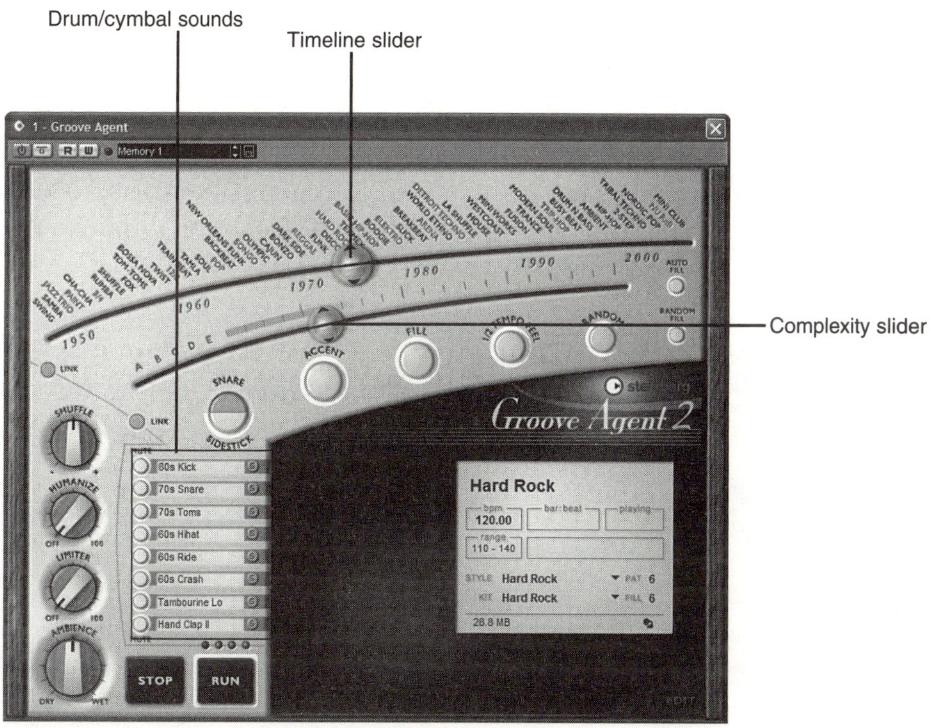

Figure 11.5 *Creating a drum groove with Groove Agent.*

You start by selecting the type of groove you want with the groove selector. This is as simple as moving the top slider (dubbed the Timeline slider) to the specific groove you want. (The grooves are arranged by era, from 1950 to 2000.) You can dial in variations of the selected groove by using the second slider (dubbed the Complexity slider). This control has dedicated A–E positions (which move from simple to complex), and then a continuously variable section that moves through variations of the chosen groove.

To break up the groove, you can click either the Auto Fill or Random Fill (or both) buttons, which insert drum fills as specified. To add a fill at any point, just click the Fill button; to add a cymbal crash, click the Accent button.

But that's not all. Don't like the selected drum sounds for this groove? Then click a drum in the instrument list and select another one. Want to add a little "sloppiness" for a more human feel? Then adjust the Humanize and Shuffle controls. Want to switch to a half-tempo feel? Then click the ½ Tempo Feel button. And so on.

Note

Learn more about VST instruments in Chapter 9.

You assign Groove Agent to a MIDI track the same way you do with any VST instrument. Click the record button, and it starts playing—and recording—automatically, according to the configuration you selected. Groove Agent may be an expensive add-on, but the results are worth it!

Editing MIDI Tracks with the Drum Editor

However you create a MIDI drum track, you can edit it at will using a special version of the key editor called the drum editor. You open the drum editor by clicking the MIDI event and then selecting **MIDI > Open Drum Editor.**

As you can see in Figure 11.6, the drum editor looks a lot like the key editor. The big difference is that instead of pitches and a keyboard along the vertical axis, you have a list of drum sounds. In addition, each drum hit is indicated by a single "diamond," instead of a bar of specific length. (That's because drum hits are just that, hits; they don't have the sustain that you get when you hold a note on another instrument.)

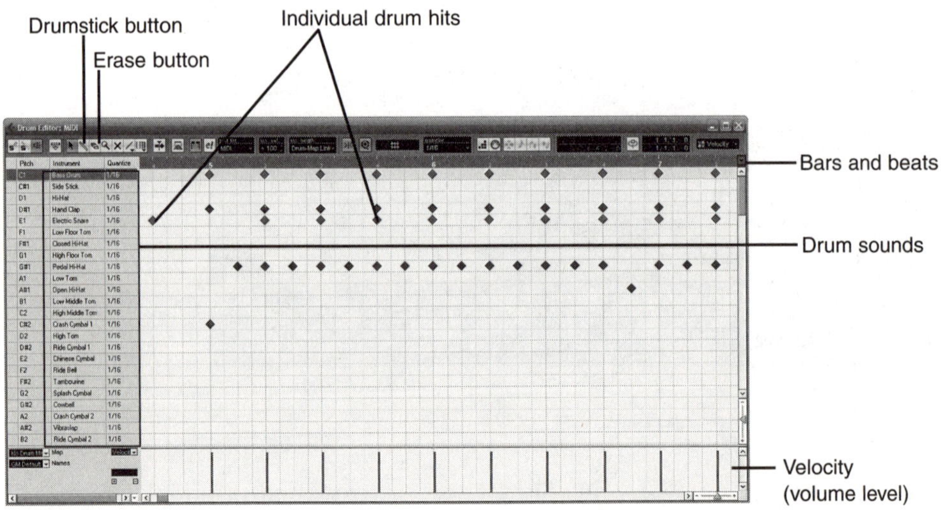

Figure 11.6 *The Drum Editor.*

Editing a drum part is as simple as clicking, dragging, and dropping. For example:

- To change a particular hit from one beat to another, grab the note with your mouse and drag it to another location on the same horizontal line.
- To reassign a hit from one drum to another, grab the note with your mouse and drag it to another instrument line; make sure you keep the note at the same horizontal position.

- To delete a note, click the **Erase** button in the toolbar and then click the note.
- To add a new note, click the **Drumstick** button in the toolbar and then click where you want the note to be—both vertically (which drum) and horizontally (which part of the measure).

When you close the drum editor, you're returned to the project window with your edits in place. As you can see, the drum editor makes it fairly easy to make changes big or small to your MIDI drum tracks.

The Least You Need to Know

- You can enhance prerecorded drum loops by editing the notes in a loop, stacking two or more loops on top of each other, stringing two or more loops together to create a longer pattern, and playing live drums on top of a loop.
- For more advanced drum track programming, invest in the optional Groove Agent VST instrument, which can create a virtually unlimited number of drum grooves.
- However you create a MIDI drum track, you can edit it using Cubase's drum editor, which looks and works pretty much like the MIDI key editor.

Part 5

Mixing and Mastering

Now that you're done recording and editing, it's time to mix all your tracks down to a stereo master—and add any desired plug-in effects and equalization. Then you're ready to export to a digital audio file, perfect for distribution on CD or over the Internet.

Chapter 12

Mixing Your Tracks

In This Chapter

- Mixing versus mastering
- Understanding the mixing process
- Setting levels
- Setting the stereo pan
- Adding equalization and effects
- Automating mixing operations

You've recorded all your instrumental and vocal tracks. You've edited all the mistakes out of the tracks, and even done a little rearranging of events to make things flow better. The musical creation process is now complete; it's time to start thinking about turning all those tracks into a finished recording.

Turning a collection of recorded tracks into a finished recording is a two-step process. The first step is to mix all those tracks so that you get the overall sound you want, complete with any necessary processing and equalization. The second step is to add master effects and export the mix to a stereo audio file, suitable for final distribution on compact disc or other appropriate media.

In this chapter we discuss the basics of the mixing process, which is a lot more involved that it sounds at first blush. In subsequent chapters we look at specific mixing techniques, such as adding equalization and plug-in effects, as well as the final mastering process.

Mixing vs. Mastering—Which Is Which?

Many novice recordists get the mixing and mastering processes confused in their minds. That's understandable; they both take place after the main recording, and involve many of the same operations. But mixing and mastering are quite different, and it helps to know which is which—and why.

So you have to mix before you master—and you have to master before you press your CDs, or distribute your music through other media. (The entire project workflow is shown in Figure 12.1.)

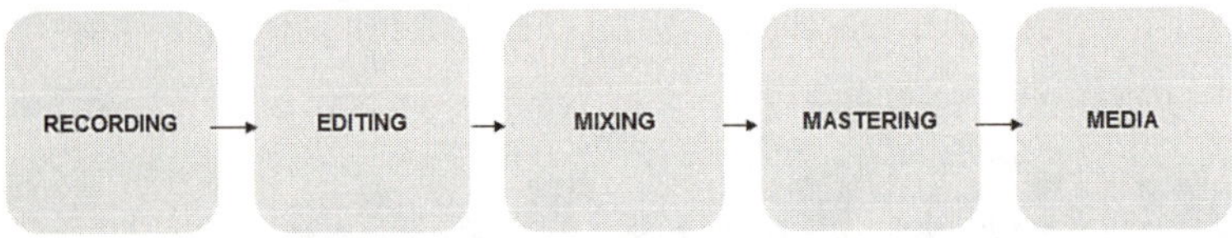

Figure 12.1 *The project workflow, from recording through mixing, mastering, and final media production.*

> **Note**
>
> Cubase also lets you create surround sound mixes, for use in video soundtracks and high-quality SACD and DVD-Audio discs. The creation of surround sound mixes, however, is beyond the scope of this book—we'll stick to simple stereo, if you don't mind.

Mixing, at its most basic, takes the multiple audio and MIDI tracks you've recorded and blends them together into a sonic whole. But there's more to it than that.

When you mix your tracks, you actually have to perform a number of related operations. These include:

- Set the relative volume levels between tracks
- Set the position of individual instruments and vocals in the stereo field
- Apply equalization to the individual tracks, to bring out desired tonal ranges
- Apply any necessary audio effects to individual tracks, such as reverb, delay, compression, and so on

That's the mixing process. The mastering process takes the next steps, including:

- Apply master equalization to all channels
- Apply any master effects to all channels
- Fade in or fade out the recording as necessary
- Save your mix to a two-channel WAV or AIFF format file

Both mixing and mastering take place within the Cubase environment—although some advanced mastering functions can also be done in other programs. The product of all this work is the final master file, which can be used to produce CDs or other media.

How to Mix a Recording

Up to this point in the process you've worked with individual tracks. During the mixing process, you start treating those individual tracks as a whole—that is, you're mixing the overall recording, not fixing individual tracks.

The mix you create will become the recording that listeners hear. Yes, that mix will include individual tracks, but no individual track is of primary importance; what's important is the overall sound, which the individual tracks mix together to create.

Creating that sound involves finding the perfect balance between all those tracks. Some tracks need to fade into the background, others need to take a more prominent position; some tracks may require additional processing or equalization, some may prove superfluous and need to be muted or deleted. That's what you do during the mixing process—adjust this track and that to create the overall sound you want.

Most mixing operations take place, appropriately enough, in Cubase's mixer window. It's here that you adjust the relative volume levels of individual tracks, as well as mute any tracks you don't want to include in the final mix. Other mixing operations utilize the track inspector, which is where you add insert and send effects and apply equalization.

Before we begin, though, a quick word on saving your work. Before you start mixing and after you've finished working with your individual tracks, you should save your work as a new file. (**Select File > Save As.**) You should then open this new file to begin the mixing process. When you complete your mix, you should save that as another new file. This way you can return to the unmixed tracks (the first file) if you ever want to create a different mix; you should thus save each new mix as a new file you can access separately. (And it wouldn't hurt to create a backup copy of your master file either; backing up your work is always a good idea.)

Tip

Before you create your mix, you have to make sure that all your individual tracks are in their final condition. That means fixing any mistakes, removing any clicks or pops, rearranging individual events, and the like. You don't want to go back and tweak individual tracks when you're supposed to be working with your project as a whole.

Setting Levels

Let's start with the most obvious part of the mixing process, the adjustment of each track's volume level. What's important here is not the volume of any individual track, but rather how each track relates to the other tracks and fits into the overall mix.

Setting the levels is deceptively easy, but actually takes quite a bit of work—and a lot of listening and trial-and-error experimenting. Here's how it goes, in general terms:

1. Open your project and display the mixer window, as shown in Figure 12.2.
2. Make the mixing window as wide as possible, to display as many individual channel strips as you can.
3. Make sure that no tracks are activated for recording, that no tracks are muted (click the individual Mute buttons to turn them off, if they're currently on), and that no tracks are activated for solo play (click the Solo buttons to turn that feature off, if it's on).
4. Rewind the project to the beginning.
5. Click the **Play** button on the transport panel.
6. As the project plays back, adjust the volume sliders for each channel. Move the sliders up to increase the volume levels; move the sliders down to decrease the volume levels.
7. Repeat until done.

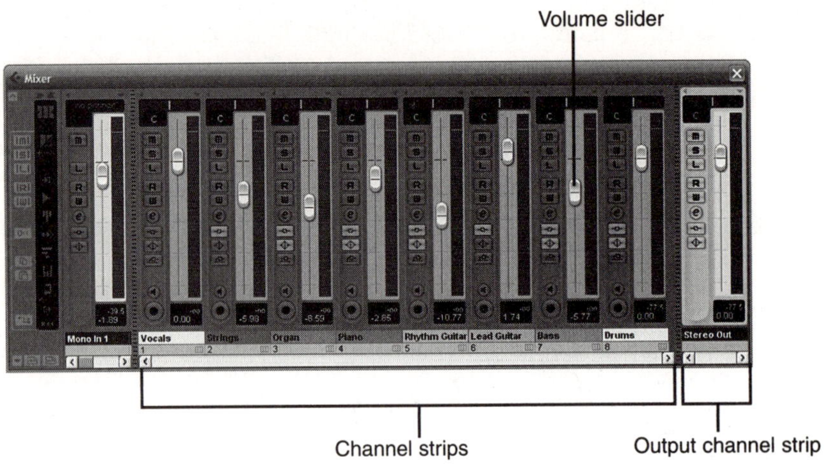

Figure 12.2 *Adjusting channel levels in the mixer.*

> **Tip**
>
> At this point in the process we're not that focused on the overall volume levels. If you want to adjust the overall volume, use the volume slider in the output channel strip.

I said that this process is deceptively simple. That's because, although moving the volume sliders is easy enough, deciding *where* to move them requires some skill—and good ears. It's impossible for me to tell you how to mix any individual recording; what sounds good to me might not be what you're aiming for at all. A collection of tracks can be mixed together in an almost infinite number of ways, and it's always surprising to hear how different mixes create such different feels. Should the rhythm guitar be buried in the background, or should it be more up front? Should the piano and lead guitar be equal in volume, or should one take precedence? Just how prominent should the snare drum backbeat be? And is the vocal clear enough in the mix, or is it too overbearing?

These are all questions that you have to address as you work through your mix. Trust me, you'll be listening to your recording *a lot* during this process; diligent mixing requires playback after playback after playback until you get things just right.

> **Tip**
>
> Don't panic if you want the volume level of any given track to change over the course of a recording. Maybe you want the lead guitar in the background during the verses, but moved up in the mix during the chorus. This is easily enough done, using Cubase's automation function; more on this in the "Automating Mixing Operations" section, later in this chapter.

What Makes a Great Mix?

As I said, it's impossible for me to provide detailed instructions on how to best mix all the recordings you might make. I can, however, provide some general advice that may or may not apply in any given situation.

- The most important track is almost always the lead vocal track. If the lead vocal gets buried in the mix, you haven't done your job. Listeners want to hear the lead vocals, which means mixing them up—or sending the other tracks to the background.
- A mix can be too busy. Too much happening in the background can detract from the lead vocal—which is, I repeat, almost always the most important part of the mix. Don't get carried away by the unlimited number of tracks that Cubase lets you work with; sometimes a simpler mix is better.
- Don't fall in love with subsidiary parts. That bass line may be happenin', but if it's too busy you may have to simplify it. No matter how cool it is, it's there to support the lead vocal, not to function as a solo track.
- Proper stereo placement is important. Seldom do you want to place important vocals or instruments hard left or hard right in the mix. Off-center placement is fine for auxiliary tracks (rhythm guitar, piano accompaniment, and so on), but for the main tracks (lead vocal, drums, bass), placement in the center of the sound field is the least distracting way to go.
- Don't make it too perfect. The best recordings are seldom the most flawless ones. When mixing tracks, I find that feel matters more than technical precision. Give me a take with a lot of energy and a few minor mistakes over one with zero mistakes and a machine-like soul; most listeners will never hear the details (and flaws) that you do in the studio.
- Remember that most people will listen to your recording in the car, or on an iPod, or on an otherwise less-than-perfect audio system. The sound you hear on your nearfield monitors will almost always be better than what most listeners will hear on their equipment. Consider burning a "pre-mix" to CD that you can play on various audio setups, to hear for yourself what the average listener will hear. In the old days, some top producers would feed their recordings through a cheap car speaker connected to the mixing console, to hear how things would sound to a teenager cruising around town; today, you might want to run your mix through a pair of cheapo computer speakers or the speakers in a laptop PC, since many people will be listening through similar devices.

Overall, it's important to think like a producer during the mixing process—not like a musician. It's the final sound that's important, not any individual part, even if you played it yourself. Be as ruthless as you need to be to cut and fade and otherwise mold the individual tracks to achieve the most effective mix.

Setting the Stereo Pan

The next part of the mixing process involves placing each instrument somewhere in the left-to-right stereo field. We're long past the age of monophonic recording; not all instruments should be *panned* hard center. You open up the mix and let the recording breathe by using the entire stereo field.

def•i•ni•tion

When you **pan** a track, you move it from one place to another in the stereo sound field.

Each track in your recording can be panned anywhere in the stereo field, from hard left to dead center to hard right. Just follow these steps:

1. Open the mixer window and initiate playback.
2. Move to the channel strip for the channel you want to pan.
3. Click the blue line in the Pan control, as shown in Figure 12.3.
4. Drag the line left or right to position this track in the stereo sound field. Alternately, enter an "LXX" or "RXX" number in the Pan field, to indicate how far off center (to the left or right) you want to place this channel.

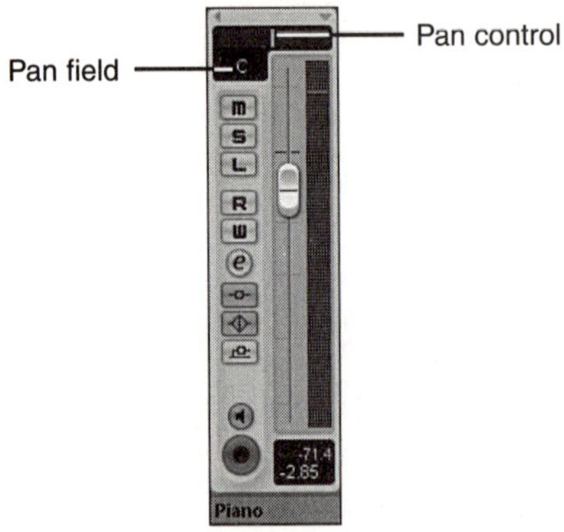

Figure 12.3 *Adjusting the stereo pan.*

> **Tip**
> To make fine adjustments to the Pan control, hold down the Shift key while dragging the blue line. To return a track to dead center, hold down the Ctrl button (Command on the Mac) and click the Pan control.

In general, you want to be subtle with your use of stereo positioning. The days of putting all the vocals in the left channel and all the instruments in the right went out with The Beatles' second American album. Hard-right or hard-left positioning can be used for effect, but otherwise should be reserved for subsidiary instruments or vocals.

Muting Unwanted Tracks

As you proceed through your mix, you'll sometimes find a track that sounded good when you recorded it but just doesn't fit in with the final recording. No problem. While you could simply delete the track, it's possible you'll change your mind at some later time—and it's tough to bring a track back from the dead. A better approach is to mute the track, which removes it from the mix but still keeps it in the track pool, so you can turn it back on again if you later decide to.

To mute a track, all you have to do is click the Mute button in the mixer or track listing, as shown in Figure 12.4. Click the Mute button a second time to unmute it.

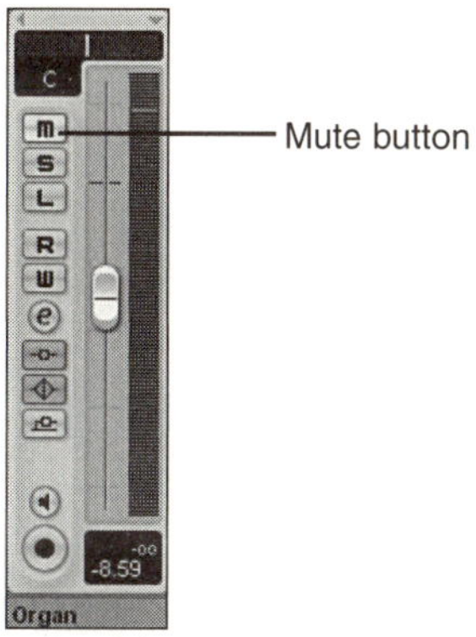

Figure 12.4 *Muting an unwanted track.*

Adding Effects

Cubase offers a variety of plug-in effects that you can apply to individual tracks in your mix, including reverb, delay, compression, and so on. You use these effects to alter the basic sound of a track, or to compensate for defects in the original recording.

The topic of plug-in effects warrants its own chapter. Turn to Chapter 13 to learn more.

Adding Equalization

After you have your vocals and instruments where you want them and at the proper volume level, you can think about applying equalization on a track-by-track basis. Equalization (or EQ) shapes the tone of a signal by boosting or lowering specific frequencies. During the mixing process you can apply different levels of EQ to individual tracks; during the mastering process you can apply EQ to the mix as a whole.

As with plug-in effects, the topic of equalization is important enough to warrant its own chapter. Turn to Chapter 14 to learn more.

Automating Mixing Operations

Mixing is complicated enough when all the settings stay constant throughout the entire length of a recording. But what do you do when the settings need to change halfway through—when you need to change a track's volume level, or temporarily add special processing?

In the old days, the final mix-down took place in real time. The final mix was recorded direct to tape, which meant the engineer had to twiddle the knobs, slide the sliders, and punch the buttons as the tape rolled. If he missed an operation, he had to rewind the tape and try it again. This made mixing a somewhat stressful process.

def•i•ni•tion

Automation enables you to program control changes into your recording, so that on playback these changes happen automatically.

Today, fortunately, the process is less stressful. Thanks to computerization, all the mid-project adjustments you make are recorded along with the audio and MIDI tracks, in a special *automation* track. When you play back the mix, the automation track is also played back, automatically making the adjustments you had recorded earlier. And when you master your mix to the final stereo file, all the automated changes take place just as if you were twiddling the knobs yourself.

Recording Automation

Automating changes to your mix is as easy as clicking a button and letting Cubase record your actions. Here's how it works:

1. Rewind your project to the beginning.
2. Click to activate the Write Automation button(s) in the mixer for the track(s) you wish to automate, as shown in Figure 12.5. You can automate one track at a time, or several at once.
3. Click the **Playback** button on the transport panel.
4. Make any necessary volume or other adjustments as the track plays.
5. Click the **Stop** button when playback has ended.
6. Click the Write Automation button(s) again to deactivate them.

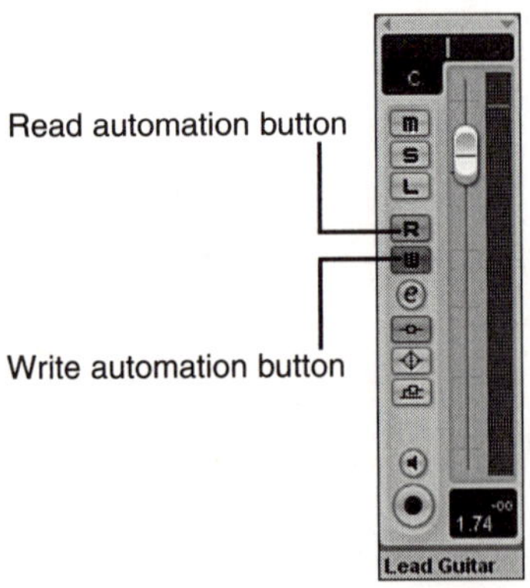

Figure 12.5 *Automating the mixing process.*

Any changes you make to that track during playback will now be recorded—volume adjustments, effect activation, in-process stereo panning, you name it. And if you messed up in any way, you can repeat these steps at any time to re-record a new automation track.

Playing Back Automated Tracks

Playing back a track for which you've recorded automation instructions is also as easy as clicking a button. Follow these steps:

1. Rewind your project to the beginning.

2. Click to activate the Read Automation button(s) in the mixer for the track(s) you automated. (Make sure the Write Automation buttons are clicked off.)
3. Click the **Playback** button on the transport panel.

Simple enough to do—and it really works!

> **Note**
>
> You'll want to make sure that you've turned on Read Automation before you master your recording to a stereo file, so that all your automation instructions are live. Learn more in Chapter 15.

Editing Automated Tracks

Instead of rerecording a flawed automation track, you can choose to edit it in the track listing. It's somewhat complicated and differs a bit depending on which parameters you automated, but it can be done.

To edit an automation track, you first have to display it. To do this, right-click on the selected track in the track listing, and then select **Show Used Automation** from the pop-up window. As you can see in Figure 12.6, the automation track displays a duplicate of the original waveform (for guidance purposes), along with a horizontal line called the *automation curve*. The automation curve reflects the status of the selected parameter.

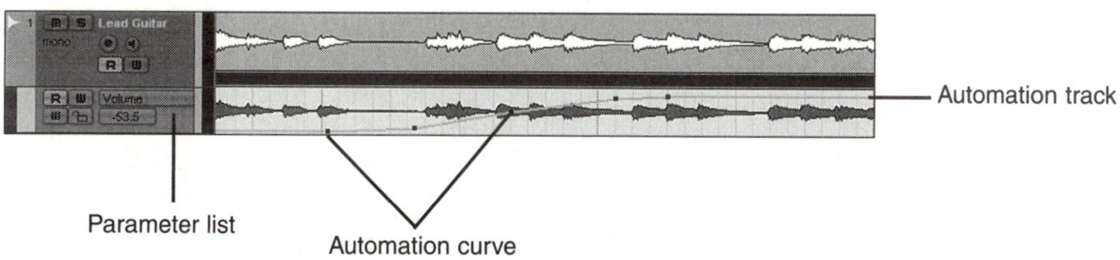

Figure 12.6 *Automating the mixing process.*

You select which parameter is displayed by pulling down the parameter list in the track listing for the automation track. You can opt to display volume, mute, insert effects, send effects, and so on.

Editing the automation track is now accomplished by dragging the automation curve up or down, as appropriate. Here's how to do it:

1. Right-click on the selected track in the track listing and select **Show Automation.** This displays the automation track.
2. Pull down the parameter list in the track listing for the automation track and select the parameter you wish to edit.
3. Click on the automation curve where you want to make a change, and then drag that point of the curve to a new position.

Some parameters (such as volume) have continuously variable curves. Other parameters (such as mute) have just two positions—on and off, as shown in Figure 12.7. Adjust each type of curve as necessary.

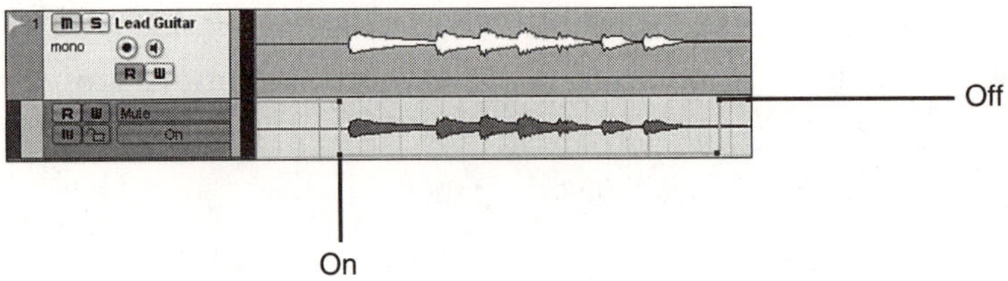

Figure 12.7 *Editing the mute automation—a simple on/off operation.*

The Least You Need to Know

- Mixing involves manipulating all your recorded tracks to achieve the desired overall sound.
- Mastering involves sending your final mix to a stereo audio file, which can then be reproduced on CD or other media.
- The first part of the mixing process is to set the volume levels for each of the tracks you've recorded.
- Next, you use the pan control to position each track within the left-to-right stereo sound field.
- Apply equalization and audio effects to each of the tracks in your mix.
- If you need to adjust your mix in the middle of a recording, use Cubase's automation controls to record your actions—and play them back automatically.

Chapter 13

Applying Plug-In Effects

In This Chapter

- Understanding how plug-in effects work
- Applying insert and send effects
- Using popular plug-in effects, including noise gate, reverb, and dynamic compression

Back in Chapter 7 you learned how to apply various types of processing to individual audio events. That's just the tip of the iceberg when it comes to audio processing, however. There is a lot more processing you can do later in the process, when you're creating your final mix. I'm talking about applying dynamic compression, adding reverb, even using various filters and modulators to alter your recorded parts in very distinctive ways.

These audio effects—and similar MIDI effects—are applied to your recorded tracks via software-based plug-ins. Cubase includes a number of these plug-in effects as part of the Cubase package; other plug-ins can be downloaded from the Internet or purchased from third parties. Performing this type of processing is one of the last things you do before completing your mix and moving on to the mastering process.

How Plug-In Effects Work

Audio effects have traditionally been added to recordings via what are called *plug-ins*. In tape-based recording, these were outboard boxes that literally plugged into the recording console; with computer-based recording, the plug-ins are software programs or utilities that perform the same functions as the traditional outboard boxes.

def•i•ni•tion

A **plug-in** is a device or effect that changes or processes the sound of a recording in any way other than equalization or volume level. Reverb, echo, and flanging are all audio effects.

Note

Cubase 4 utilizes new VST3 plug-in technology. VST3 effects automatically adjust their number of audio busses for the type of channel in which they're inserted (mono, stereo, and so on) and include a silence detection function that only processes audio when there is actually a signal present. Cubase 4 includes more than 30 new VST3 plug-in effects, as well as a bevy of older SX3-style plug-ins updated to VST3 technology.

Cubase follows this paradigm by offering a variety of plug-in effects, from simple reverb to complex filtering and modulation. Each plug-in effect you select is inserted into the audio signal path at a given point, and affects the audio signal from that point onward. The effect is applied in real time, which means that the audio processing requires a fair amount of computing horsepower. Because the processing is in real time, and is applied after the original audio signal enters the system, the original audio is not altered by the effect—only the resulting sound is changed.

Where to Apply Plug-In Effects

When you choose to apply a plug-in effect, you also have to choose where in the process to apply it. As shown in Figure 13.1, you can apply plug-in effects at five different points in the recording process:

- Added to the input bus as the recording is being made, so that the recorded track includes the effect processing. (These are called *input insert effects*; they work pretty much like regular insert effects, and are best used for adding real-time compression when recording lead vocals.)
- Directly to the recorded audio event—*not* to the entire track. (This is known as *offline processing*, which we discussed in Chapter 7.)
- Inserted into the signal path just after the original channel input and before equalization and volume are applied. (These are called *insert effects*, and are applied to an entire track.)
- Added to the end of the signal path as separate effects tracks; the final audio is routed to the effects track as the final step in the process. (These are known as *send effects*, and are applied to an entire track.)
- Inserted into the master output bus during the mastering process, after the individual tracks have been mixed to a stereo signal. (These are known as *master insert effects*, and are applied to the entire mix, not individual channels.)

Caution

Audio processing effects (found on the **Audio > Process** menu) can not be applied as insert, send, or master insert effects; these effects are only available for offline processing. For insert/send/master insert effects, the only effects you can use are plug-in effects.

To simplify things, just remember that insert effects apply to your inputs and send effects apply to your outputs. In addition, input insert effects are applied directly to a track when you're recording, and master insert effects are applied at the end of the process, to your entire recording.

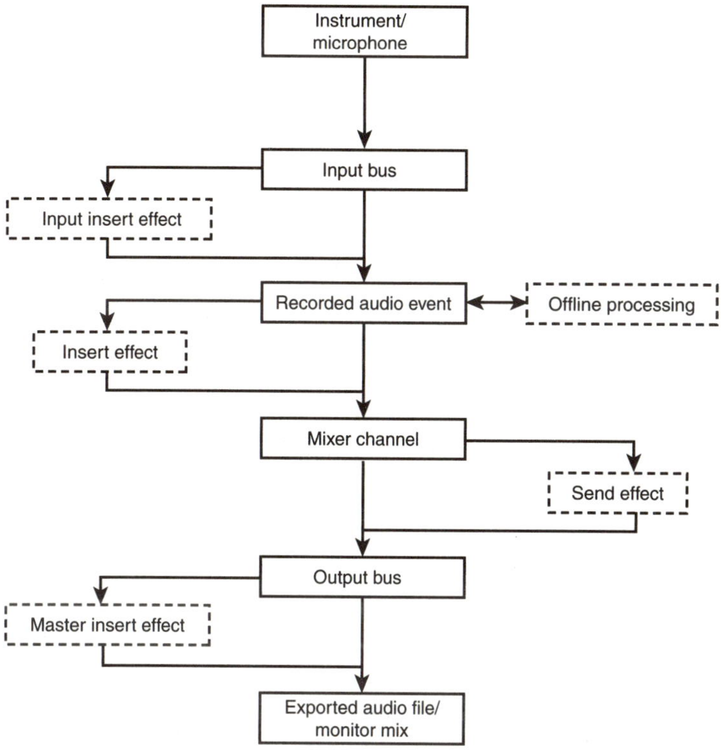

Figure 13.1 *The different points where effects are added in the recording process.*

Let's look at an example of an input insert effect. Imagine that you want to apply some compression to a lead vocal track. The signal input from the microphone is routed through the selected plug-in, which applies the compression effect, and then sent back through the input bus as normal. The signal recorded on disc includes the effect processing.

Now consider an example of how a regular insert effect works. Let's say you want to apply some distortion to a guitar track you've just recorded. The audio from the event is routed through the selected plug-in, which adds a distortion effect to the signal. The now-distorted signal continues through the path, on to the output bus and ultimately to the monitor mix (or, when you're ready, the final mix). Note that the original recorded event remains unchanged in the track listing, altered not at all by the process; the effect is applied to the signal after the event is played.

Compare this type of insert effect to a send effect—for this example, adding reverb to a vocal track. With a send effect, the audio stays in the signal path until it reaches the output bus, where it is sent to the selected plug-in. The processed signal is then available to be sent to the monitor mix, or to the final mixdown.

Master insert effects are similar to insert effects, but applied to the final mixed-down stereo signal. As an example, imagine that you're adding a compression effect to your entire mix. The stereo signal is routed through the compression plug-in and back to the output bus for final output.

Caution

The primary drawback to adding plug-ins to the signal path is that each one requires a fair amount of computer processing. When you start stacking effect upon effect, the CPU power required increases—which ultimately slows down even the fastest computer.

Choosing Which Type of Effect to Use

Okay, so now you can figure out where to apply the various types of effects—but how do you decide *which* of these effects to use? Admittedly, it's a tad confusing, but it all comes down to how much computer horsepower each operation takes and what type of effect you're applying.

Let's start by making a distinction between real-time or "online" processing, versus offline processing. Online effects—which include insert, send, and master effects—are calculated and processed by your computer in real time, and require tons of processing power. If you apply too many online effects at the same time, your computer will slow down considerably, and might even freeze up. (Naturally, the newer and more powerful your computer, the less of a problem this is.)

In contrast, offline effects (which we discussed in Chapter 7) are processed before you initiate playback or mixing, and thus use up none of your computer's precious processing power. To reduce the load on your PC, then, you should choose offline effects over online ones whenever practical.

And, just to confuse things even more, all insert effects (including input inserts and master inserts) require more processing power than send effects. Don't ask why; it's a technical thing.

Okay, right now you're probably somewhat bumfuzzled about what effects to apply when. Well, there are actually some simple guidelines you can use to help you make your processing decisions:

- Use *input insert effects* for adding compression when recording vocal tracks.
- Use regular *insert effects* for filters, choruses, phasers, noise gates, compression, and other dynamic effects.
- Use *send effects* for equalization, reverb, delays, and modulation effects.
- Use *master insert effects* for any effects you want to apply to your entire mix—typically compression, reverb, and equalization.
- Use *offline processing* for any of Cubase's audio processes (on the **Audio > Process** menu), as well as for those effects you want to apply to only a section of a track.

Less bumfuzzled now? I certainly hope so!

> **Tip**
>
> One of the cool things about insert and send effects is that you can easily switch the effect in and out, as the effects are processed in real time. Initiate playback with the effect switched off, then switch it on so you can hear the effect of the effect—and make any adjustments to the effect as necessary.

Applying Plug-In Effects

As you just learned, Cubase lets you apply plug-in effects as either insert or send effects. (You can also apply audio effects directly to audio events, as we discussed in Chapter 7.) Now let's learn how to apply each type of effect.

Adding an Input Insert Effect

Input insert effects are added to the beginning of the signal path as a recording is being made. This means that the processed sound is recorded to disk; once added, you can't remove an input insert effect.

To add an input insert effect while recording, follow these steps:

1. In the mixer, click the **Show/Hide Input Channels** icon in the common panel to display the input pane.
2. In the input pane, click the **Edit** button for the input bus (*not* the selected track) you're using to record, as shown in Figure 13.2.

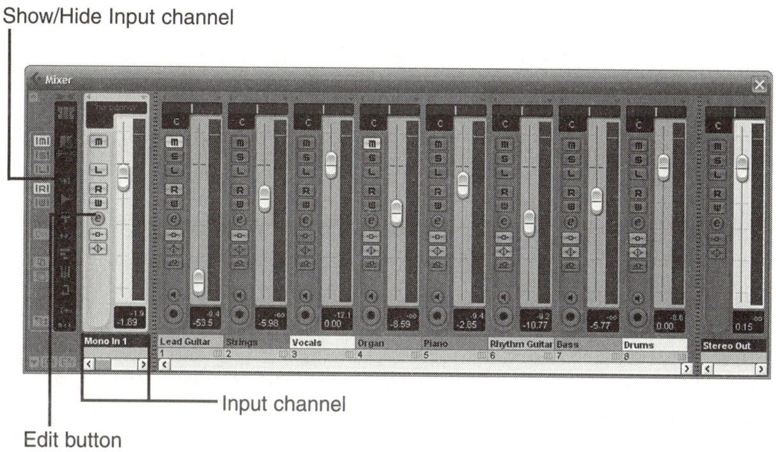

Figure 13.2 *Getting ready to add an input insert effect directly to the input bus.*

3. This displays the VST Input Channel Settings dialog box, shown in Figure 13.3.
4. Click the first **Effects** slot to display the list of available effects.
5. Select an effect from the list.
6. The control panel for that effect now appears in a separate window. Configure the effect as necessary, then close the window. (You can reopen the effect control panel at any time by clicking the **Edit** button in the insert effects slot.)
7. To activate the insert effect, make sure the blue Inserts State button is activated (displays blue).

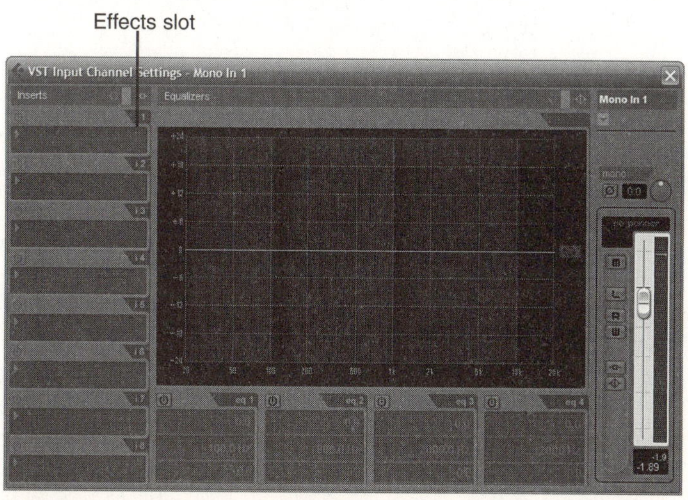

Figure 13.3 *Adding an input insert effect.*

Adding an Insert Effect

Regular insert effects are added to the signal path just after the original channel input, which means that the audio is routed through the effect—affecting everything that comes after that point in the process. Inserts require the most processing power of any type of audio processing or effect.

To add an insert effect, follow these steps:

1. In the project window's track list, select the track to which you want to apply the effect.
2. In the track inspector, click the **Inserts** control. This expands the Inserts panel to show slots for eight insert effects, as shown in Figure 13.4.
3. Click the **Effects** control in the first insert effects slot to display the list of available effects.
4. Select an effect from the list.
5. The control panel for that effect now appears in a separate window. Configure the effect as necessary, then close the window. (You can reopen the effect control panel at any time by clicking the **Edit** button in the insert effects slot.)
6. To activate the insert effect, make sure the blue Inserts State button is activated (displays blue).

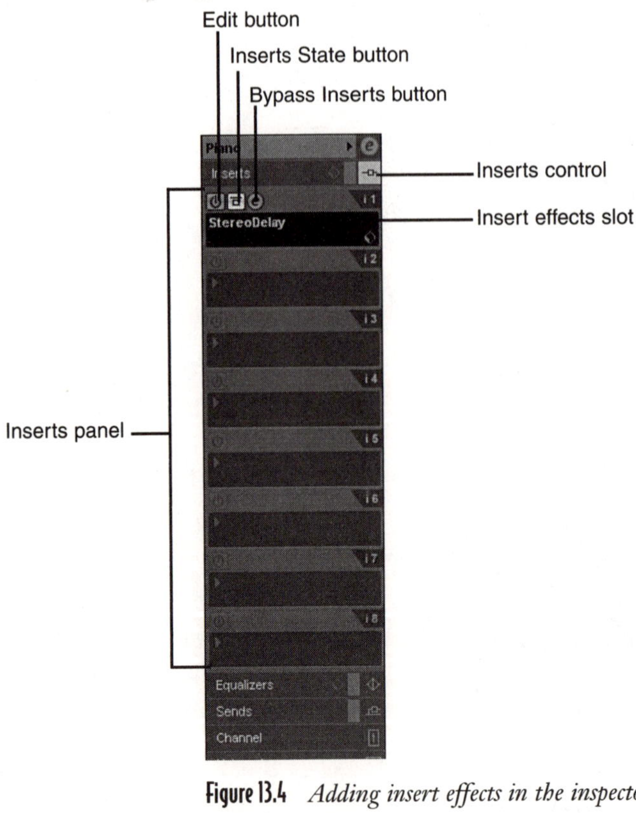

Figure 13.4 *Adding insert effects in the inspector.*

Repeat this process to add additional effects to that channel. The effects will be applied in the order they're listed in the inspector.

> **Tip**
>
> To bypass an insert effect—that is, to turn it off without actually removing it—click the **Bypass Inserts** button. (A yellow button means that the insert is being bypassed.)

Adding a Send Effect

Send effects are added at the very end of the signal path, and thus are best suited for effects such as reverb and delay. That said, a send effect requires slightly less processing power than a similar insert effect.

Applying a send effect is a little more complex than adding an insert effect. You first have to create an FX track in the track list, and then apply that effect to the Send Effect panel in the inspector. The benefit of this method is that you can control the mix of the effect and the original audio, making the resulting audio either "dryer" (less effect) or "wetter" (more effect).

Here's how to do it:

1. Select **Project > Add Track > FX Channel.**
2. When the Add FX Channel dialog box appears, as shown in Figure 13.5, pull down the Configuration list and select **Stereo.** (Alternately, you can select to apply the effect only to the right or left output channel.)

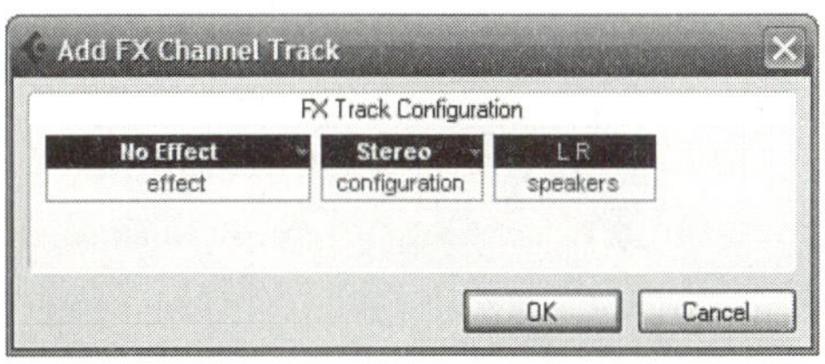

Figure 13.5 *Creating a new FX Channel track.*

3. Still in the Add FX Channel dialog box, pull down the Plugin list and select the effect you want.
4. Click **OK.**
5. Cubase displays the new FX track in the track list, as shown in Figure 13.6, and opens the control panel for the selected plug-in.
6. In the track list, select the track to which you want to apply the send effect.
7. In the track inspector, click the **Sends** control. This expands the Sends panel to show slots for eight send effects.
8. Click the **Effects** control in the first send effects slot to display the list of available effects.
9. The FX track should be displayed in this list; select it.
10. To activate the send effect, make sure the blue Sends State button is activated (displays blue).

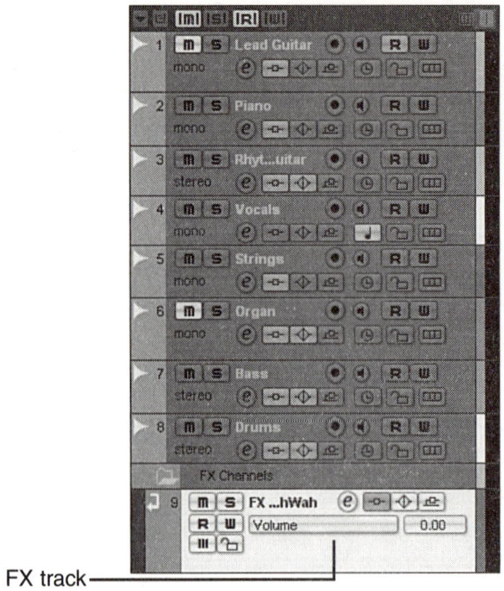

Figure 13.6 *Working with send effects and an FX track.*

Adding a Master Insert Effect

Master insert effects work just like regular insert effects, but are applied to the final mixed-down stereo signal. This results in the plug-in effect processing the entire mix, not just an individual track. For this reason, the most common master effects are reverb, echo, compressors, limiters, and so on—effects that need to be applied to all tracks equally.

Here's how to apply a master effect:

1. In the mixer, click the **Edit** button for the master output bus, as shown in Figure 13.7.

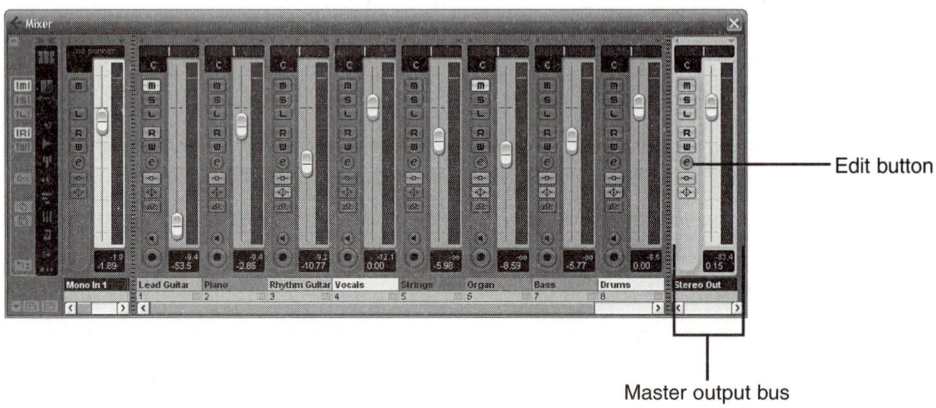

Figure 13.7 *Getting ready to add master insert effects directly to the output channel.*

2. This displays the VST Output Channel Settings dialog box, shown in Figure 13.8.

3. Click the first **Effects** slot to display the list of available effects.
4. Select an effect from the list.
5. The control panel for that effect now appears in a separate window. Configure the effect as necessary, then close the window. (You can reopen the effect control panel at any time by clicking the Edit button in the insert effects slot.)
6. To activate the master insert effect, make sure the blue Inserts State button is activated (displays blue).

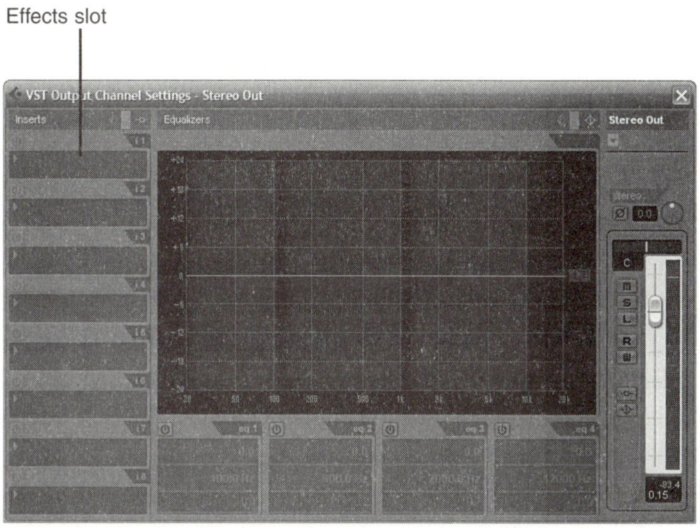

Figure 13.8 *Adding a master insert effect.*

> **Tip**
>
> For all insert effects, the first six effects slots apply to the signal before the fader control; the last two slots apply after the fader. Use these last two slots for any effects you want to continue after the main level has been faded out or turned down, such as a trailing echo or reverb. Similarly, these are the slots to be used for any dithering effect. (Dithering is an important part of the mastering process, as you'll learn in Chapter 15.)

Using Popular Plug-Ins

If you're like me, you'd like some specific instructions on how to apply certain types of effects. Obviously, space does not allow for an in-depth tutorial for every single audio process and effect that Cubase offers, but we can work our way through some of the most popular audio effects. In particular, I'll show you how to apply a noise gate, dynamic compression, and reverb.

Tip

Additional plug-ins can be found at various Internet sites, including Camel Audio (www.camelaudio.com), db audioware (www.db-audioware.com), mda-vst (www.mda-vst.com), Pluginz.com (www.pluginz.com), SoundDesigners (www.sounddesigners.biz), and Synth Zone (www.synthzone.com/cubase.htm).

Note

One common use of a noise gate is to remove breathing noises on a vocal track, when the vocalist isn't singing. It's also common to use a noise gate to cut off the ringing sound after a snare drum or tom tom has been played.

Reducing Noise with a Noise Gate

A noise gate is a plug-in effect that silences a track when the volume falls below a specified level. As soon as the signal level exceeds the set threshold, the gate opens to let the signal through. This is a great way to remove hiss or noise from a track when an instrument or vocalist is silent. (The thinking is that the hiss is somewhat hidden when the instrument is playing, but very audible when the instrument is silent.)

Cubase 4 includes the new Gate noise gate plug-in. You should apply this plug-in as a traditional insert effect on a specific track. As with most VST3 plug-ins, the easiest way to apply the noise gate is to select a preset configuration; here's how it works:

1. In the project window's track list, select the track to which you want to apply the noise gate.
2. In the track inspector, click the **Inserts** control.
3. Click the **Effects** control in the first insert effects slot and select **Dynamics > Gate.** The control panel for the Gate plug-in now opens, as shown in Figure 13.9.
4. Click in the name field at the top of the window. This opens the Preset browser, shown in Figure 13.10.
5. In the Viewer pane, double-click the preset that best matches how you intend to use the noise gate.
6. Close the Gate control panel; the plug-in effect will now be automatically applied to the selected track.

Figure 13.9 *The Gate noise gate plug-in.*

Alternately, you can adjust the controls within the Gate control panel to manually configure the noise gate:

- **Threshold** determines the level at which the noise gate is activated.
- **Attack** sets the time it takes for the gate to open.
- **Hold** determines how long the gate stays open.
- **Release** sets the amount of time it takes for the gate to close.

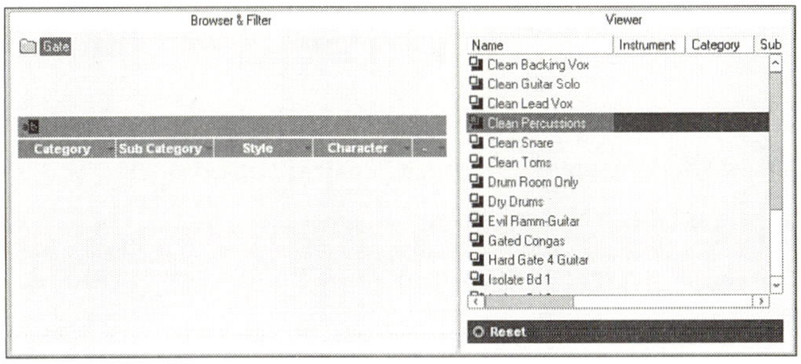

Figure 13.10 *Preset configurations for the Gate plug-in.*

Adding Presence with Reverb

Almost every recording today features some amount of *reverberation*, which makes your recording sound bigger. Reverb can be recorded naturally (by non-close mic'ing in a big, "live" room), in which case you don't need to read this section. It can also be added via audio processing after the fact, which you need to do if your recording is too dry-sounding.

> **def•i•ni•tion**
>
> **Reverberation** is the persistence of sound in a room or other space, after the original sound has ended, caused by sound reflections that decrease in intensity over time. Reverb can be created naturally (in a room with hard surfaces, for example), or added digitally to a dry recorded sound.

Cubase 4 offers several reverb plug-ins, of which my favorite is RoomWorks. Let's take a look at how to apply this plug-in to an individual track as a send effect.

1. Select **Project > Add Track > FX Channel.**
2. When the Add FX Channel Track dialog box appears, pull down the Configuration list and select **Stereo,** then pull down the Effect list and select **Earlier VST Plug-ins > Reverb > RoomWorks.** Click **OK.**
3. Cubase displays the new FX track in the track list and opens the RoomWorks control panel, shown in Figure 13.11.
4. Click the name field at the top of the window (default selection: Default Program) and select the setting that best matches the reverberation effect you're trying to achieve.
5. Return to the track list and select the track to which you want to apply the send effect.
6. In the track inspector, click the **Sends** control to expand the Sends panel for the selected track.
7. Click the **Effects** control in the first send effects slot and select **FX 1-RoomWorks.**

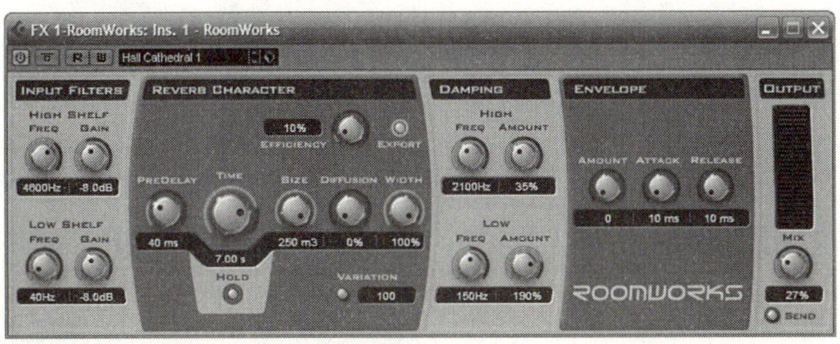

Figure 13.11 *The RoomWorks reverb plug-in.*

Tip

Many engineers and musicians prefer to fatten their recordings with delay or echo effects instead of reverb. That's because reverb isn't very clean; you can have multiple reflections from multiple surfaces. In contrast, delay creates a single copy of the original sound, placed precisely after the original. It's worth experimenting with both effects to see which you like best.

Alternately, you can adjust the controls within the RoomWorks control panel to manually configure the reverb effect:

- **Predelay** sets the delay between the direct sound and the reverb output. (A short predelay makes the reverb effect more natural sounding.)
- **Time** sets the length of the reverb time, in milliseconds.
- **Size** determines the size of the simulated room. (A bigger room produces a more pronounced reverb sound.)
- **Diffusion** affects the character of the reverb tail. (Higher diffusion is smoother, while lower diffusion can be clearer.)
- **Width** controls the width of the stereo image.
- **Mix** determines the balance between the dry (unprocessed) and "wet" reverb signal.

Creating a "Hotter" Recording with Dynamic Compression

Many contemporary recordings make liberal use of dynamic *compression*. When a recording is compressed, the dynamic range is made narrower—soft sounds are made louder, and loud sounds are made softer.

def•i•ni•tion

Compression is the process of reducing the dynamic range of a recording to create a punchier sound, typically achieved via use of a compressor or limiter plug-in.

Unless you're recording for the audiophile market (or are an audiophile yourself), you'll probably want to apply some amount of compression to your recordings. The average listener tends not to like large swings between super-soft and super-loud passages; in fact, some equipment simply can't reproduce wide dynamic ranges. (Soft passages get lost in the equipment's built-in distortion, or masked by ambient room noise.)

Cubase offers a number of ways to add compression to your recordings. The easiest approach is to use the Compressor plug-in as a master insert effect. Here's how to do it.

1. In the mixer, click the **Edit** button for the master output channel, which displays the VST Output Channel Settings dialog box.
2. Click the first **Effects** slot and select **Dynamics > Compressor;** this displays the Compressor control panel, shown in Figure 13.12.
3. Click in the name field at the top of the window to open the Preset browser.
4. In the Viewer pane, double-click the preset that best matches the type of compression you need.
5. Close the Compressor control panel; the plug-in effect will now be automatically applied to your master output.

Figure 13.12 *Cubase 4's Compressor plug-in.*

Alternately, you can adjust the controls within the Compressor control panel to manually configure the compression effect:

- **Threshold** determines the level where the compressor kicks in. (Signals above the threshold level are affected by the compression; signals below the threshold level are not processed.)
- **Ratio** determines the amount of gain reduction applied to signals over the threshold level.
- **Make-Up** is used to compensate for any output volume loss caused by use of the compressor.
- **Attack** determines how fast the compressor will respond to signals above the threshold level.
- **Hold** sets the time the compression will affect the signal after the threshold is exceeded.
- **Release** sets the amount of time it takes for the gain to return to its original level when the signal drops below the threshold level.
- **Analysis** determines whether the input signal is evaluated according to peak or RMS levels. Turn counterclockwise (peak) if your recording has lots of sudden attacks, as with drums and highly rhythmic material. Turn clockwise if your recording has few transients, as with vocals, ballads, and smoother songs.

Tip

Recordings that have been compressed often sound "hotter" when played over the radio or on a lower-quality audio system, which explains the appeal. This is because the entire recording can be played at louder levels without worrying about transient volume spikes.

Too Much Compression is a Bad Thing

To my ears, much of today's popular music overuses dynamic compression. When you over-compress a recording, there is little or no difference between the softest and loudest sections of the song; the volume level stays pretty much in one place from the start to the finish.

This type of single-level recording might be fine for the dance floor (and radio programmers also like it), but it's just one more way to dehumanize modern music. When you listen to musicians performing live—electric or acoustic, it doesn't matter—you hear a broad range of dynamics. Great musicians use dynamics for effect, contrasting whisper-quiet sections against full-on attacks. When you compress a recording, you lose this contrast; everything sounds the same.

Of course, there are good reasons to employ some degree of compression. As I noted, radio programmers like compressed recordings, since many of their listeners are listening in an automotive environment full of ambient noise (the car's engine, other passengers, even the sound of the outdoors filtering in through an open window). If a station plays music that's too soft, listeners will simply switch stations. In this situation, some degree of volume equalization is a necessity.

In the home, however, especially on a quality audio system, this degree of compression is uncalled for. Unfortunately, many engineers, producers, and even musicians are fooled into thinking that an overly compressed recording sounds more "hot" to the listener. (This false impression comes from the fact that the recording can be mastered louder, knowing that there won't be any transient highs to worry about.) When a fine recording is overcompressed, however, it's the listener—particularly the audiophile listener with a high-quality audio system—who is cheated. Not everyone listens to their music on an iPod or car stereo system; why compromise your recording by playing to the lowest common denominator?

The Least You Need to Know

- Plug-ins are used to apply various types of effects (such as compression, reverb, and noise gating) to your audio and MIDI tracks.
- Input insert effects are added to the "live" signal coming through the input bus while you're recording.
- Offline processing is applied directly to the recorded event, and uses less CPU power than other types of processing.
- Insert effects are inserted just after the original channel input.
- Send effects are added to the end of the signal path as separate effects tracks.
- Master insert effects are applied to your final stereo mix via the master output bus, not to individual tracks.

Chapter 14

Equalizing the Mix

In This Chapter

- Understanding frequency, boost, and Q levels
- How to add EQ in Cubase
- Applying EQ settings to particular instruments
- Avoiding common EQ mistakes

The sound of an instrument or vocal stretches across a large band of frequencies. Even if a singer sings just one specific pitch at a specific frequency, that pitch is colored by harmonics and resonant sounds that exist at other frequencies. And, of course, few recordings consist of a musician singing or playing just one pitch.

When an instrument or vocal doesn't sound quite right to your ears, or doesn't cut through in the mix, then it's time to start thinking about adjusting the volume level of specific frequencies reproduced by that instrument or vocalist. A subtle boost or decrease of a given frequency can make a vocal sound warmer, give a snare drum more "crack," clean up a muddy bass guitar, or make a lead guitar cut through the backing instruments.

This adjustment of specific frequencies on a recorded track is called *equalization*, or *EQ*. Equalization is the secret weapon of the savvy recording engineer, and can make or break the sound of a recording. It's also the last part of the mixing process; after you've applied EQ, you can move straight to mastering.

How EQ Works

Equalization shapes the tone of a signal by boosting or cutting selected frequency ranges. Each track you create in Cubase can be equalized separately; the mixer includes a built-in *parametric equalizer* that lets you adjust four different frequency ranges.

> **def•i•ni•tion**
>
> A **parametric equalizer** is a type of equalizer device or plug-in in which the range of frequencies affected by level boosts or cuts is adjustable.

When you add EQ to a track, there are three settings you have to specify—the frequency you want to boost or cut, the amount you want to boost or cut that frequency, and the "Q" level. Let me explain.

Frequency

The first setting is fairly simple. Of the entire 20–20,000 Hz frequency range, you can pick any given frequency to boost or cut. We'll get into what effects result from fiddling with certain frequencies, but for now it's enough to know that you can choose to boost the volume of the 500 Hz frequency or cut the one at 8,000 Hz.

Boost/Cut

Next, you specify how much you want to boost or cut that frequency. Volume level is measured in decibels (dB), and that's how you specify the boost/cut level. Cubase lets you boost or cut the frequency up to 24 dB—that's a +/-24 dB range for each frequency you equalize.

Q

Finally, we come to the mysterious Q setting. Well, it's not that mysterious—it's just an odd name. The Q level specifies the width of the frequency range that is effected. With a very high Q level, your boost/cut is applied pretty much to the selected frequency, without overly affecting adjacent frequencies. A very low Q level widens the range of frequencies affected by the EQ.

Without getting too technical, the Q level corresponds to a set number of octaves that are affected by the EQ boost/cut. For example, a Q of 0.7 affects a bandwidth of two octaves; a Q of 1.4 affects one octave; and a Q of 2.8 affects just a half octave. That's why a lower Q number affects a wider frequency range.

> **Tip**
>
> Many engineers believe that the "magic Q" setting is 1.0, which corresponds to a 1 ⅓-octave range. This happens to be the bandwidth that best matches how different instruments cover the different frequency ranges. For more melodic instruments, you can broaden the frequency range covered by using a lower Q number; for less melodic instruments, such as drums, you can use a higher Q number.

For example, Figures 14.1 and 14.2 both show equalization graphs for a 10 dB boost at 1,000 Hz. Figure 14.1 has a high (12.0) Q level, which dictates a narrow EQ range; Figure 14.2 has a low (1.0) Q level, which dictates a much wider EQ range. As you can see, the high Q level in Figure 14.1 results in a very fast ramp up to the 10 dB boost, while the low Q level in Figure 14.2 has a much longer and more gradual ramp up to the 10 dB boost. With the low Q level, a much wider range of frequencies are affected by the equalization.

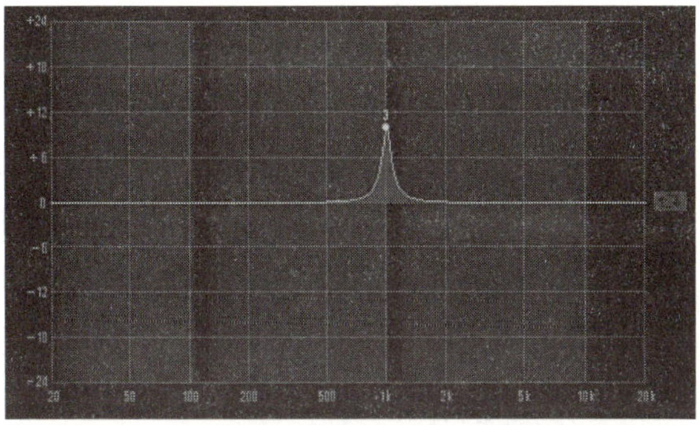

Figure 14.1 *Boosting 1,000 Hz by 10 dB with high (12.0) Q.*

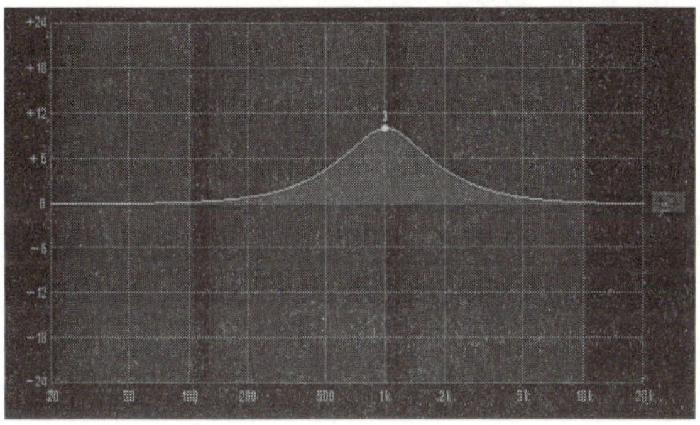

Figure 14.2 *Boosting 1,000 Hz by 10 dB with low (1.0) Q—a much gentler curve.*

> **Note**
>
> Cubase lets you apply EQ to up to four frequency ranges for each channel. The EQ is applied separately to each channel, so you can apply much different EQ to the electric guitar track than to the vocal track, for example.

> **Tip**
>
> When you're working with a recording project, you can add EQ at any point in the process—even when you're laying down the initial tracks. That said, I prefer to add EQ after the recording has been made and other effects have been added; this way you're equalizing the final sound you'll hear, after all the other recording tricks have been applied.

Adding EQ in Cubase

There are three different ways to add EQ in Cubase. They all add the exact same EQ, and in pretty much the same fashion; which method you use depends on how you like to work.

EQ in the Channel Settings Window

The easiest way to adjust EQ is in Cubase's Channel Settings window. You open the Channel Settings window for a given channel by selecting that track in the track listing, then clicking the Edit button at the top of the track inspector.

As you can see in Figure 14.3, the parametric equalizer rests in the middle of the Channel Settings window. There's a big frequency graph at the top of this section; below are four panels for the four EQ bands you can adjust.

Within each EQ band panel are three controls. The top control (Gain) selects the amount of boost or cut to apply to that frequency. The middle control selects which frequency to adjust; and the bottom control selects the Q level. You can enter precise values into each control, or use your mouse to click and drag a point on the frequency curve in the graph.

> **Tip**
>
> To adjust the Q level in the graph, press the Shift key while clicking the selected point, and then move your mouse up or down to increase or decrease the level.

> **Tip**
>
> If you know the precise frequency you want to boost or cut, it's easier to enter the frequency into the value field directly.

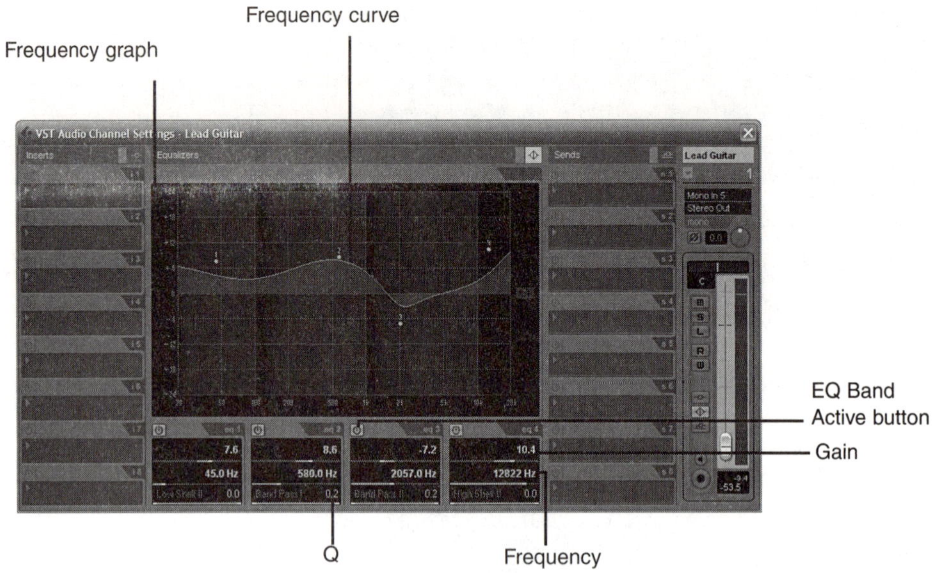

Figure 14.3 *The parametric equalizer in the Channel Settings window.*

Here's the easy way to do it:

1. Start with the lowest frequency you want to equalize.
2. Click the **EQ Band Active** button for the first EQ setting control to turn it on.
3. Enter the frequency you want to adjust into the Frequency control.
4. Enter the amount of boost/cut you want to apply into the Gain control.
5. Enter the desired Q level into the Q control.
6. Repeat steps 2 through 5 for each additional frequency range you want to adjust.

EQ in the Extended Mixer

If you're using the mixer in extended view (as discussed in Chapter 3), you can make these same EQ adjustments there. As you can see in Figure 14.4, the extended mixer provides two ways to display/adjust EQ settings—EQs (enter values only) or EQs Curve (enter values or adjust pop-up sliders, with an EQ curve at the top of the display). The same general approach applies, whichever EQ display you select. In both views, the top (or first) parameter is the boost/cut (Gain), the middle is the frequency, and the bottom is the Q level.

> **Tip**
>
> To select the EQ view in the extended mixer, click the down arrow at the bottom right of the extended panel.

EQ in the Track Inspector

Finally, the track inspector for each track includes an Equalizers panel. Click the **Shows Active Equalizers** button to display the panel, as shown in Figure 14.5. The four bands are displayed from hi to low; within each band, the controls are, from top to bottom, boost/cut, frequency, and Q level.

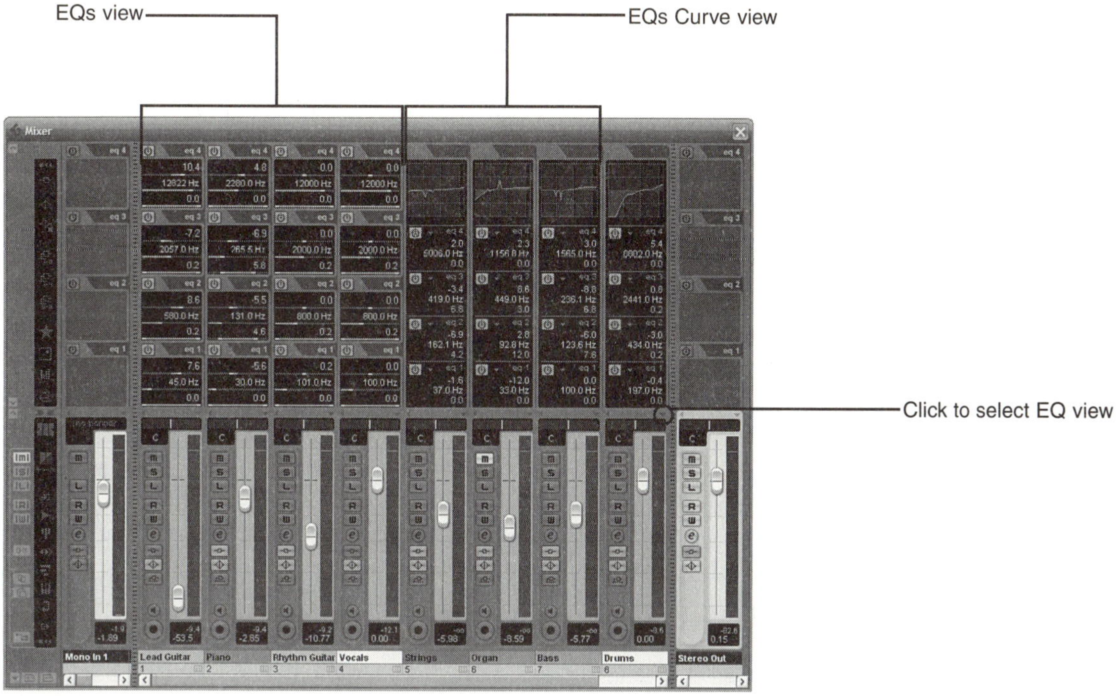

Figure 14.4 *Two ways to adjust EQ in the extended mixer.*

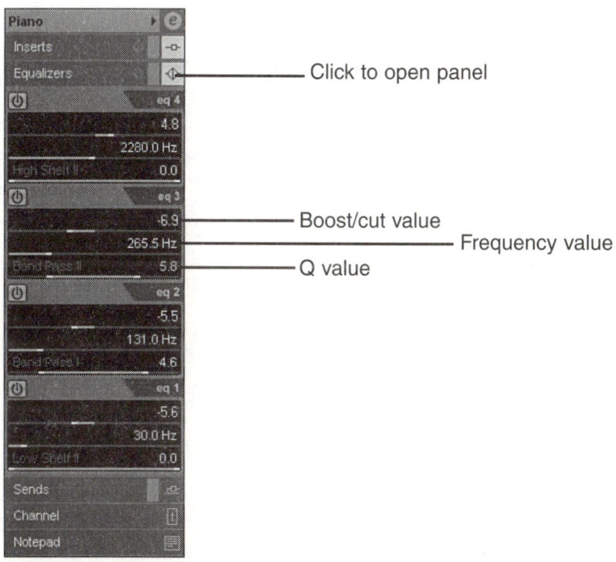

Figure 14.5 *The Equalizers panel in the track inspector.*

If you like, you can also display the EQ curve by right-clicking the **Equalizers** panel and selecting **Audio Equalizer Curve.** As you can see in Figure 14.6, this is an editable curve, just like in the Channel Settings window; click any point on the curve to adjust the EQ.

Tip

To bypass a particular EQ setting click "off" the green power button for any band in the equalizer.

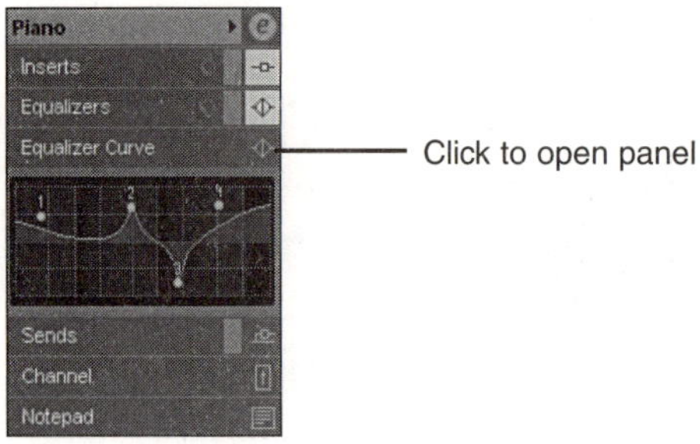

Figure 14.6 *The Equalization Curve panel in the track inspector.*

Using EQ Presets

When you use the Channel Settings window to adjust equalization, Cubase provides some handy preset EQ levels to work with. These EQ presets are a good starting point for basic equalization; you can always tweak them for your personal use. To access these EQ presets, click the **Preset Management** button above the equalization graph.

Tip

Cubase 4 also comes with a number of VST plug-in effects you can use to apply EQ. These include the GEQ-10, GEQ-30, and StudioEQ plug-ins; they all offer a bit more precision than does Cubase's built-in EQ function. You apply these EQ plug-ins as you would any other insert or send effect.

Common Equalization Settings

With all this talk of boosting and cutting frequencies, I've neglected one important discussion—which frequencies should you boost and cut? This leads me into the whole topic of which instruments utilize which frequency ranges. Of course, examining this topic fully would require a book or two and maybe even a degree in acoustical physics, so I'll try to focus on the important points in as practical a fashion as possible—which means providing some guidance for applying EQ for specific types of tracks.

Before I start, however, know that there are no golden rules when it comes to EQ. What works in one situation might sound horrible in another. That's because there are so many factors involved—the individual instrument (or vocalist), the microphone used, how the instrument was recorded, the room in which the recording was made, you name it. And that's not even taking into account personal taste. So you should take the following advice with a grain of salt, and let your own ears tell you what what's right and what's wrong.

Equalizing Vocal Tracks

In general, you want to apply as little EQ as possible to your vocal tracks. When working with vocals, EQ should be used only if the voice has some specific defects you need to fix, or if you're trying to achieve a particular effect, or if the vocals are getting buried in the mix. To this end, you should try to work with as narrow (high) a Q setting as possible, to avoid distorting the overall sound of the vocalist.

That said, here are some tips on how to use EQ for best effect on your vocal tracks:

- Reduce audible noise in the vocal track by cutting all frequencies below 60 Hz.
- If the vocalist has a soft, wispy sound, try cutting by about 7 dB at 100Hz.
- To add warmth and fullness to a vocal track, try a gentle boost in the 100–200 Hz band.
- To reduce nasality, try cutting in the 1,000–2,000 Hz range.
- To reduce harshness, cut the 2,500–4,000 Hz range.
- To improve projection and help the vocal cut through the mix, add a slight boost around 2,500–3,000 Hz (for men) or 3,000–3,500 Hz (for women). Also, try boosting around 500 Hz (men) or 1,000 Hz (women).
- To add presence to a vocal and also help it cut through the mix, try a slight boost around 5,000 Hz.
- To make the vocal sound a little brighter, apply a slight boost above 6,000 Hz.
- To reduce sibilance, try cutting in the 6,000–10,000 Hz range.
- To add some "air" to the vocal, add a wide (low Q) boost between 14,000–16,000 Hz.

Tip

Backing vocals sit better in the mix if you slightly roll off the bass frequencies.

In addition to applying EQ, the other important effect to apply to a vocal track is de-essing, which reduces sibilance—those hard, spitty s's, z's, and ch's. When you use a de-esser, you can then add back upper mids and highs during the EQ process, which helps to push the vocals above the other tracks in the mix. To this end, Cubase 4 includes the SPL DeEsser plug-in, found at **Earlier VST Plug-ins > Dynamics > DeEsser.**

Equalizing Acoustic Piano Tracks

A well-recorded acoustic piano shouldn't require much equalization. That said, here are a few tips to create a more prominent piano sound:

- To add a fuller bottom, boost the 60–120 Hz range.
- To improve clarity, add a slight boost at 2,500 Hz.
- To add airiness, boost the 8,000–15,000 Hz range.

Carving EQ Holes

There are two main reasons to apply EQ—to adjust the timbre of the sound, as we've been discussing, and to make room for certain instruments (or vocals) in the mix. This second approach is called carving EQ holes, as you use equalization to "carve out" a hole that a specific instrument can sit in.

The most common use of EQ carving is to make vocal tracks stand out. Since vocal intelligibility relies on frequencies in the 1,000–4,000 Hz range, if you cut this range in other instruments, such as guitars and keyboards, you reduce the overlap with the vocals. This pretty much gives this range to the vocals alone, which makes them easier to hear and understand in the mix.

Another use of EQ carving is to reduce competition among similar instruments. A good example of this is the bass guitar and bass drum, which both compete in the lower frequency ranges. To make the bass guitar a little more prominent and the bass drum a little kickier, try cutting the bass guitar at 60 Hz and boosting it at 100 Hz, and then boosting the bass drum at 60 Hz and cutting it at 100 Hz. This reduces the competition between the two instruments, and makes the bottom of your mix a little less muddy.

Equalizing Acoustic Guitar Tracks

As with acoustic pianos, a well-recorded acoustic guitar should stand pretty much on its own with little additional EQ necessary. Still, if you find your acoustic guitar fading back into the mix, consider these changes:

- To reduce string squeaks, roll off all frequencies below 60 Hz.
- To reduce muddiness and boominess, cut the 80–150 Hz range.
- To reduce harshness, apply a cut between 1,000–3,000 Hz.
- To add sparkle to the sound, use a boost between 5,000–10,000 Hz.

Equalizing Electric Guitar Tracks

There's lots of equalization you can apply to electric guitar tracks, depending on the type of sound you want to achieve:

- Remove low frequency rumble by rolling off all frequencies below 100 Hz.
- To improve the sound of direct-injected rhythm guitars, try a large boost between 3,000–6,000 Hz.
- Reduce a boomy sound by cutting between 100–250 Hz.
- Fatten up a thin sound by boosting between 100–250 Hz.
- Create a fuller sound by boosting in the 150–400 Hz range.
- Reduce a boxy sound by cutting in the 250–500 Hz range.
- Improve clarity by boosting in the 900–3,500 Hz range.
- Add bite to a lead guitar by boosting between 2,000–6,000 Hz.
- Remove high-frequency hiss by rolling off all frequencies above 4,000 Hz.

Tip

To separate two rhythm guitars in your mix, boost one at 3,000 Hz and the other at 4,000 Hz, which should give them slightly different tonal textures.

Equalizing Bass Guitar Tracks

Bass tracks are often problematic. If your bass sounds too muddy and indistinct, try some of these EQ tricks:

- Remove rumble by rolling off all frequencies below 100 Hz.
- Improve articulation and add a little fret noise by boosting in the 1,000–2,000 Hz range.
- If the bass is too prominent in the mix, roll off the overtones between 7,000–12,000 Hz.
- Create a warmer sound by cutting in the 12,000–18,000 Hz range.
- For ballads, try boosting both the 100 Hz and 500 Hz frequencies, and cutting at 300 Hz and 12,000 Hz.
- For a more aggressive sound, boost the 1,000–2,000 Hz range and apply a cut at 200 Hz.
- For an early Beatles-like bass sound, add a slight boost around 100 Hz.
- For a "twangy" country & western sound, apply a slight boost at 100 Hz and 1,000 Hz, and a large cut between 200–250 Hz.
- For the James Jamerson Motown sound, apply a slight boost at 100 Hz and 200 Hz, and a large cut at 5,000 Hz.

Equalizing Drum Tracks

Some engineers will spend all day trying to get the "perfect" drum sound. The key is to equalize each of the drum mics separately; each type of drum and cymbal has different sonic characteristics and EQ needs. Here are some tips:

- For the bass drum (sometimes called the "kick"), apply a slight boost between 80–100 Hz, cut aggressively between 200–500 Hz, and apply a slight boost at 2,500 Hz.
- For dance-oriented music, add an additional boost to the bass drum at 4,000 Hz.
- For death metal and similar styles, create a clickier bass drum sound by adding a large boost at 10,000 Hz.
- For the snare drum, add slight boosts between 100–300 Hz, 1,000–3,000 Hz, 5,000–8,000 Hz, and 9,000–15,000 Hz.
- For a fatter snare sound, apply a cut in the 150–300 Hz range and then boost the lower and higher frequencies.
- For the toms, add a slight boost between 80–100 Hz, a cut between 300–500 Hz, and boosts between 5,000–8,000 Hz and 9,000–12,500 Hz.
- For the hi-hat cymbals, apply a big cut between 60–120 Hz and a slight boost between 7,000–10,000 Hz.
- If the hi-hats are too bright, apply a cut at 9,000 Hz.

What *Not* to Do: Common EQ Mistakes

Now let's look at some common equalization mistakes—and provide a bit more advice on what to do and what not to do when you're applying EQ.

First, know that many rookie engineers make the mistake of applying EQ solely while listening to a track solo. Although this is a good way to get started, it ignores the fact that the sound of any instrument on a recording is dependent on the sound of *all* instruments in the mix. Start EQ'ing solo, but then listen to how that track sounds with all the other tracks activated.

In addition, any changes you make to one instrument in the mix will affect how the other instruments sound. Boosting the bass guitar, for example, will have a big effect on the clarity of the bass drum. This is another good reason not to make EQ changes without considering the rest of the mix—and to consider carving EQ holes when necessary.

Next, you should try to boost less and cut more. That's because the ear is used to hearing a reduction in musical energy, due to the way sound-absorbing objects and material interact with the sound. In general, a 6 dB boost sounds about the same as a 9 dB reduction. That means it's better to reduce unwanted frequencies than it is to boost desired ones.

Similarly, you can make a desired frequency stand out by cutting frequencies on either side of it. Instead of applying a boost at 1,000 Hz, for example, try cutting at 900 Hz and 1,100 Hz.

It's also important to know that it's easy to be too subtle with your EQ. Not many people can hear changes below 2–3 dB. That said, lots of subtle changes can be very effective in shaping the overall mix, even if the average listener can't hear the individual changes.

Listeners can hear big changes, of course—which is why you also shouldn't be overly aggressive in applying EQ. Boosts or cuts of 9 dB or more should be avoided, when at all possible.

Finally, know that all the EQ in the world can't cover up a bad recording. If the recording was made with good levels using a quality instrument, well-tuned, in a good-sounding room, you won't need much EQ. On the other hand, if the recording was made with too little gain using an out-of-tune instrument in a room full of unwanted reflections, you can spend all day working on the EQ and not be able to save it. Start with a great recording, and the rest of your work will be a lot easier.

The Least You Need to Know

- Equalization works by boosting or cutting the volume level of specific frequencies or frequency ranges.
- Cubase lets you adjust three EQ settings—frequency, amount of boost or cut, and Q level (how wide a range is affected).
- You can adjust EQ in the Channel Settings window, in the extended mixer, and in the track inspector.

- If you use the Channel Settings window to adjust EQ, you can utilize Cubase's preset EQ settings—or save your own settings as presets.
- Always factor the effect of EQ on the entire recording; EQing one track will make all the other tracks sound a little different, too.
- EQ is a great tool, but it's not a magic bullet; it can't make a horrible recording sound like a great one.

Chapter 15

Mastering the Final Recording

In This Chapter

- Converting MIDI tracks to audio tracks
- Applying master effects and EQ
- Exporting your mix to a stereo audio file
- Exploring other mastering options

Now we come to the final part of the recording process, where we take everything you've done up to this point and prepare it for distribution. This process is called *mastering*, and it creates the master files that end up on a shiny new compact disc or uploaded to the Internet.

The mastering process starts when you convert all your MIDI tracks to standard audio tracks. You then take your final, final, *final* mix and apply any master effects or equalization necessary. (These are effects and EQ that are applied to the entire recording, not just a single track.) Finally, you export your mix as a stereo digital audio file, in whatever format is appropriate to your method of distribution. Then you're done.

This process sounds fairly simple, and it can be. It can also be a tweaker's heaven, as the sign of a truly professional recording is the quality of the mastering. To this end, many home-brew musicians take their files to a professional recording or mastering studio for the final mastering. I'll talk about this option, as well as the rest of the process, as we move through this final chapter.

Converting MIDI Tracks to Audio Tracks

Recording with MIDI is great. But all a MIDI track records is MIDI instructions, which don't copy directly to a digital audio file or CD. If you want to include MIDI tracks in your final recording, you first have to convert those tracks to standard audio tracks.

> **Note**
>
> Unlike pure MIDI tracks, VST tracks *do* copy directly to audio files during the mastering process, and don't have to be manually converted. (This is one more good reason to use VST instruments in your projects.)

So before you begin your final mastering, you have to convert all your MIDI files to audio files. This process is a little kludgy, especially as you have to convert each track separately. Here's how it goes:

1. In the project window, select **Project > Add Track > Audio** to create a new audio track.
2. When the Add Audio Track dialog box appears, select either **Mono** (to record a mono MIDI track) or **Stereo** (to record a stereo MIDI track), then click **OK.**
3. In the track list, go to the MIDI track you want to convert and click to activate the **Solo** button, as shown in Figure 15.1. Make sure that the Record and Monitor buttons for this track are deactivated.

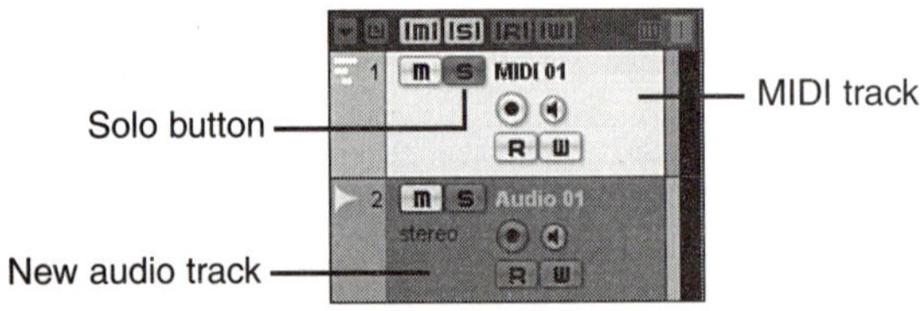

Figure 15.1 *Converting a MIDI track to an audio track.*

4. Make sure that the output for the MIDI track is routed to the correct MIDI instrument/synthesizer.
5. In the new audio track, click the **Record Enable** and **Monitor** buttons to activate them.
6. In the transport panel, click the **Play** button and then move to the mixer and adjust the level sliders for the new audio track to avoid clipping.
7. When you have the levels properly set, go to the ruler and position the cursor at the beginning of the MIDI track you want to convert.
8. In the transport panel, click the **Record** button.
9. When the entire MIDI track has played through, click the **Stop** button.
10. Repeat this entire process for all the MIDI tracks in your project.

> **Caution**
>
> Make sure you turn off Cubase's click track before you do your MIDI-to-audio conversion; the click is generated by MIDI, and if activated could be recorded along with the selected MIDI track.

What you now have is an audio track that mirrors your original MIDI track, with the selected MIDI instrument playing. From this point on in the mixing process, you should mute the original MIDI track (by clicking that track's Mute button in the track list) and perform all future mixing, EQ, and effects processing on the new audio track.

> **Tip**
>
> You'll probably need to take another listen to your mix after you've converted MIDI tracks to audio tracks. That's because the conversion isn't always perfect; sometimes volume levels get changed, or sonic characteristics get subtly altered. Fortunately, you can go back and tweak the volume levels for the newly created audio tracks, as well as apply any desired audio effects and EQ.

Applying Master Effects and EQ

Now we come to the subject of master effects and equalization. As noted previously, these are effects and EQ that you apply to your entire mix, not just to individual tracks. The effects and EQ are inserted into the output bus, and included in the export to the final stereo file.

Why would you want to apply effects and EQ globally, like this? There are several good reasons.

First, you may want to apply a specific effect to the entire recording. Maybe you want your song to sound as if it were recorded in a concert hall; the simple solution is to apply reverb as a master effect. The same thing with dynamic compression, which can be used to make a recording sound more "hot." Compress the entire recording, and you make the soft parts louder and guard against unwanted transients.

Second, EQing the entire mix lets you tweak the sonic qualities of the entire recording. If you want your song to sound bright and poppy, then add some EQ on the top end. Want a boomier bass sound? Then add some EQ to the low end. You get the picture.

Tip

Want to fade out the entire recording at the end of a song? Then use the read/write automation techniques you learned about in Chapter 12 while sliding down the master fader in the output bus during playback. The output bus fader affects all the tracks in your project, and automating puts the fade in the mix.

Adding Master Insert Effects

We discussed master insert effects in Chapter 13, so I won't repeat all that information here. Basically, you add these master effects at the very end of your project, to the output bus. The effects are applied to all the tracks that feed through to the final file export.

Adding Dithering

If you're mastering for compact disc, there is one master insert effect that's pretty much a necessity. *Dithering* helps to reduce the perceived noise in your recording, especially when you record in a 24- or 32-bit environment and then create a 16-bit master for CD. What dithering does is add a low level of random noise to your project, but in a way that masks actual noise and is virtually inaudible to the listener. The technology involved is complex, although the procedure for applying dithering is quite simple, thanks to Cubase's inclusion of the UV22hr plug-in.

def•i•ni•tion

In audio terms, **dithering** is the introduction of digital noise into a recording. (The term "dithering" means different things in different professions; for example, when talking about video, dithering is a technique for filling the gap between two pixels with another pixel that averages the values of the first two pixels.)

Here's how to do it:

1. In the mixer, click the **Edit** button for the master output bus.
2. When the VST Output Channel Settings control panel appears, as shown in Figure 15.2, click the final Inserts effects slot and select **Earlier VST Plug-ins > Other > UV22hr.**

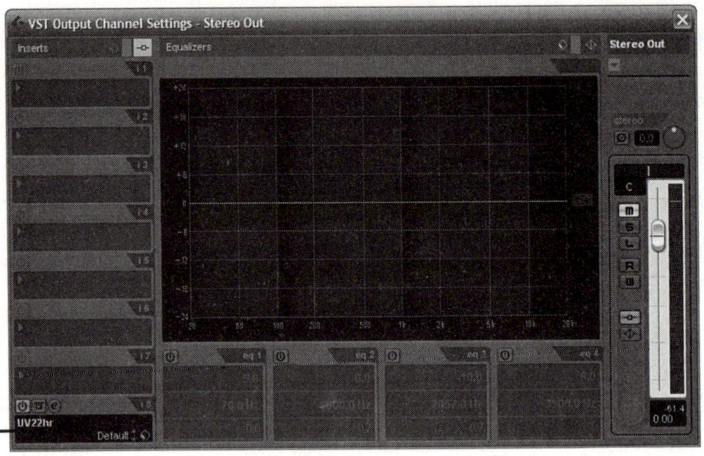

Figure 15.2 *Adding a new master insert effect to the VST Output Channel Settings dialog box.*

3. When the UV22hr control panel opens, as shown in Figure 15.3, click the **Normal, Autoblack,** and **16** buttons.
4. Close the control panel and make sure the blue Inserts State button is activated for the output bus in the mixer.

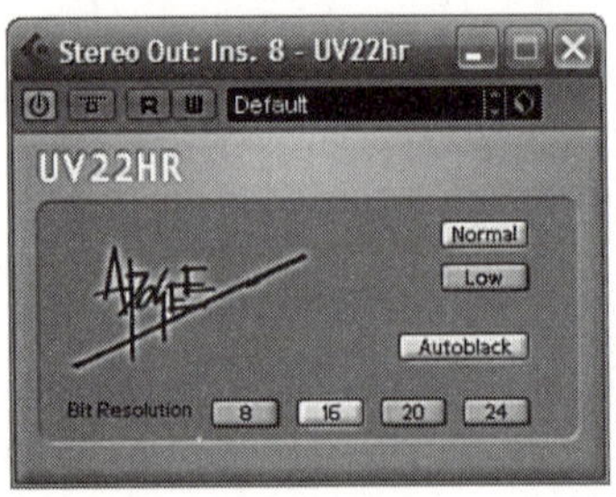

Figure 15.3 *Configuring the UV22hr dithering plug-in.*

Adding Master EQ

> **Note**
>
> Applying EQ during mastering is just like applying it during the mixing process, as you learned in Chapter 14.

You apply master EQ pretty much the same way you add master effects, to the output bus in the mixer. Remember, any EQ changes you make are applied to *everything* in the final mixdown. Here's how to do it:

1. In the mixer, click the **Edit** button in the output bus strip.
2. When the VST Output Channel Settings window appears, as shown in Figure 15.4, use the equalizer controls to apply the desired EQ.
3. Close the VST Output Channel Settings window when done.

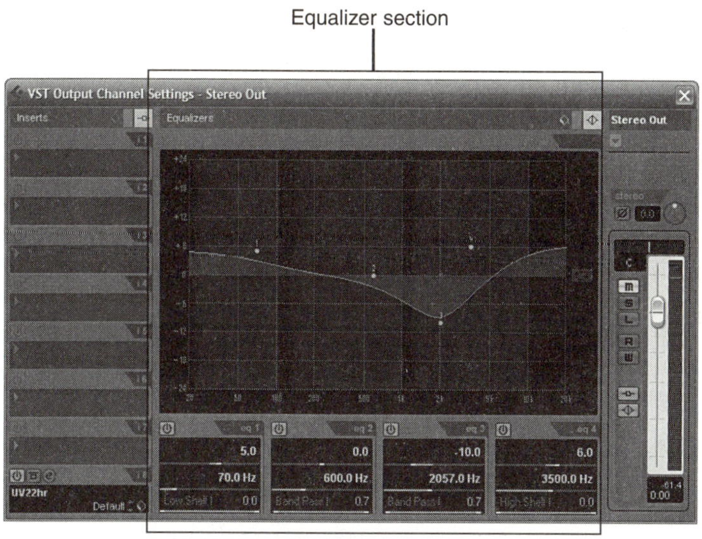

Figure 15.4 *Adding equalization in the VST Output Channel Settings window.*

Exporting to an Audio File

When everything else is done—when you've converted your MIDI tracks to audio tracks, added all your master effects, and applied your master EQ—then you can finally export your project to an audio file. It is this audio file that you'll use to distribute your music. If you're making a CD, you send the audio file to the disc pressing plant (or import it into the CD creation software on your own PC). If you're distributing your song over the Internet, you upload the audio file to a website. The final audio file is the end result of the entire recording process.

Exporting to an audio file is relatively easy—click a few buttons, make a few selections in a dialog box, and sit back and let Cubase do all the work. But those selections you have to make are important, especially the one where you choose which audio file format you want to export to.

> **Note**
>
> Cubase 4 also lets you export to a surround sound file, which is useful if you're creating television or movie soundtracks, or mastering for the SACD or DVD-Audio formats. The whole surround sound process is too involved to cover in this book, as it involves panning and placement in a 360-degree field.

Choosing the Right File Format

Let's talk file formats. Cubase lets you save your project in a number of different formats; which format you choose depends on how you want to distribute your recording.

I could complicate things by providing the specifications of all the different formats, along with the pros and cons and other such info. Instead, I'll make it simple for you.

If your final distribution medium is compact disc, you want to mix down in either the WAV (Wave) or AIFF format. Use WAV if you're recording on a Windows system; use AIFF if you're recording on a Mac. Both formats easily convert to the CDDA format used on all commercial compact discs (and do so automatically when you burn a disc using a CD-burning program).

If, instead, you intend for your music to be downloaded over the Internet, you want to mix down in either the MP3 (MPEG 1 Layer 3) or WMA (Windows Media Audio File) format. MP3 files can be played on virtually all computers, but have slightly lower audio quality than the WMA format. WMA files are higher quality, but aren't compatible with Apple iPods. (In addition, only Cubase 4 can save to the MP3 format; Cubase Studio 4 lacks this feature.)

As you might have noticed, I didn't include all of Cubase's available file formats in this table. That's because some file formats, although quite nifty on their own, just aren't that practical in the real world. For example, Ogg Vorbis and Windows Media Audio Pro files (sometimes called WMA Lossless) are great for storing CD music in digital home entertainment systems. But these formats create files that are still too large for normal Internet downloading, and you don't want to compromise a compact disc recording even a smidgeon by introducing any type of compression, even the lossless kind. (Which is why we use WAV and AIFF for CD mastering—both are uncompressed formats.)

Bottom line: If you're making a CD, use either the WAV (Windows) or AIFF (Mac) format. If you're preparing a song for Internet download, use the MP3 format. (MP3 is more universal than WMA.)

Export Options

Whichever format you export to, you have a few options to choose from during the export process. It's important to choose the right options, of course, so let's take a look at what you're likely to encounter.

When you're saving to WAV or AIF format, the key decisions you'll need to make concern the sample rate and bit depth. Assuming that you're mastering for CD burning, select a sample rate of 44.100 kHz and a bit depth of 16-bit. If you intend to submit your files to an outside house for professional mastering, use a bit depth of 32-bit instead.

If you're saving to the MP3 format, your export decisions will be slightly different. In fact, about the only thing you need to configure is the bit rate, which you do with the Bit Rate fader. The higher the bit rate, the better the audio quality and the larger the file size (and the longer it will take for listeners to download). Choose a lower bit rate and the file size will decrease (speeding up those download times), to the detriment of audio quality. You can experiment with which settings you prefer, but a good compromise is 128 kBit at 44.100 kHz.

Make your decisions up front, then get ready to export.

Exporting the File

For all the preparation you have to do, you'd think that the export process itself would be extremely convoluted. It's not. In fact, here's all you have to do:

1. Make sure that you've converted all your MIDI tracks to audio tracks, and muted any tracks you don't want to appear on your final recording.

2. In the ruler, Ctrl-click where you want the beginning of the recording to be.
3. Still in the ruler, Alt-click where you want the end of the recording to be, as shown in Figure 15.5. (These two steps define the length of your recording.)

Tip

You probably don't want your recording to end immediately at the end of the last note. It's a good idea to leave a second or two of silence at the end of the track, so you have a little breathing room before the next recording on the CD—unless you want your tracks to run together, that is.

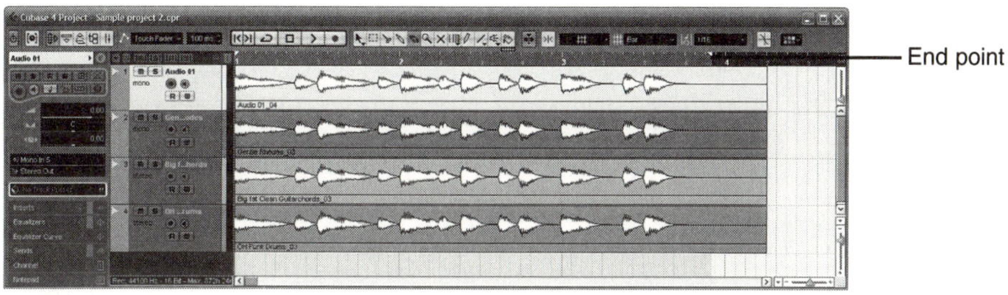

Figure 15.5 *Setting the end point of your recording.*

4. Click to activate the **Read Automation** buttons for all the tracks that include mixing automation.
5. Select **File > Export > Audio Mixdown.**
6. When the Export Audio Mixdown dialog box appears, as shown in Figure 15.6, click the **Choose** button to navigate to the folder where you want to store the file.
7. Enter a name for the file into the File Name box.
8. Pull down the Files of Type list and select the file type you want to save—Wave File or AIFF File if you're mastering to CD, or MPEG Layer 3 File if you're uploading to the Internet.
9. Select the appropriate bit rate/depth and sample rate options, as discussed in the previous section.
10. Click the **Export** button.

Note

If your project includes certain types of VST instruments, you'll need to perform the export in real time, to let the instruments "play" during the process. Read the instructions for your VST instrument for more details; if you need real-time exporting, check the Real-Time Export option in the Export Audio Mixdown dialog box.

Cubase now begins exporting your mix to an audio file. This may take a few minutes, but then you're done. You probably want to play back the newly created file in Windows Media Player or any similar audio player program to hear what it sounds like. If you're satisfied with the results, you can then distribute the file, as you intended.

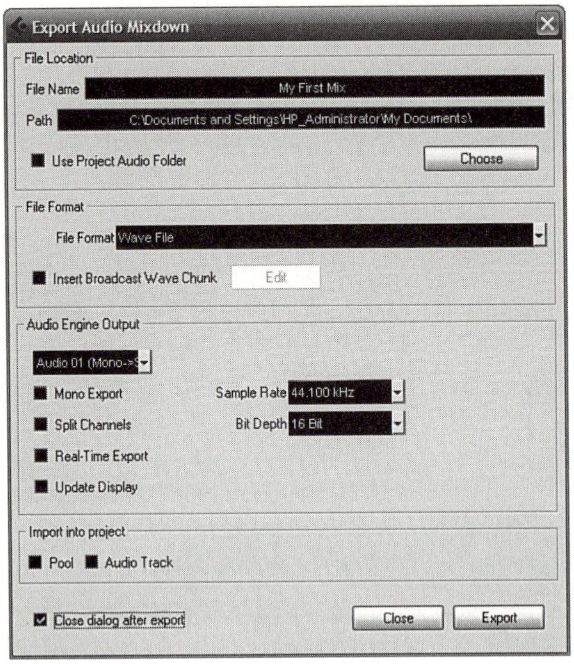

Figure 15.6 *Saving as a WAV file—selecting appropriate mixdown options in the Export Audio Mixdown dialog box.*

Burning Your Own CDs

Many independent musicians create their recordings with Cubase and then burn their own CDs for sale at gigs or over the Internet. Although just about any digital audio player (such as Windows Media Player or iTunes) can be used to create CDs, you probably want to use a program geared for professional CD burning. These programs burn CDs to official Red Book specifications, and offer a variety of useful features not found in end-user-oriented programs.

For example, Cakewalk Pyro not only lets you create and edit track playlists, but also lets you specify the amount of pad time between tracks and adjust the volume level of individual tracks. This last feature is extremely useful in creating a consistent volume level among all the tracks on your CD; depending on your recording/mixing/mastering skill, you might need this helping hand to normalize the volume level for tracks recorded at different times and at different levels.

When you're shopping for a pro-level CD-burning program, check out Cakewalk Pryo (www.cakewalk.com) and Sony CD Architect (www.sonymediasoftware.com). Pyro is perfect for the home recordist and sells for $39; CD Architect is a more full-featured program that sells for $120.

Also good are Steinberg's WaveLab or the less-expensive WaveLab Essential (www.steinberg.net). You might know these as mastering programs, but they can also burn Red Book CDs and DVDs, as well as create and print CD jackets and labels. They're good choices if you're already using one or the other to master your recording.

Other Options for Mastering Your Recording

Cubase makes it relatively easy for you to turn your multi-track recording into a two-channel stereo file. You can even apply some basic effects and EQ to this final two-channel mix, to make your recording sound as good as possible for distribution on CD or over the Internet.

As good as all that is, however, it may not be good enough. Many professional musicians, even those that make their recordings in home studios, hand off the mastering process to other programs (or other people) that provide more mastering options than offered by Cubase.

Third-Party Mastering Programs

Cubase is a digital recording and mixing program. It isn't a dedicated mastering program. As such, it's limited to some degree in how it processes two-channel audio files.

Not to fear, however. Numerous manufacturers (including Steinberg) offer dedicated mastering programs. These programs let you perform all sorts of audio tweaking on your stereo files, or (in many cases) offer almost-magical one-button mastering solutions. These programs make it easy to punch up the sound of your stereo master files, or perform any fine editing that may be necessary.

The most popular of these mastering programs include BIAS Peak (www.bias-inc.com), Sony Sound Forge (www.sonymediasoftware.com), and Steinberg's WaveLab and WaveLab Essential (www.steinberg.net). You can use any of these programs in conjunction with Cubase. Just export your mixes to WAV or AIFF files as described earlier in this chapter, and work with the WAV/AIFF files in the mastering program.

In addition, T-RackS (www.t-racks.com) and Ozone (www.izotope.com) are VST plug-ins that include various mastering tools, such as paragraphic equalizers, compressors, limiters, exciters, reverb, and more. They work just like any other Cubase plug-ins; you use them as master insert effects in the output bus.

Tip

Personally, I'm a big fan of Sony's Sound Forge, which I use to master all my Cubase recordings. Sound Forge comes with a Wave Hammer tool that serves as a combination dynamic compressor/volume maximizer. In most instances, Wave Hammer provides one-button mastering/optimization, assuming you like the default presets. I find it really punches up my recordings without requiring a lot of technical wizardry on my part. (And, as an added bonus, Sound Forge comes with a copy of Sony's CD Architect software—which makes the program's $300 price a little more tolerable.)

Professional Mastering

Making your own recording is one thing; creating your own master is another. Many musicians gladly pay a few hundred (or thousand) bucks to let a professional mastering studio turn their tracks into professional recordings. A professional mastering engineer does this sort of thing for a living, and knows exactly how to punch up and prepare a recording to best effect. Most professional recording studios offer mastering services, and there are many studios that only do mastering work.

Depending on the studio, you may need to provide your entire Cubase project or just your exported stereo WAV/AIFF files. Consult with the mastering engineer beforehand so you'll know what they need—and maybe save yourself a little work in the process.

Making a Magical Master

What makes for a superbly mastered recording? Mastering is a subtle art, but there are some key points to keep in mind.

First, remember that mastering is not the same as mixing. Mastering happens after the mixing process, so don't try to fix any mix problems at this stage. If the mix is bad, go back and remix it—and then begin the mastering process.

It's important to enter the mastering process with your ears as fresh as possible. You're used to listening to track-oriented details during mixing; during mastering, you should be listening to the whole recording, not individual tracks. Sometimes it helps to put some real time (days, if not weeks) between the mixing and mastering operations. It may also help to do your mastering at a different facility than where you did your mixing. It certainly pays to listen to your master on a different set of speakers, not only to freshen your ears but also to get a different perspective on the sound of the thing.

Naturally, you shouldn't attempt to master your recording using only a set of headphones. Although you *might* be able to record and mix with headphones (not that I'd advise it, mind you), you definitely need a good set of speakers to hear the subtleties in the master recording. Speakers, yes; headphones, no.

When mastering, you need to keep the entire album in mind. That is, you want the individual songs to fit comfortably with one another, in terms of volume level, equalization, and general tonal quality. This is where you pull out your master insert effects and master EQ, to create the best sonic match between the different songs.

That said, any changes you make during the mastering process should be subtle ones—tweaks rather than dramatic changes. You don't want to alter your mix, you want to improve upon it. That means giving the bass just a hair more definition, or making the high end just a tad more crisp. This is not the point to decide to change the entire sound of a song; if you don't like what you're hearing, stop mastering and do a remix instead.

And Now You're Done ...

Mastering your files for CD or Internet distribution concludes your Cubase project, and this now concludes this book. If you've followed along, you've learned how to wear many hats—you've been a musician, a recording engineer, a mixing engineer, and a mastering engineer. That's a lot of work for one person to do, but the results are worth it. Whether you're recording in your spare bedroom or in a professional studio, you know now what it takes to make a professional-sounding recording. That all this activity takes place within a relatively low-priced software program that you run on a personal computer makes it all the more remarkable.

So take your newfound knowledge, your developing skills, and your musical ideas, and do something with them. Yes, you'll put in some long hours, but everything worthwhile is worth a little work. Make the best-sounding recordings you can—and share them with the world. That's what Cubase lets you do.

The Least You Need to Know

- If you recorded any MIDI tracks, you first have to convert them to standard audio tracks. (You don't have to do this if you used VST instruments.)
- You should apply any master effects (such as dithering) and equalization to the output bus.
- You export your mix—including all read/write automation—to a stereo audio file.
- If you're mastering for a CD, export to WAV (Windows) or AIFF (Mac) formats; if you plan on distributing your song over the Internet, save to MP3 format.
- Many musicians use a dedicated mastering program to create their final masters; others utilize professional mastering studios to do the work.
- However you do it, mastering should be a subtle process that enhances your original mix without dramatically altering it.

Appendix A

The Complete Idiot's Recording Glossary

0 db Zero decibels, a common reference point for discussing sound levels. Levels above 0 dB are expressed as positive (+1 dB), and levels below 0 dB are expressed as negative (–1 dB).

¼" jack A type of audio connector used to connect professional microphones and electric instruments to computers or mixers.

⅛" jack A type of audio connector used to connect consumer-grade equipment to computers or portable audio players.

acoustic instrument An instrument without pickups or built-in electronics that requires a microphone for recording.

acoustical foam A type of sound-absorbing foam used to deaden recording studios.

acoustics The science that deals with sound and its physical properties.

active speaker A loudspeaker with a self-contained power amplifier. Most studio monitors (and all computer speakers) are active speakers.

ADSR Acronym for attack, decay, sustain, and release—the four stages of an audio waveform.

ADT Acronym for automatic double tracking, a precursor to modern chorus effects that adds the effect of a second vocal or instrumental track played in unison with the original. (Originally devised by recording engineer Ken Townshend for Beatles' recordings.)

AIFF A type of digital audio file used on the Macintosh platform. AIFF files (along with the Windows WAV files) deliver the best-quality sound, and are used to export final recordings in Cubase.

ambience The acoustics, reverberation, and reflections of a room or other space.

ambient mic'ing Also known as *distant mic'ing*, the placement of one or more microphones at a distance of several feet from the performers or their amplifiers. The opposite of *close mic'ing*.

amplification See *gain.*

amplitude The height of a sound wave. The larger the amplitude, the louder the sound.

analog recording A traditional form of recording where the recorded waveform maintains the general shape of the original waveform.

arpeggiate To play the individual notes of a chord one after another, instead of all at once.

arpeggiator A MIDI plug-in that automatically arpeggiates the notes of a chord.

ASIO An acronym for audio stream input/output, a standard for sound card drivers that offers high performance and low latency.

attack The very beginning of a note or sound.

attack time When using a compressor, the time it takes for gain reduction to occur in response to the attack of a note.

attenuate To reduce the level of a signal.

audio recording A traditional recording of audio waveforms. When played back, the original waveform is reproduced. In contrast, a *MIDI recording* consists of electronic note instructions, not waveforms.

automation A feature that lets a recording engineer program control changes into the recording, so that on playback these changes happen automatically.

baffle A sound-absorbing panel used to prevent sound from entering or leaving a certain space. Baffles are used in recording studios to isolate certain acoustic instruments or vocalists.

balance The relative volume levels of various instruments, tracks, or channels.

balanced connector See *XLR connector.*

bandpass filter A filter that passes a band or range of frequencies but rejects frequencies outside the band.

bandwidth A range of audio frequencies.

beats per minute Abbreviated as *bpm*, the number of musical beats occurring in one minute; a method of measuring tempo.

bi-directional microphone Sometimes called a "figure-eight microphone," a microphone with a pickup pattern to sound arriving at the front and rear of the microphone, but not at the sides.

bit depth See *bit rate.*

bit rate Also known as the *bit depth* or *sample depth*, the number of bits transferred in one second by a digital audio device. The higher the bit rate, the higher quality the recording.

bleeding When the sound of one instrument or track unintentionally mixes in with another.

board See *mixer.*

boomy A sound or mix that emphasizes lower frequencies.

booth See *recording booth*.

bottom Another term for low frequencies, typically those below 125 Hz.

boxy A sound or mix that emphasizes mid frequencies.

bpm See *beats per minute*.

breakout box A device that provides a variety of audio inputs and outputs for a computer. Breakout boxes can have both audio and MIDI connections, and typically connect to a computer via either USB or FireWire.

bright A sound or mix that emphasizes higher frequencies.

burn To copy files to a CD or DVD.

bus A signal path that feeds into or out of a program or device, such as a mixer. An input bus feeds into the device; an output bus feeds out of the device.

cardioid microphone A microphone with a pickup pattern that is strongest from the front, less strong from the sides, and weakest from the rear.

channel (1) A signal path. (2) An individual track within a Cubase project. (3) In the final audio file, one of the sides of a stereo recording.

chorus An audio effect in which a single sound source is made to sound like several, through the use of time delay and detuning.

clean A sound that is free of noise, distortion, and other effects.

click (1) The sound made by a *click track*. (2) In some forms of music, such as death or speed metal, the non-boomy part of a bass drum sound.

click track A metronome-like click that sounds on every beat of each measure, in time to the selected tempo. Click tracks are used during recording to help all the musicians play to the same steady beat.

clipping The introduction of distortion into an audio signal by playing it too loud—above the 0 dB level.

close mic'ing A recording technique where the microphone is placed very close to the instrument being mic'ed. This technique yields a great deal of presence and detail, while avoiding leakage from other sound sources and minimizing the room's natural acoustics.

compressed (1) An audio recording with a restricted dynamic range. (2) A type of digital audio file where "unnecessary" pieces of the original waveform are removed, to create smaller files; this typically results in lower sound quality.

compression The process of reducing the dynamic range of a recording to create a punchier sound. Typically achieved via use of a compressor or limiter.

compressor Also known as a *dynamic compressor*; this is a device or plug-in that reduces the dynamic range of a program by limiting the volume peaks and boosting the lowest volume levels.

condenser microphone A type of microphone that is powered by an outboard power source (called *phantom power*). Condenser mics are more sensitive than dynamic mics. Condenser mics are particularly suited to recording vocals.

console See *mixer*.

control room A new feature in Cubase 4 that lets professional studios create a separate monitor mix. See also *recording booth*.

control surface An outboard mixer that connects to a computer and interfaces with the Cubase software.

DAW See *digital audio workstation.*

dB See *decibel.*

de-esser A device or plug-in that removes excessive sibilant sounds (s's, ch's, and so on) by compressing frequencies in the 5,000–10,000 Hz range.

dead Having little or no reverberation; *dry*.

decay The trailing section of a waveform; the last sounding part of a note.

decibel The means of measuring loudness. In audio recording, the 0 dB level is the loudest level possible before the signal clips.

delay The time interval between a signal and its repetition.

DI See *direct injection.*

diaphragm In a microphone, the thin, flexible membrane that vibrates in response to sound waves to produce electrical signals.

digital audio workstation Also known as a *DAW*, a standalone system for digital recording that contains a mixer and hard disk recorder.

digital recording A newer form of recording where the original analog waveform is represented by a series of digital ones and zeros. With digital recording, the recorded signals can be easily edited and processed using programs such as Cubase.

digital signal processing The act of somehow altering the original recorded signal using digital techniques.

direct injection Also known as *DI*, the process of recording an electric instrument, such as an electric guitar or bass, directly to the mixing board, without using an instrument amplifier.

directional microphone A microphone that is sensitive to sounds coming from a particular direction, typically directly in front of the mic.

distant mic'ing See *ambient mic'ing*.

distortion A change to the original audio waveform, typically caused by overloading the input signal, that causes a raspy or unclear sound quality.

dithering The introduction of low-level digital noise into a recording.

doubling The process of combining the original audio signal with a copy of the signal, delayed by 15 to 25 milliseconds. Doubling typically produces a fatter sound than a pure signal.

drum editor In the Cubase program, a utility that enables the editing of MIDI drum tracks.

drum machine A synthesizer or soft synth that creates drum sounds and patterns.

dry A sound or track without any effects or reverberation; the opposite of *wet*.

DSP See *digital signal processing*.

dynamic compressor See *compressor*.

dynamic microphone A type of microphone that records via electromagnetic induction, using a small diaphragm that vibrates under sound pressure.

dynamic range The loudness spectrum of a recording, from the softest passage to the loudest.

echo The delayed repetition of a sound or signal, typically at least 50 milliseconds after the original sound. Echo is typically cleaner than reverb, as it doesn't include any unwanted reflections in the sound.

echo chamber In vintage recording studios, a hard-surfaced room or enclosed space containing a playback speaker and microphone, used to create and then record reverberation.

edit To modify, copy, or delete sections or parts from a recording.

effects In general, any device or plug-in that changes or processes the sound of a recording in any way other than equalization or volume level. Reverb, echo, and flanging are all audio effects.

engineer See *recording engineer*.

envelope The rise and fall in amplitude of a note. The envelope consists of four stages—attack, decay, sustain, and release, otherwise known as *ADSR*.

EQ See *equalization*.

EQ hole A frequency range that is deliberately cut to make room for a similar-sounding voice or instrument in the mix.

equalization A means of shaping a recorded tone by boosting or cutting specific frequencies or frequency bands.

equalizer A device or plug-in that changes the frequency of a recorded signal.

event A distinct recorded part, typically from a single instrument or microphone. In Cubase, there are separate audio events and MIDI events, depending on what type of recording was made.

event display That part of the Cubase interface, on the right side of the project window, that displays all recorded events for each of the available tracks.

expander A device or plug-in that increases the dynamic range of a signal.

fade in The process of gradually increasing the volume of a signal from zero to the desired level.

fade out The process of gradually decreasing the volume of a signal from the starting level to zero.

fader A slider that typically controls volume level.

fat A sound that has a warm, full sound. Sometimes accomplished by doubling.

feedback The return of a portion of the output signal to the device's input. When overused, this creates a squealing sound.

filter A device or plug-in that removes frequencies from a sound or waveform above or below a certain frequency.

FireWire Also known as IEEE 1394, a type of computer connection used for high-speed data transfer.

flanging An effect in which a delayed signal is varied in its delay time and then combined with the original signal. The resulting sound is a kind of hollow swishing.

frequency The number of cycles per second of a sound wave, measured in *hertz*. High frequencies have higher pitches, and low frequencies have lower pitches.

frequency response A measure of the sonic properties of a signal, typically represented as a graph.

FX Short for *effects*.

gain (1) Also known as *amplification*, the ratio between the input power and the output power, typically expressed in decibels. (2) Sometimes used to refer to an increase or decrease in volume level.

gate See *noise gate*.

hard disk recording Digital recording that is made to a hard disk drive.

harsh An unpleasant sound that peaks in the upper midrange area, typically between 2,000 and 6,000 kHz.

headroom A margin of safety between the current signal level and the maximum signal level before clipping occurs.

hertz Abbreviated *Hz*, a measure of frequency or pitch that describes the vibrations of an audio signal, in cycles per second.

high-cut filter Also known as a *low-pass filter*, a filter that passes frequencies below a given frequency and cuts all frequencies above that level.

high-pass filter Also known as a *low-cut filter*, a filter that passes frequencies above a given frequency and cuts all frequencies below that level.

hot Recording audio signals at a high level, at or slightly above the 0 dB clipping point, causing a mild distortion to occur.

hum An undesired low-pitched sound (typically around 60 Hz) that is heard along with the audio signal.

Hz Abbreviation for *hertz*.

input box See *breakout box*.

input bus The signal path that feeds into a program or device.

input insert effects Plug-ins or audio effects that are inserted into the signal path of the input bus as a recording is being made.

insert effects Plug-ins or audio effects that are inserted into the signal path after the original input and before equalization and volume are applied.

inserts See *insert effects*.

inspector See *track inspector*.

jack The female end of an audio cable.

key editor In the Cubase program, a utility that enables the editing of MIDI notes by pitch or duration.

kHz Abbreviation for *kilohertz*.

kilohertz Abbreviated *kHz*, a measure of frequency or pitch that describes the vibrations of an audio signal, in thousands of cycles per second; 1 kHz is equal to 1,000 Hz.

latency The amount of time between a signal arriving at a sound card and when it comes out of the speakers. Low latency results in almost immediate response to any input; high latency means that what you play and what you hear are separated by a noticeable period of time.

leakage The spill of one instrument's sound into another instrument's microphone.

level The strength or volume of an audio signal, typically measured in decibels.

limiter Also known as a *peak limiter*, a device or plug-in that dictates a maximum volume level; any sounds louder than this level are automatically lowered in volume to match (but not exceed) the peak level.

list editor Within the Cubase program, a utility that enables the direct editing of MIDI instructions.

live A sound or recording that has reverberation.

loop A short audio sample, typically repeated multiple times to create a longer track in a recording.

loop library A collection of audio loops or samples, typically distributed on compact disc.

loop-based recording A recording constructed primarily from repeated audio loops.

low-cut filter See *high-pass filter*.

low-pass filter See *high-cut filter*.

mask To cover up one sound with another.

master EQ Equalization applied to the entire recording via the output bus.

master insert effects Plug-ins or audio effects inserted into the master output bus during the mastering process, after the individual tracks have been mixed down to a stereo signal.

mastering The process of readying a final mix for distribution on other media. In Cubase, this process includes the export of the mix to a stereo digital audio file of some sort. Ideally, the mastering process should involve all the songs in an album, so that they are tonally and dynamically balanced when played sequentially.

mastering engineer A recording engineer who specializes in the mastering process.

mastering studio A small recording studio—often just a recording booth—devoted to the mastering process.

meter A device that indicates signal level; in Cubase's mixer, meters display the current volume level.

mic See *microphone*.

microphone A device that converts acoustic sound waves into electronic form.

MIDI Acronym for musical instrument digital interface, a standard that dictates how various electronic instruments (such as synthesizers) communicate with each other and with computers and computerized mixers.

MIDI instrument A synthesizer or synthesizer program (*soft synth*) that reproduces the sounds of one or more acoustic or electric instruments. A MIDI recording must be fed through a MIDI instrument in order to play a sound.

MIDI keyboard A keyboard instrument that has MIDI input and output, and can be used to record MIDI tracks. Some MIDI keyboards have built-in synthesizers, some don't.

MIDI recording A recording of a musical performance translated into a series of instructions on how to play each note, such as pitch, duration, and volume level. A MIDI recording does not include a reproducible waveform; the MIDI instructions must be played through a MIDI instrument to create an audio recording.

midrange That range of frequencies between 200 and 2,000 Hz.

Mike The author's first name. (The short form of microphone is *mic*, not Mike.)

mixer (1) A hardware device that accepts multiple microphone and audio inputs, mixes the sound from these inputs, and sends the signals to a recording device. Also known as a *board*, *console*, *mixing board*, or *mixing console*. (2) That part of the Cubase interface that functions as a virtual mixer.

mixing (1) The process of putting together all the tracks in a recording project to make a pleasing overall recording. (2) The process of combining two or more tracks into a single audio channel, or of combining three or more tracks into a stereo signal.

mixing board See *mixer*.

mixing console See *mixer*.

mixing down See *mixing*.

monitor Another name for the small powered speakers used in most recording studios.

MP3 Short for MPEG layer 3, a type of digital audio file that uses compression technology to create smaller-sized files. The most common file format for Internet music downloads.

muddy A sound or mix that lacks clarity.

multitrack recording The process of recording on multiple channels within a single recording.

music notation program A type of software program that enables the creation of musical scores, using traditional music notation, on a personal computer. Cubase's score editor is a rudimentary music notation program.

mute To silence a track or signal.

nearfield monitor A small speaker designed for listeners located very close to the speaker, as in a recording booth.

noise Unwanted sound.

noise gate A device or plug-in that shuts down a signal when its volume falls below a given level. Typically used to eliminate unwanted noise between notes.

normalize Similar to compression, the process of boosting the highest level of a recording to the maximum level short of clipping (0 dB), and then raising the volume level of the rest of the recording by the same proportion.

offline processing Audio processing that takes place offline, before playback or mixing. Offline processing is applied to individual audio events.

omnidirectional microphone A microphone that is equally sensitive to sounds coming from all directions.

online processing Audio processing that takes place in real time during playback or mixing.

outboard equipment Signal processors or other devices that are not software based.

output bus The signal path that feeds out of a program or device.

overdub To record a new musical part on an unused track, or to replace an existing section of a recorded track.

pan (1) To place a sound at a specific point in the stereo sound field. (2) To move a sound from one place to another in the stereo sound field.

parametric equalizer A type of equalizer in which the range of frequencies affected by level boosts/cuts is adjustable.

passive speaker A loudspeaker that requires external amplification. Almost all home audio speakers are passive speakers.

patch A particular instrument sound produced by a synthesizer or sampler.

peak limiter See *limiter*.

phantom power The outboard power supplied to condenser microphones.

play list A list of the sections of a recording, organized into a desired play order. Play lists are created within the play order editor.

play order The order in which various sections of a recording are played back, as determined by a user-created *play list*.

play order editor In the Cubase program, a utility that enables the rearrangement of various sections of a recording. Used primarily for organizing loop-based recordings.

plug The male end of an audio cable.

plug-in A device or software program that inserts into the signal path and performs some useful function. Most Cubase plug-ins add audio or MIDI effects to a recording.

polyphonic synthesizer A synthesizer that can play multiple notes at one time.

pop filter See *windscreen*.

presence The aural characteristic of an instrument being "up front" in the listening environment.

processing The act of somehow altering an audio signal or track.

processor See *signal processor*.

producer In a traditional recording environment, the person in charge of the recording session. Not to be confused with the recording engineer, who actually makes the recording.

project How Cubase refers to all the tracks and takes that make up a larger recording.

project window That part of the Cubase interface that displays the track list, track inspector, and event display.

punch in/punch out The process of overdubbing a recording beginning and ending at specific points.

Q The means of defining the width of a frequency band affected by equalization.

quantize The correction of rhythms in a MIDI recording, achieved by snapping the MIDI notes to specific rhythmic values.

RAM Acronym for random access memory; the memory capacity of a personal computer, typically measured in gigabytes (GB).

record (1) To store an audio or MIDI event in a permanent form. (2) As a noun, those old vinyl discs that preceded CDs.

recording booth Also known as the *control room*, a small room, typically adjacent to a recording studio, where the actual recording takes place. The recording booth typically contains the mixing board and the tape or hard disk recorder. Many recording booths are large enough to accommodate a small audience.

recording engineer The person who runs the recording board and captures the recording during a recording session.

recording studio A room where musicians sing and play their instruments during the recording process. Recording studios can be any size, from a spare bedroom to a large dedicated hall.

Red Book A standard for burning music CDs.

reflected sound Sound waves that reach the listener after being reflected from one or more surfaces (walls, ceilings, and so on).

release The final portion of a sound's envelope, where the sound falls from its sustain level back to silence.

release time In a signal processor, the time it takes for the gain to return to normal from its processed level.

remix To perform another mixdown with different edits or mixing parameters.

reverb See *reverberation*.

reverberation Also known as *reverb*, the persistence of sound in a room or other space, after the original sound has ended, caused by sound reflections that decrease in intensity over time. Reverb is a "dirtier" sound than echo, as it includes multiple reflections instead of a single repeated sound. Reverb can be created naturally (in a room with hard surfaces, for example), or added digitally to a dry recorded sound.

reverberation time The time it takes for reverberation to decay to 60 dB below the original level.

rhythm tracks The collective name for the recorded tracks of the rhythm section—drums, bass, rhythm guitar, keyboards, and other percussion.

ribbon microphone A type of microphone in which the conductor is a long metallic ribbon, similar to a filament in a light bulb, suspended in a magnetic field. Ribbon mics are very fragile and sensitive to loud sound pressure levels.

sample (1) In Cubase, another way of referring to an audio or MIDI event. (2) A short recording of a musical instrument, used by certain types of synthesizers or samplers to play back MIDI events and reproduce the original sampled sound.

sample depth See *bit rate.*

sample editor In the Cubase program, a utility that enables the editing of audio waveforms of individual recorded events.

sample rate The frequency at which bits of data are recorded in digitizing a sound. Higher sample rates result in more accurate digital reproduction of the original signal.

sampler A device that plays back (and sometimes records) sampled sounds.

sampling The recording of a short sound event into a sampler or computer.

Score Editor In the Cubase program, a utility that enables the creation and editing of MIDI tracks using traditional music notation.

send effects Plug-ins or audio effects added to the end of the signal path as separate effects tracks; the final audio is routed to the effects track as the final step in the process.

sends See *send effects.*

sequencer A device or software program that records a stream of MIDI events and plays them back as instructed.

sibilance In a vocal recording, excessive peaks in the frequency response in the 6,000 to 10,000 Hz range, typically due to an overemphasis of *s*, *sh*, and *ch* sounds. A vocal recording with excessive sibilance is referred to as "essy," and can be corrected with a "de-esser" plug-in.

signal A varying electronic voltage that represents sound.

signal path The route a signal travels from input to output in the recording process.

signal processor A device or plug-in used to deliberately alter a signal in a controlled manner.

signal-to-noise ratio Sometimes referred to as S/N ratio, the ratio (in decibels) between an audio signal and a noise signal. A low S/N ratio indicates a noisy recording; a high S/N ratio is considered quiet, because the audio signal is much louder than the background noise.

soft synth A software-based synthesizer; a virtual synthesizer.

sound pressure level Abbreviated SPL, the acoustic pressure of a sound wave, measured in decibels. A way to measure the loudness of a sound.

stacking tracks The process of recording several performances of a musical part on separate tracks, so that the best portions of each performance can be identified on playback.

stereo An audio recording with distinct left and right channels.

studio See *recording studio.*

sustain (1) That portion of the envelope of a sound in which the level is constant. (2) The ability of a sound to continue without noticeably decaying.

sweetening The addition of brass, strings, and other instruments to previously recorded rhythm and vocal tracks.

synthesizer A musical instrument that generates sound electronically, and that allows changes to the sound parameters (via filters, oscillators, and so forth) to create new sounds.

take One recorded performance of a song or part. Many recording sessions consist of multiple takes, the best of which is used for the final recording.

tempo The speed of the beat in a song or composition.

threshold (1) In a compressor or limiter, the level above which compression or limiting takes place. (2) In a noise gate or expander, the level below which gating or expansion takes place.

time warp A Cubase feature that enables the shrinking or stretching of an event or track, or of individual notes within an event, without changing the song's pitch.

track (1) An individual recorded channel or part in a Cubase project. (2) An individual song on a compact disc. (3) As a verb, the process of making a recording, as in "tracking the band."

track inspector That part of the Cubase interface, on the left side of the project window, that displays information and controls for the currently selected track.

track list That part of the Cubase interface, in the middle of the project window, that lists all the tracks available in the current project.

transient An unusually high-amplitude, rapidly decaying, peak signal level.

transport panel That part of the Cubase interface that contains the main transport controls—play, rewind, fast forward, record, and so on.

transpose To change the pitch of an event or track.

unidirectional microphone See *directional microphone.*

upper midrange That range of frequencies between 2,000 to 6,000 Hz.

USB Acronym for Universal Serial Bus, a type of computer connection used for high-speed data transfer.

velocity How loudly a note is played; another word for volume.

virtual instrument A software program that emulates a physical instrument.

vocoder A device that combines a vocal signal with an instrument signal to create a mechanical-sounding vocal.

VST An abbreviation for Virtual Studio Technology, a standard developed by Steinberg for virtual instruments and plug-in devices.

VST instrument Also known as *VSTi*, a virtual instrument used to play back MIDI tracks.

VST3 New plug-in technology utilized in Cubase 4.

VSTi See *VST instrument*.

warm (1) Describing a mix or track with good bass and sufficient low frequencies. (2) Describing a mix or track that sounds spacious, with good reverberation.

warp tab When working with Cubase's time warp feature, a point in an audio sample that corresponds to a major attack. Warp tabs can be moved within the sample to fix off-beat passages, or to subtly change the feel of a recording.

WAV A type of digital audio file used on the Windows platform. WAV files (along with the Macintosh AIFF files) deliver the best-quality sound, and are used to export final recordings in Cubase.

waveform A graph of an audio signal's sound pressure over time.

wet A sound or track that contains reverberation or ambience.

windscreen Also known as a *pop filter*, a screen placed between a vocalist and a microphone that filters out pop or wind disturbances before they strike the microphone diaphragm.

WMA Abbreviation for Windows Media Audio, a Microsoft proprietary format for digital audio files, a compressed format that offers slightly better sound than the comparable MP3 format.

XLR connector XLR is the abbreviation for Xtended Locking Round, also called a *balanced connector*. A three-pin connector used in professional audio situations, typically to connect a microphone to the mixer or control surface. XLR connectors use phasing technology to deliver a cleaner signal with less interference than similar ¼'' cables.

Appendix B

New Features in Cubase 4

Cubase 4 is the latest version of Steinberg's Cubase recording software. It's available in two flavors—the professional Cubase 4, and the less-expensive (and less fully-featured) Cubase Studio 4. If you haven't yet upgraded to the new version, you should consider doing so.

New Cubase 4 Features

Cubase 4 offers many subtle and not-so-subtle improvements over prior versions of the program. The most noticeable of these improvements include the following:

- **Revised interface.** The controls and displays in the Cubase 4 interface are a little less three-dimensional than those in Cubase SX3. The interface is also a tad darker than before. These changes help to highlight the selected controls, which appear much brighter than the surrounding elements.
- **VST3 plug-in technology.** Perhaps the most important change in Cubase 4 is the introduction of new VST3 plug-in technology. VST3 plug-ins automatically adjust their number of audio busses to the channel to which they're assigned, and include a silence detection function that lets them process audio only when there's a signal present. (This helps reduce the system processing load.) Cubase 4 includes more than 30 new VST3 plug-ins for all types of audio processing.
- **New channel equalizer.** One of the most important applications of VST3 technology appears in the built-in parametric equalizer, which incorporates state-of-the-art EQ technology.
- **New VST instruments.** Cubase 4 comes with a completely new collection of VST instruments. HALionOne, Prologue, Spector, and Mystic are all new to Cubase 4; Embracer and Monologue are carryovers from the previous version.

- **VST instrument tracks.** In previous versions of Cubase, the only way to use a VST instrument was to apply it to a MIDI track. Cubase 4, however, includes new VST instrument tracks that are optimized for the use of VST instruments. You should use a VST instrument track when you want to play a VST instrument "live" in your recording.
- **Track presets.** Whether you're recording to VST instrument, MIDI, or regular audio tracks, Cubase 4 makes it easier to create and configure new tracks via the means of track presets. Each track preset includes EQ and effect settings specific to the type of instrument selected; it's kind of a "fast pass" approach to track configuration.
- **Control Room.** If you use Cubase in a professional recording environment, you can use the new Control Room feature to create multiple monitor mixes, and control where those mixes are sent. (Figure B.1 shows a typical Control Room diagram.)

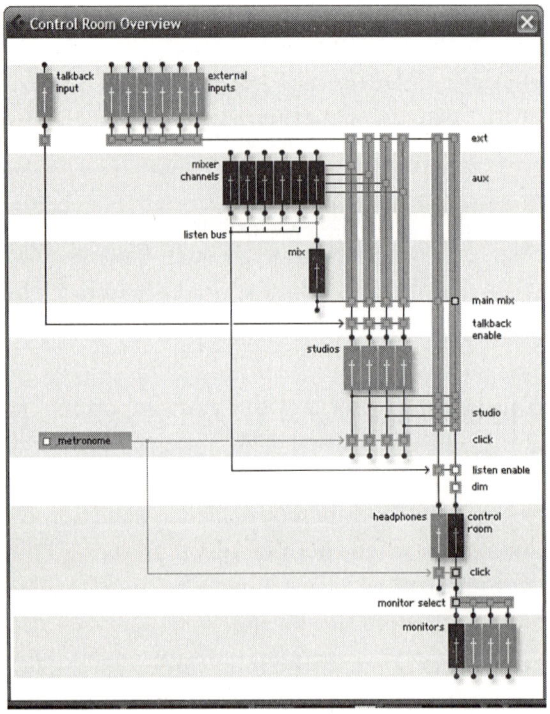

Figure B.1 *The Cubase 4 Control Room overview.*

- **MediaBay file management.** Cubase 4 includes a new centralized media file management system, dubbed MediaBay. As you can see in Figure B.2, the MediaBay lets you view and select all your audio and MIDI files, instrument and plug-in presets, video data, and project files in a single location. (MediaBay is part of what Steinberg calls its StudioFrame universal sound management system, which also includes Cubase's new track presets and ready-to-play sounds.)

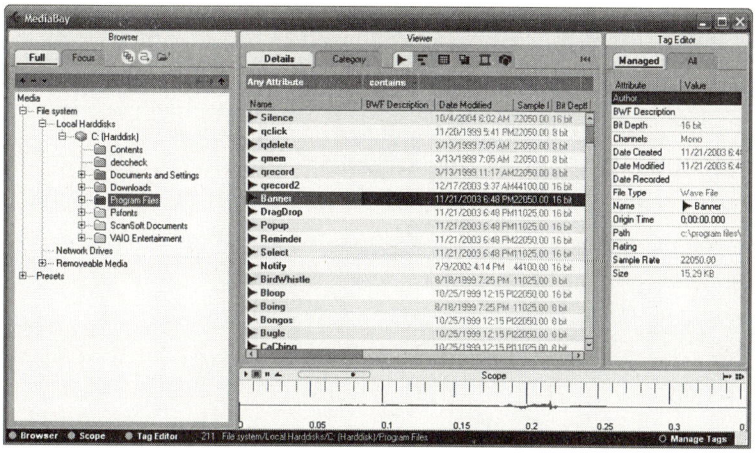

Figure B.2 *The Cubase 4 MediaBay file management system.*

- **Score Editor.** The Score Editor interface has been substantially revamped, with fewer extraneous toolbars and more commands integrated into the main menu system. There are also two new score fonts included—"Jazz" and "Classical," which supplement the original "Legacy" font.
- **Improved audio and MIDI setup.** It's now a lot easier to set up your system for both audio and MIDI inputs. Configuration controls have been both simplified and centralized, and Cubase 4 does a better job of detecting what equipment you have installed on your system.

All in all, these are very important reasons to upgrade from any older version of Cubase to the new Cubase 4—especially since Steinberg has discounted upgrade pricing available.

Differences Between Cubase 4 and Cubase Studio 4

The Cubase family now includes two programs—Cubase 4 and the less-expensive Cubase Studio 4. As you might expect, Cubase Studio 4 isn't quite as fully featured as its more expensive sibling.

The following table details the differences between the two versions of the program.

Cubase 4 vs. Cubase Studio 4

	Cubase 4	Cubase Studio 4
Intended users	Professional music production facilities	Composers, musicians, home project studios
Price (U.S.)	$999.99	$499.99
Audio recording	Yes	Yes
MIDI recording	Yes	Yes
VST virtual instrument recording	Yes	Yes
VST instruments included	6	2 (HALionOne and Prologue)
VST3 plug-in technology	Yes	Yes
VST plug-ins included	66	47
SoundFrame and MediaBay	Full	Limited
Control Room	Yes	No
Surround sound recording	Yes	No
New channel EQ	Yes	No
Physical inputs and outputs	256	128
Mixer views	3	1
External instruments and effects	Yes	No
Advanced Tempo Editor (including TimeWarp)	Yes	No
MIDI devices with editors and user panels	Yes	No
Studio connections	Recall + Audio	Recall only
Full printed manual	Yes	No

In other words, Cubase Studio 4 will do the job for most home studio recording. But if you're working in a professional studio, or need the more complete feature set, Cubase 4 is worth the additional cost.

Index

Numbers

A

B

C

D

E

F

G

H

I

N

O

X-Y-Z